*Imagining Japan*

# Imagining Japan

*The Japanese Tradition
and Its Modern Interpretation*

ROBERT N. BELLAH

*University of California Press*

BERKELEY    LOS ANGELES    LONDON

University of California Press
Berkeley and Los Angeles, California

University of California Press, Ltd.
London, England

© 2003 by the Regents of the University of California

Library of Congress Cataloging-in-Publication Data
Bellah, Robert Neelly, 1927–
   Imagining Japan : the Japanese tradition and its modern interpretation
/ Robert N. Bellah.
      p.   cm.
   Includes bibliographical references and index.
   ISBN 978-0-520-23598-4 (pbk.)
   1. Japan—Civilization.   2. Japan—Intellectual life—1868–.
I. Title.
DS821 .B4353   2003
952.03—dc21                                          2002003307

Manufactured in the United States of America
12   11   10   09   08   07
10   9   8   7   6   5   4   3   2

The paper used in this publication meets the minimum requirements of
ANSI/NISO Z39.48–1992 (R 1997) (*Permanence of Paper*).♾

# Contents

# Introduction
## *The Japanese Difference*

Understanding Japan has preoccupied Japanese intellectuals for centuries and Westerners ever since the discovery of Japan in the sixteenth century. In the recent past the effort to understand Japan, variously to imagine it, has become, if anything, more frenetic than ever.[1] If one is overly influenced by the welter of popular publications coming from within or outside of Japan on this subject, then one will be tempted to adopt either the latest Japanese self-interpretation, which comes in several closely related versions, but which can be summarized under the common term *nihonjinron* (the discourse about the Japanese), or one of the several Western interpretations that emphasize the exotic nature of Japan or its formidable combination of "tradition" and "modernity," views that are closely related to "Orientalism." These usually turn out to be not two temptations but one, for both of them emphasize Japanese uniqueness, Japanese exceptionalism, or Japanese particularism.

Although much of this writing is superficial, it is not my point that either the Japanese or the Western versions are wholly mistaken. Much contained in them is undoubtedly true. Nor does the weakness of this literature derive only from the fact that it emphasizes uniqueness but lacks a comparative perspective. There often is a comparative perspective but comparisons are used only to show how different Japan is, and has always been, from everybody else. It will be one of the purposes of this Introduction to locate Japan within a comparative spectrum, and not outside it; for the Japanese, like all peoples, are indeed unique, but they represent a set of possibilities within the normal range of human culture and society.

Although I will discuss some of this recent literature in this Introduction, the essays collected in this volume are largely concerned with an earlier period. The Japanese or Western "discourse about the Japanese" of recent

1

years has taken place within a relatively benign international atmosphere in which Japan is considered an advanced industrial society and accepted as such in a variety of international organizations. During the 1980s there was some talk in the West of the Japanese threat to dominate the world economy for its own exclusive advantage, but since the collapse of the Japanese bubble economy at the beginning of the 1990s, there has been much less talk of that sort. If anything, Japan has been treated as something of an economic basket case, which should get its act together in order to emerge from its economic doldrums. None of this is particularly frightening, though the pressures are real enough.

The period with which most of the chapters in this volume are concerned was much more ominous: the years before and after 1945, the defeat of Japan at the end of World War II and the first occupation of Japan by a foreign military power. In that period Japanese identity was a matter of life and death, and the ways in which Japan was imagined were strongly contested. Watsuji Tetsurō and Ienaga Saburō, the figures treated most extensively in this book (in Chapters 2 and 3, respectively), though they wrote about many of the same subjects, could hardly be more different in their assessment of the Japanese tradition. Much recent *nihonjinron* literature reiterates, often with less subtlety and insight, what Watsuji had already said in the 1930s and early 1940s and much of the criticism of it reiterates what Ienaga said in the late 1940s and the 1950s. Maruyama Masao, treated briefly in Chapter 4, which is devoted to him (I will have more to say about him later in this Introduction), enormously influential in the decades right after 1945 but largely ignored today, is perhaps the most penetrating mind to appear in twentieth-century Japan and has his own interpretation of the Japanese experience. The issues with which the essays collected in this book are concerned, then, are still very much on the table in Japan and the world today, but Japan has not produced intellectuals of the stature of Watsuji, Ienaga, and Maruyama in recent years.

## PREVIOUS WORK

Before I turn to the main task of this Introduction, namely, to develop a comparative framework adequate to make sense of Japan, it may be helpful for me to make a brief autobiographical digression, especially since many readers will think of me primarily as a student of American society and religion and have no knowledge of my prior interest in Japan. I might begin by mentioning the connection with Japan of one of my best-known contributions to American studies, namely, my 1967 essay, "Civil Religion in

America."[2] The first version of what was to become that essay was delivered as a Fulbright lecture in the Spring of 1961 during my Fulbright year in Japan, soon after the Inaugural Address of John F. Kennedy, which plays a significant role in the essay. It was not an effort to speak to an American audience, but rather to explain to the Japanese, who had been so sternly lectured to by the Occupation authorities on the critical importance of the separation of church and state, why no American president could be inaugurated without mentioning God in his inaugural address. So my first tentative approach to American studies was from the point of view of Japan, and some acute reviewers have seen an East Asian perspective in all my work on the United States, work that emphasizes informal thought and practice as much as legal and institutional structures.

My doctoral dissertation, which was completed in 1955 and published in 1957 as *Tokugawa Religion*, was an effort to think of Japan not as "different" or the "Other" in any absolute sense, but as sharing similarities and differences with other modern societies in a comparative framework.[3] In the first chapter of the book I used two sets of what Talcott Parsons called "pattern variables," a scheme that he developed from Max Weber's typology of social action, to describe Japanese society as characterized by the pattern variables of particularism (as opposed to universalism) and achievement (as opposed to ascription). By particularism I meant that in Japan considerations of relational context usually took precedence over considerations of abstract and universal principle. And by achievement I argued that in Japan persons were evaluated more in terms of what they could do than of what status they occupied. The latter point was more controversial than the former in terms of the general understanding of Japan, particularly in the Tokugawa period when social status was of great importance. But I argued that in the actual practices of life achievement was highly valued. As an example I gave the instance of a peasant boy, Tomita Kokei, who, when starting off from his home to attend the Confucian school in Edo, heard footsteps and turned around to see his mother running after him. He asked what was the matter and she replied, "If you do not succeed you need not return home."[4] Since I described American society as characterized by the pattern variables of universalism and achievement, I was arguing that Japan was at this most general level as similar to as it was different from my own society.

But my effort to characterize Japan in terms of sociological variables was only introductory to the main purpose of the book, which was to argue that, though there was nothing like the Protestant Reformation that could have inaugurated modernity in Japan, there were functional equivalents of aspects of Protestantism that made the Japanese more capable than most other non-Western societies of responding effectively to the challenge of modernization when it came. In this case, where I was extending Weber's argument on religion and capitalism beyond what he had written, I was not arguing for Japan's uniqueness, but for some basic similarities to the West.[5] It was just concerning this point that Maruyama Masao believed I had gone too far. Maruyama, Japan's leading social scientist at the time, criticized me for eliding too easily the differences between Japan and the West and for being insufficiently aware of the negative aspects of the Japanese tradition, and of Tokugawa society in particular. I will return to some reconsiderations of the Tokugawa period below.

My view of Japan in comparative perspective was developed further in a series of lectures that I delivered at International Christian University in Tokyo in the spring of 1961 under the title "Values and Social Change in Modern Japan," in which I developed a more critical perspective on aspects of the Japanese tradition, partly in response to Maruyama.[6] In those lectures I described a series of Japanese efforts to attain a transcendental perspective, beginning with Shōtoku Taishi in the seventh century, continuing with the major figures of Kamakura Buddhism in the thirteenth century, especially Shinran and Dōgen, touching on Tokugawa Confucians such as Ogyū Sorai, and concluding with Christians since the Meiji period, particularly Uchimura Kanzō. I pointed out how in each case the moment of transcendence was quickly submerged. The particularistic "ground bass" of Japanese society that I had described in *Tokugawa Religion* reasserted itself, soon drowning out the transcendental melody that had appeared in the upper register. I did not use the term nonaxial, which S. N. Eisenstadt would use in his book *Japanese Civilization*, but the germ of that idea was present in those lectures.[7] Although a comparative framework is implied in all the essays contained in this book, none of them returns to a consideration of a basic framework for thinking about Japanese culture and society in a comparative perspective as did *Tokugawa Religion* and "Values and Social Change in Modern Japan."[8] I want to use the rest of this Introduction to develop such a framework.

## MODERNITY AND ITS PRECURSORS

In both popular and scholarly discourse the distinction between societies that are "modern" from those that are "traditional" is hard to avoid, yet the current usage of the modern/traditional dichotomy is so riddled with untenable and unexamined presuppositions that it is virtually useless. The stereotypical contrast of a rapidly changing modernity with a stagnant and unchanging traditional society, an idea that, unfortunately, owes more than a little to Max Weber, is surely wrong. But something about modernity makes it different from earlier social conditions, and it has been sociology's task from the beginning to try to explain what that something is. It would not be an exaggeration to say that sociology began as an effort to explain modernity to itself. In so doing it was necessary for the founders of sociology—certainly for Marx, Weber, and Durkheim—to think systematically about what came before modernity in order to understand how modern societies are different from all preceding ones. Weber's notion of a development from societies based on kinship and neighborhood, through societies organized by bureaucracy or feudalism, to modern capitalism was a version of a story told in different ways by Marx and Durkheim as well. Coming out of this sociological tradition, my own effort to situate modernity in relation to what preceded it was first set forth in my 1964 article on religious evolution.[9]

In my version, drawing directly from Weber, religion played an important role in the emergence of modernity. Weber began his study of religion in 1904 with his famous *The Protestant Ethic and the Spirit of Capitalism*. It is clear, however, that we must consider not only that essay but the place of the Protestant ethic argument in Weber's work as a whole. He believed that ascetic Protestantism was an indispensable catalyst for the emergence of a new form of society that he called "modern capitalism"—but which he saw as a new kind of civilization, not just a new kind of economy. Although circumscribed markets had existed for millennia within what Randall Collins calls "agrarian-coercive societies," never before the Reformation in the West had ideological, political, and economic resources crystallized to form such a new kind of civilization.[10] Once established, however, capitalism became a worldwide phenomenon, even though taking different forms in different civilizational areas. Thus Protestantism, though occurring in only one tradition, was, indirectly but crucially, an indispensable precondition for the cross-cultural emergence of modernity.

In searching for the root causes of modernity and why it arose first in the West, Weber embarked on the most ambitious set of comparative studies ever undertaken. In the course of his study of the great traditions he came to believe that religious events in the first millennium B.C. were of critical importance. Within each of the world religions that emerged at that time arose prophets or saviors who radically rationalized previous forms of what Weber tended to call "magical religion." In each case the emergent figure (Confucius, the Buddha, the Hebrew prophets, Socrates, Jesus) preached a systematic form of ethical conduct quite different from the diffuse ritual and sacramental practices that preceded them. By calling these new symbolic forms "rationalized" Weber was pointing to the fact that they were more coherent, more cognitively and ethically universalizing, more potentially self-critical (reflexive), and more disengaged from the existing society than what preceded them. Karl Jaspers, Weber's close friend and student, called the period of the emergence of these religions, the first millennium B.C., the "Axial Age."[11] S. N. Eisenstadt speaks of the world religions as axial religions and of their related civilizations as axial civilizations.[12] If one follows Weber's argument that religion is the indispensable catalyst for the emergence of modernity, as I do, then one can see that the axial religions, even though they emerged millennia before modernity, were its indispensable precondition.

In my 1964 article I proposed a simplified way of looking at the shape of religious evolution. I argued that whereas tribal and archaic religions were primarily this-worldly in orientation, which is what Weber, perhaps unwisely, meant by the word magical, the axial religions were world-rejecting (and thus, for Weber, crucially, magic-rejecting), although they differed as to whether this rejection was to be worked out within the world (ethically), or as far as possible outside the world (mystically). It was the leverage of axial religion in a transcendental reference point, outside the world so to speak, that made it possible to criticize and in principle to revise the fundamental social and political premises of existing societies. Whereas in tribal and archaic societies self and society were seen as embedded in the natural cosmos, the axial religions and philosophies made it possible in principle for the self to become disembedded from society and society from the given world of nature. It should be remembered, however, that in its radical consistency axial religion was never more than the religion of a minority; the majority continued to entertain beliefs and practices continuous with archaic or even tribal religion, which is what Weber meant by the return to the garden of magic.

With the Protestant Reformation the belief in a radically transcendent God had dramatic this-worldly consequences: the consistent demands of an axial ethic were to be expected from everyone and in every sphere of daily life. An entirely new degree of disembeddedness of self from society and society from nature became possible. But in the subsequent development of modernity, though the this-worldly dimension remained dominant, its transcendental basis became transformed into immanentism, thus returning the modern world in a much different way to the this-worldly immanentism of preaxial times. The new form of immanentism, however, did not lead to a reembeddedness of self and society in the cosmos but rather to ever-increasing degrees of differentiation and disembeddedness. Weber clearly observed this transition, but viewed it almost entirely negatively. The modern world of rationalization would run on its own bureaucratic and economic energies without any transcendental sanction, would become an iron cage.[13] Thus, although Weber was the modernization theorist par excellence, his was a dark view, not at all a triumphalist one, of where modernity is heading.

Let me try to place Japan within this evolutionary framework. In *Japanese Civilization* S. N. Eisenstadt speaks of Japan as a nonaxial civilization. It is not that Japan has not been exposed to axial religions and civilizations. Since at least the seventh century Japan has been deeply influenced by Buddhist and Confucian ideas, as well as by Indian and particularly Chinese civilization. And since the sixteenth century Japan has been influenced by Christianity and Western civilization. But in the face of these religious and civilizational influences the Japanese have not rejected their preaxial civilizational premises; instead they have continuously revised them without abandoning them. Outside cultural influences have been appreciated and understood with intelligence and sensitivity, but then used to bolster the nonaxial premises of Japanese society rather than to challenge them.

Because the Japanese have been aware of axial principles, have understood them thoroughly, and yet have rejected them, preferring instead to adapt them to the reformulation of their own archaic heritage, and because they have done so with dynamism and an openness to change so that they have not been "traditional" in the pejorative sense of the term, Eisenstadt argues that they should be called nonaxial rather than preaxial. Yet there is one sense in which Japanese civilization can be called preaxial. The underlying premises of Japanese society, though they can be reformulated with great sophistication, cannot be challenged. They are off the board, so to speak, when it comes to serious discussion of fundamental change. When in my essay "Values and Social Change in Modern Japan" I spoke of the Japanese "ground bass," I was referring to this preaxial element in Japanese culture; when I spoke of the "tradition of submerged transcendence," I was referring to the presence of axial traditions in Japan—Buddhist, Confucian, Christian, Marxist—that never quite succeeded in replacing the preaxial premises of Japanese culture. This is a first approximation in placing Japan in a comparative framework, one that relies heavily on Eisenstadt, but it needs more specificity.

## THE FORMATION OF AN ARCHAIC STATE

The treatment of Japan so far in terms of cultural, and even specifically religious, traditions could be criticized as too "culturalogical," that is, as treating culture as an autonomous causal variable rather than as one always embedded in social structures and, more particularly, structures of power. Although Eisenstadt's *Japanese Civilization* has far more to say about structures of power than I have so far mentioned, it will be helpful to turn to another extremely valuable analysis of the Japanese case, Johann Arnason's *Social Theory and Japanese Experience*, to reflect on the ways in which power and culture have interacted in Japanese history from the beginning.[14] Arnason suggests that it is key to understanding the Japanese case to see that it was in a process of state building when it first emerged on the historical stage. What preliterate Japan, that is Japan before the sixth century A.D., was like can only be reconstructed from archaeology and later, often problematic, written accounts. It appears that Japan had been divided into a large number of what can probably be called chieftainships (the Chinese records referred to them as "kingdoms" because that is how they thought of peripheral peoples), who were gradually being united by a paramount chieftainship located in the Yamato region of central Japan. Sometime, probably not long before the sixth century, this paramount chieftainship developed into an early state, something that could be compared to the state created by King Kamehameha I in the Hawaiian Islands at the end of the eighteenth century.[15]

Finally by the seventh and eighth centuries, when the evidence, though still problematic, becomes much more extensive, what one can observe is the conscious creation of an archaic state, using resources from the considerably more advanced civilization of the Chinese mainland to do so. By an early state I mean a paramount chieftainship that is just moving beyond a tribal confederation to establish a centralized government. The fact that even in the seventh century there was no fixed capital suggests just how tenuous this early state really was. It was not until 710 that a "permanent" capital was established at Nara (though it was only seventy-five years before it was abandoned for another capital). But it was from the rather fragile early state structure of the sixth century that the effort to establish a full-scale archaic state began. The effort is associated with the name of Shōtoku Taishi (Prince Shōtoku, 574–622). He sent large-scale embassies to China in 607, 608, and 614. These ambassadorial visits involved much more than diplomacy. Buddhist monks, scholars, artists, and artisans studied for a year or even several years, bringing back a wide range of material and ideal cultural artifacts on their return to Japan. Undoubtedly elements of Chinese culture had been imported from China or the Korean peninsula for centuries—rice agriculture had been spreading in Japan since several centuries before the Christian era—and Buddhism, which was probably not unknown even earlier, was officially received at the Yamato court in 552, but the kind of systematic importation that took place under Shōtoku's regency was unusual. Many simple societies in history have acquired the culture of more advanced neighbors but in almost every such case it has been because they had been conquered by such a neighbor. It has often been remarked that Japan's deliberate self-transformation without the experience of conquest was repeated in the late nineteenth century when it was not Chinese but Western culture that was imported on a grand scale.

It is important to note that the transformation of Japan in the seventh and eighth centuries was in considerable part a response to changes in China, namely, the unification of the country after four centuries of disunity, first under the brief Sui Dynasty in 589, followed soon thereafter by the long-lasting T'ang dynasty beginning in 618. Although it is tempting to think of Japan as an "insular" culture developing in its own way relatively independent of the rest of the world, this has never been true. Significant changes in mainland East Asia, usually China, and later in the world at large, have always had important repercussions in Japan.

Stanley Tambiah, working primarily on Southeast Asia, has developed the idea of a "galactic polity" that helps to understand what was going on in East Asia at the time.[16] An empire such as the T'ang focuses on an exemplary center, with regional administrations replicating the center. Military and political control in such premodern empires was seldom intense, but even when physical control of peripheral areas weakened, the influence of the exemplary center often persisted. The Sui and the early T'ang, for example, invaded Korea in an effort to make it a Chinese province. They were finally militarily unsuccessful, but the effort produced a unified Korea under the domination of the kingdom of Silla, which forced the T'ang to accept it as a tributary but autonomous state, at the same time that it undertook an internal restructuring on the T'ang model. Vietnam was administered by China through most of the T'ang Dynasty, directly if loosely, and here too a Chinese model of state and society was imposed that long outlasted direct Chinese control.[17] Neither the Sui nor the T'ang ever attempted an invasion of Japan, though Japanese contingents were involved with one or another Korean kingdom during the struggles with the T'ang. But the powerful exemplary influence of T'ang China, felt in Central Asia in the west and Manchuria in the north as well as in Korea and Vietnam, had a major impact on Japan. This would not be the last time that changes on the mainland would have profound consequences for Japan.

I want to emphasize that the state being established was not an axial state that the contemporary Sui and T'ang Chinese models would have suggested—the resources for that degree of transformation simply did not exist in Japan—but an archaic state, typologically similar to that of the Shang Chinese state of the second millennium B.C. There are two indices, one structural, one cultural, that I would use to suggest why the new Japanese state that emerged in the seventh and eighth centuries was archaic and not axial. On the structural side, although a centralized state on the Chinese model was established, with a bureaucracy that administered land and tax registers and a conscript army, the hold of the great aristocratic lineages (the descendants of earlier tribal chieftains) was not broken. The Chinese idea of a bureaucracy staffed on the basis of merit as measured by an examination system never took hold. Bureaucratic offices were soon appropriated by lineages as their permanent possessions. The old *uji* (clan) system was undoubtedly reconstructed, but the principle of lineage was never broken through.

On the more cultural side, the radical (axial) implications of the Chinese conception of monarchy were rejected. Some notion of aristocratic descent from the gods was undoubtedly ancient in Japan as it was in many early societies, and the status of lineages could be judged by the status of the gods from whom they claimed descent in the polytheistic pantheon. That the Yamato chief claimed descent from the sun goddess was an expression of this kind of archaic logic. The Chinese notion that the emperor is the son of heaven could be apparently seamlessly adopted in Japan, but with one major problem. It is exactly what made the Chinese case axial that a polytheistic pantheon had been replaced by an emphasis on a heaven that judged rulers according to ethical standards and could transfer "the mandate of heaven" in cases where the ruler failed to live up to such standards. To replace divine descent by an ethical notion of the mandate of heaven would have been for the Japanese to move from an archaic to an axial conception of rule. Such a move, though available ever since Confucian doctrines were first understood, was never made.

Another aspect of the archaic quality of the Japanese state that was taking shape in this early period was the survival and reorganization of the preexisting religious cult. While in rural areas quite ancient cults have survived in all the advanced civilizations, in early Japan there was an effort to preserve and rationalize the older religious forms that would considerably later be referred to by the Sinified name of Shinto (the way of the Gods). Although in remote parts of the country early forms of ritual practice have survived for millennia, what would later be known as Shinto was a dynamic reformulation of indigenous beliefs and practices occurring as part of the state building of the seventh and eighth centuries and should not be confused with some timeless past before the introduction of Chinese influences. Indeed Chinese influences were essential in the reformulation of the native tradition. The two primary documents of Shinto, the *Kojiki* of 712 and the *Nihongi* of 720, were modeled on Chinese dynastic histories, even though they began with an account of the age of the gods. Undoubtedly the form they took was itself partially influenced by ideological considerations with respect to the Yamato ruling family and other aristocratic lineages and was thus part of the state-building process. In short, autochthonous and Chinese culture existed in a dynamic relationship in the newly forming archaic state and neither can be fully understood without the other.[18]

Buddhism is indeed one of the great axial religions, emphasizing the tension between the existing world and ultimate reality, one of the key marks of axial religion, as strongly as any known religious tradition ever has, but we must not imagine that the statues, texts, and rituals that were being gradually introduced to Japan at this early period added up to any such entity as we would envisage with the modern term "Buddhism." Although the transcendental Buddhist beliefs may have been appreciated by some Japanese intellectuals, as the remark attributed to Shōtoku that "the world is a lie; only the Buddha is true" would indicate, the primary meaning of Buddhist beliefs and practices in early Japan was not axial but archaic. It was the magical power associated with Buddhist artifacts and rituals that was most desired, and it was Buddhist devotion as providing good fortune for the ruling house and the aristocratic lineages that brought it into favor.

During the Nara period (roughly the eighth century) six schools or lineages of Mahayana teaching were established, each with one or more temple-monasteries devoted to its study. For a long time, these were referred to by scholars as the six Nara sects (*shū*). It is now generally accepted that shū cannot be translated as "sect" except perhaps in Tokugawa and recent times. The translation "schools" is not entirely adequate either, but at least it gives the notion that these were nonexclusive teaching traditions— a monk could be inducted into more than one—and being trained in one did not mean lack of knowledge and interest in others. The newly emerging Japanese state in the Nara period was modeled on T'ang China; its fundamental ideology was Confucian. Confucian texts provided the basis for the education of officials, court ritual was largely Confucian, and the emperor was conceived of as the son of heaven in Confucian terms (an idea thought to be perfectly consistent with continued belief in his descent from the sun goddess). Yet the idea of the mandate of heaven was rejected. Confucianism explained natural disasters and military setbacks as caused by the failure of imperial virtue, and if they became serious enough, as justification for a change of dynasty. Because this possibility was not open to the Japanese, they turned to the Buddhists for alternative explanations of such disasters. Thus the temples could provide defense against the occurrence of such untoward events; and when they did occur, they provided both explanations of them in terms of the acts of evil spirits or demons and propitiatory rituals to mitigate their consequences.[19] In accordance with T'ang precedent, Buddhist monks and nuns were regulated by state law, with ordinations strictly limited to authorized ordination platforms, only one of which was in Nara. While state control of ordination and the necessity to provide spiritual assistance to the state did limit the independence of the monastic community, or *sangha*, still the Nara schools developed considerable sophistication in their traditions and provided support for serious Buddhist practice for monks and a growing number of lay followers as well.

Early in the ninth century after the capital had been moved to Heian-kyō (present-day Kyoto), an entirely new form of Buddhism that would become pervasive for many centuries was introduced by the monk Kūkai after he had returned from China in 806. In Japanese Buddhist studies this is called Esoteric Buddhism, but is also known as Vajrayana Buddhism or Tantric Buddhism, best known today from its Tibetan form. Ryūichi Abé in an important recent study has argued that Kūkai should not be seen in the first instance as the "founder of the Shingon school," though he was later considered to be such, but as the person who introduced a whole new form of Buddhism, Esoteric Buddhism, which saw itself as a new "vehicle" (*yana*), that is, the Vajrayana, that included and superseded Mahayana, just as Mahayana had included and superseded Hinayana.[20] That Kūkai could have succeeded in this enterprise virtually single-handedly is a tribute to his stature both as a thinker and as a monastic politician. He persuaded the six Nara schools to accept the legitimacy of his new teaching and begin the process of integrating it with their older Mahayana traditions and he persuaded the imperial court to integrate Esoteric ritual at the heart of its annual ritual cycle.

One must not neglect to mention the other figure normally paired with Kūkai, Saichō, who had returned from China in 805 and who really was, quite self-consciously, the founder of the Tendai school.[21] Saichō had studied Esoteric Buddhism in China but had not reached nearly so advanced a stage as Kūkai, with whom he studied after his return to Japan. Doctrinally Saichō was intermediate between the older Nara schools and Kūkai because he believed that Tendai, focusing on the Lotus Sutra, was the only true Mahayana teaching and that the older sects (all of whom acknowledged the importance of the Lotus Sutra) were virtually Hinayana teachings. Without ever giving up its stress on the Lotus Sutra, Tendai did become in later centuries a major channel for the dissemination of Esoteric Buddhism. Institutionally, however, it was Tendai that insisted on its separate identity. Although a tradition tracing its origin to Kūkai did develop as the Shingon school, Shingon, which is really another way of saying Esoteric Buddhism, permeated all subsequent teaching traditions. The spread of Esoteric Buddhism and its fusion with Exoteric teachings led to important institutional changes.

Kūkai's teaching, as Abé has shown, brought a whole new level of Buddhist practice and embodiment into Japan. In this teaching Vairocana (Dainichi, "Great Sun") Buddha was the Buddha's dharma body. Unlike the humanly incarnated Buddha, Sakyamuni, or the heavenly Buddhas such as Amida, Vairocana Buddha did not use "skillful means," or teachings adapted to the condition of the believers, but rather taught the unmediated truth through every element in the universe. Indeed the universe was seen as a form of writing, a supreme mantra, although it required the appropriate practice to be able to "read" it. Kūkai's Esoteric Buddhism can be seen both as a new level of doctrinal sophistication and as a reappropriation of an archaic form of spirituality.

Thomas Kasulis has described Kūkai as "philosophizing in the archaic."[22] Kasulis's point is that while philosophy is usually seen as antithetical to myth, as holding up the mythical to critical inspection, Kūkai used Buddhist philosophy to defend an archaic structure of thought. At one point Kasulis speaks of Kūkai as engaging in the "philosophizing *of* the archaic," which seems to be a good description of a long line of Japanese thinkers.[23] They have used the materials of an axial tradition (in this case Buddhist, but in many cases Confucian as well), to justify a nonaxial position, often in a way that shows them thoroughly at home in the axial way of thinking. This might be called using the axial to overcome the axial, just as some Japanese thinkers early in World War II sought to "overcome the modern."

At the core of both Shingon and Tendai traditions is *hongaku* (original enlightenment) thought, namely, the idea that all beings are already enlightened and their only task is to realize it.[24] This position was not an unusual one in the tradition of Mahayana Buddhism in China and it became even more widespread in Japan, but it is one that comes close to affirming the world as it is rather than holding it in tension with ultimate reality, thus undermining the axial core of Buddhist thought. As Ienaga Saburō puts it, the essential Buddhist logic of negation was overridden (this point is further discussed below in Chapter 2).

It might be noted that Confucianism and Buddhism, for opposite reasons, lent themselves to an archaic reinterpretation. As has often been noted, among the axial religions and philosophies, Confucianism has the heaviest "archaic mortgage," to use Eric Voegelin's term, in that it emphasizes the sacredness of kinship to an extraordinary degree, as well as respect for the authority of rulers. What makes Confucianism axial is the recognition of a transcendent heaven exercising a moral judgment over the rulers of this world. But ignoring that element of the teaching, as Japanese Confucians normally did, left most of the remaining Confucian views quite consistent with a particularistic archaic ethic. Buddhism, by contrast, pushed world-denial further than any other axial tradition. But it pushed it so far that in one important Mahayana teaching, namely, the idea that *samsara* (this world of suffering) *is nirvana* (enlightened release from this world), which was meant as a paradoxical declaration calling on the believers to open themselves to the possibility of enlightenment, could easily turn into a teaching of world acceptance consonant with an archaic worldview.

What is impressive about seventh- and eighth-century Japan was the degree of creativity and innovation displayed at both the structural and the cultural level. New institutions were set up wholesale, including a legal system based on Chinese models that would long endure, though not unchanged. Not only were the major traditions of continental thought, Buddhist, Confucian, even Taoist, thoroughly explored, but also the tradition of native myth and ritual was profoundly reconstructed. If Japan remained, as, given the materials at hand, it probably had to remain, archaic in terms of its underlying social and cultural premises, then it was an extremely dynamic archaism, indeed a newly constructed archaism, that was at issue.[25] Far from a continuous "native" culture simply absorbing new cultural imports without being affected by them, the entire structural and cultural package of Nara and early Heian Japan was newly created from the ground up, using native and foreign materials to be sure, but reorganizing everything to form a distinctly new pattern.

One further feature of the Japanese pattern that became evident from early in the period of the great transformation was a system of rule that Maruyama Masao calls the *basso ostinato* of Japanese politics, using a musical metaphor similar to but more restricted in meaning than my use of ground bass.[26] This is a pattern of thinking of government always from the point of view of those serving from below rather than from the point of view of those ruling from above. This could be interpreted as an archaic feature indicating that the governing function has not yet been clearly differentiated from the rest of society, though if this is the case it points to a pattern that is even prearchaic. The result in which Maruyama is interested is the tendency in different ways but at almost every period of Japanese history for effective rule to devolve to levels below, sometimes well below, those in titular authority. This pattern is clearest in the case of the imperial family itself, which, except perhaps briefly in the late seventh century, almost never ruled directly, but always through those who "served" it, who held the real power.[27] Two consequences of this pattern are evident. One is the difficulty of placing responsibility for political actions or, in certain circumstances, finding anyone who will take responsibility for action when it is needed. Another was the impossibility of applying the mandate of heaven theory of responsible government to the highest levels of authority who practically never had themselves taken significant action. If the theory could be applied at all it had to be applied to the effective rather than the titular rulers. While this pattern created difficulties at many points in Japanese history, and was clearly frustrating to Maruyama who wanted to establish the idea of responsible constitutional government in Japan, it was also highly flexible and even dynamic, encouraging initiative from below rather than the stagnation of authority from above. So, as usual in Japan, what might be thought of as "primitive" has had powerful creative and innovative potentialities.

## MILITARY RULE

Arnason refers to the creation of an archaic state from the seventh to the ninth centuries, with the help of Chinese models adapted for Japanese use, as an example of primary state formation.[28] The last official embassy to China was sent in 838. All contact was not lost, but the Japanese government felt official embassies were no longer safe in a period when the power of the T'ang Dynasty was collapsing. The end of official embassies was symptomatic of the fact that the period of intense institution building with the help of Chinese models was over.

What followed has been interpreted as the disintegration of the centralized state on the Chinese model and the resurgence of particularistic Japanese patterns. While this is not entirely wrong, more recent interpretations have stressed the spread of new social and cultural forms from the originally quite limited area of the old Yamato heartland to the rest of the archipelago. Growth in the agricultural economy, in part stimulated by the opening up of new lands for rice cultivation, went hand in hand with the slow but continuous increase of trade. Provincial elites nominally holding title from the imperial court were becoming ever more independent and relying on their own military power for protection.

But the warriors and the court were not the only major institutional players in medieval Japan. A third "influential party" (*kenmon*) was the great shrine/temple complexes that grew up in Japan from early Heian times.[29] The erosion of the T'ang model of the Japanese state during the long centuries of the Heian period (roughly ninth to twelfth centuries) was nowhere more evident than in the religious institutions. Effective legal control of monks and nuns did not last much beyond the ninth century. As the shrine/temple complexes grew in wealth and power, high offices within them were monopolized by the offspring of aristocratic lineages who were promoted much more rapidly than the normal course of study would allow. As land holdings increased and military might supplied by "armed monks" (seldom ordained monks, but retainers of the complexes) grew, these institutions became virtually states within a state.

Allan Grapard has given us a superb study of one of the largest and most powerful of these complexes, the Kasuga Shrine/Kōfukuji Temple complex in Nara.[30] Grapard emphasizes the degree of interpenetration of "Shinto" and Buddhist elements, each requiring the other to make sense, in what he calls a combinative rather than a syncretic pattern. The shrine dates back to the eighth century and its deities were ancestral or tutelary deities of the Fujiwara family, the most powerful of the aristocratic lineages, closely related by marriage to the imperial line. Kōfukuji served as a memorial temple for the spirits of departed members of the Fujiwara family. The temple continued to be one of the main centers of the Hossō school of Nara Buddhism, but permeated with Esoteric teachings as well. By the Kamakura period the complex had become the biggest landholder in Japan, effectively controlling Yamato Province, the heartland of the ancient dynasty. Naturally the abbot was normally a Fujiwara. Though ostensibly devoted to the imperial lineage through its reverence for the Fujiwara family so closely related to it, the complex had become a power so great that neither the court nor rising military groups could easily impose their will on it.[31]

Although great religious complexes such as the Kasuga Shrine/Kōfukuji Temple could be seen simply as exploiters of peasant labor because of the land rents upon which they depended, they did, in turn, supply the populace of the province with cultural meaning through a grand ritual cycle and religious understandings of time and place. The idea of a Pure Land was brought down to earth through the notion that the shrine/temple complex was itself a "Pure Land in this world" (*gense-jōdo*). According to Grapard, Kasuga was seen as "a sort of paradise on earth," a vision appearing in "the texts, paintings, rituals, and theatrical performance created at the multiplex over centuries."[32]

With the growth of the shrine/temple complexes and the pervasive influence of Esoteric Buddhism, the understanding of the imperial institution shifted gradually from a Confucian to a Buddhist one. In the Nara period the essentially Confucian state used Buddhism and its already associated native forms of worship to bolster its power. By the eleventh and twelfth centuries the idea of "the oneness of kingly law and Buddhist law" (*buppō ōbō ichinyo*) had developed, an idea that gave equal weight to both sides of the equation. Indeed the kingly law and the Buddhist law were said to be like the two wheels of a cart or the two wings of a bird: one could not survive without the other. Such was the degree to which the amalgam of Exoteric and Esoteric Buddhism ( the so-called *kenmitsu-taisei*, with its closely associated "Shinto" components very much part of the picture) had enveloped Japanese society by medieval times.[33]

As military power on the peripheries grew, especially in the northeast in the Kantō region, the area around present-day Tokyo, the possibility of a new locus of power appeared, leading to what Arnason, whose views on primary state formation we have found helpful above, calls "secondary state formation." In 1185 the process of secondary state formation was actualized in the founding of the Kamakura shogunate, a system of military rule that in some respects is comparable to European feudalism, with its headquarters in Kamakura, far from the old capital of Kyoto. But the imperial court in Kyoto was not displaced; it continued to wield some degree of power and a considerable degree of influence. Thus the primary state formation was not abandoned, but continued in reduced circumstances alongside the new secondary state formation. Although the Japanese case was in many ways unique, it has more similarities to the West than to China. In China the primary state formation, which was completed under the Ch'in and Han although it was recreated several times with significant innovations, remained faithful to its original pattern until the twentieth century, and no secondary state formation occurred. But in the West, after the fall of the Roman Empire, the rise of feudalism was an example of secondary state formation, that is, not the creation of a state from tribal beginnings, even though tribal peoples were involved, but the formation of new states after the collapse of, but to some degree on the basis of, an old one. And though the Roman emperor and his court did not survive in the West as the emperor did in Japan, the shadow of the older empire remained in the form of the Catholic Church with its monarchical leader, the pope, residing, significantly enough, in the old imperial capital, and wielding, if not power, then more than a little influence.

The Kamakura shogunate added new structures to the old state forms rather than replacing them, developing in the warrior (*bushi*) class a consciousness of its own importance and its right to a significant share of the agricultural surplus. I cannot here give the Kamakura regime the attention it deserves but can only comment on two significant moments that occurred during it. One of these was its successful defense of Japan against the attempted Mongol invasions of 1274 and 1281, successful in considerable part due to typhoons that destroyed the enemy ships, but nonetheless mobilizing the country in its own defense and thus contributing to its sense of common identity. The other is the emergence during the thirteenth century of the founders of several new Buddhist movements that would dominate popular Buddhism ever after.[34] These new forms of Buddhism both recovered the radical "logic of negation," to use Ienaga's term, of original Buddhism and opened the door to new ways in which world denial could be collapsed into world affirmation.[35] The most significant thing about the "new" forms of Buddhism was their emphasis on exclusive practices such as reciting the name of Amida Buddha or the title of the Lotus Sutra or "just sitting" in Zen meditation.[36] These exclusive practices in some cases broke through the Esoteric/Exoteric system characteristic of earlier forms of Japanese Buddhism, though the capacity of the older forms to reappear even in the "new" sects should not be underestimated.

The whole subject of Kamakura Buddhism has been revolutionized since the following Chapter 1 was written.[37] The new work particularly stresses that "old Buddhism," that is the Nara and Heian schools, continued to be vital and productive, participating in their own way in the new trends of the Kamakura period, and that the movements we think of as "new" were responding in complex ways to long-standing tendencies and problems in the older traditions. The use of the term "reformation," particularly if it carries Protestant Christian overtones, has been strongly criticized. In Chapter 1 I use the term reformation in a generic sense, indicating that Kamakura Buddhism is in no significant way parallel to the Protestant Reformation. Japan's relative geographical isolation—the Tsushima Strait is much wider than the Straits of Dover—protected it from foreign conquest and may have contributed to the capacity of the archaic religious tradition to resist radical reformation. In any case the Japanese state was not shattered by foreign conquest and the moment of religious transcendental insight, though not without significant consequences, never resulted in radical reform.

The very extent to which the Japanese economy was growing in both the Kamakura and its successor Ashikaga shogunates contributed to the increasing centrifugal tendencies, as outlying feudal lords became strong enough to assert their independent power, and the jerry-rigged combination of primary and secondary state formations proved incapable of maintaining centralized control. By the early sixteenth century the country was more or less continuously at war, and the period is referred to, on the analogy with pre-Ch'in China, as the Period of the Warring States (*Sengoku Jidai*). The result of these incessant wars was the emergence of three successive unifiers at the end of the sixteenth century—Oda Nobunaga, Toyotomi Hideyoshi, and Tokugawa Ieyasu. In 1600 the third, Ieyasu, founded a military regime of unprecedented strength and stability, lasting unchallenged until the confrontation with the West in the mid-nineteenth century. It is worth considering for a moment the radical implications of Nobunaga's assault on the inherited institutional pattern.

Nobunaga used a term for the realm, *tenka* (literally, all under heaven), which had been used by the Ashikaga shoguns, but he gave it a radical twist. In Chinese terms, the *tenka* included ruler and people and legitimated the ruler by the at least tacit acceptance of the people. Nobunaga identified the *tenka* with his own person and with his sheer military power, taking as his motto *tenka fubu*, which Neil McMullin translates as "Rule the Realm by Force."[38] Not only did Nobunaga eliminate the last of the Ashikaga shoguns, but it was not clear by the time of his early death whether he might not have eliminated the imperial court as well. Unlike his two successors, he based his legitimacy on himself, not on some assumed delegation from above. Although he did not live to make clear the ultimate shape he would have given the polity, he did carry out one transformation of epic proportions: the destruction of the independent power of Buddhism. Even in the late sixteenth century when Sengoku daimyo had built up centers of regional power greater than ever before, some of the great shrine/temple complexes could still rival them. In addition, the followers of the Honganji school of Jōdo Shinshū had created a new form of military power, founded more on the alliance (*ikki*) of independent farmers and local samurai than on the landed estates of the temple complexes. In any case, when Nobunaga set out to unify the country he faced three great opponents, the other daimyo, the shrine/temple complexes, and the Honganji federations. The fact that two of these were Buddhist organizations indicates how powerful Buddhism still was. While Nobunaga succeeded in reducing most of the daimyo, he utterly destroyed his Buddhist opponents. His military success against them was by far not the only reason for the subsequent decline of Buddhism from its formerly central influence on Japanese culture, but it was a significant factor in that decline.[39] In any case after Nobunaga burned the great temple complex on Mt. Hiei and slaughtered all its inhabitants it was clear that the era of "kingly law and Buddhist law" was over. Whatever *tenka* was and whatever form it would take in Nobunaga's successors it was something very different from what had existed before. As one court noble lamented after the destruction of Mt. Hiei, "the bird has lost a wing, the cart a wheel."[40]

According to Herman Ooms in his book *Tokugawa Ideology*, all three unifiers sought religious legitimation independent of the imperial court, even though Hideyoshi and Ieyasu accepted court office.[41] Nobunaga and Hideyoshi each claimed divine status for himself, Nobunaga perhaps going the farthest, constructing a palace designed as a microcosm of the universe with himself at the pinnacle and with quarters for the emperor when he was to come to pay tribute to Nobunaga. Nobunaga's self-divinization was cut short by an early death, but Hideyoshi lived long enough to see his own cult flourishing throughout the country. Ieyasu was deified only after his death. There is nothing surprising in the divinization of human beings in an archaic culture—one has only to think of divinized heroes in ancient Greece or the divinization of rulers in the Hellenistic and Roman Empires. And the divinization of human beings has continued up to the twentieth century: remember the great shrine to the Meiji emperor in Tokyo, but also the shrine to the spirit of General Nogi, who, with his wife, committed ritual suicide on the day of the Meiji emperor's funeral in 1912. What is surprising is not so much the self-divinization of the great unifiers as the fact that they toyed with the idea of surpassing or at least rivaling the emperor.

It is a tribute to the mystique of the imperial line that it survived at all in the Period of Warring States, for its resources were extremely limited and it was treated with little respect by the rival warlords. Yet even the greatest of them hesitated to replace the imperial line. In thinking about the relation of culture and power it is worth remembering that sheer naked military power has probably never been exercised in Japan so directly as by the three great unifiers. Their military control was so absolute that it would have been no problem for them to abolish the imperial house. The survival of the imperial line in such a situation can only be seen as a triumph of powerless culture in the face of military power of doubtful cultural legitimacy.

An occasion that could have posed a severe threat to the imperial line is reported by Ooms on the basis of "soft" evidence, namely, that one of Ieyasu's closest advisors suggested in 1615 that the imperial family be confined to Ise, the shrine of the sun goddess, where it would perform only ritual duties, and Ieyasu would take the title of son of heaven, on an equal level with the emperor.[42] That Ieyasu, while severely limiting the prestige and influence of the imperial family, not only did not take that advice but apparently never considered simply extirpating the imperial line speaks volumes about the Japanese pattern.

Another kind of rival to the unification of Japan under warrior rule came from religious groups. It is well known that the unification of the country was accompanied by the persecution of Christian converts, a persecution that was begun by Hideyoshi and completed by the first three Tokugawa shoguns, ending with the brutal repression of the Shimabara rebellion of Christian peasants in Western Kyushu in 1637–38. It is less well known that Pure Land and Nichiren sects that had descended from the Kamakura period and had become well entrenched in several parts of the country were also persecuted by the unifiers. Nobunaga had been particularly brutal in putting down the Honganji federations, peasant groups organized on the basis of their fervent Pure Land belief and who refused to admit the legitimacy of any rulers other than the emperor or the leaders of their own sect. Some extreme followers of the teachings of Nichiren refused to accept the legitimacy of any rule other than that of the Buddha.[43] If Pure Land and Nichiren followers were suspect for nurturing a loyalty to authorities beyond this world, so especially were Christians, and though the Pure Land sects and (most of) the Nichiren sects could be brought to heel, Christianity had to be destroyed.[44] Archaic culture is remarkably tolerant of religious diversity except when its own basic premises are called in question. Axial religions can be tolerated so long as they downplay their radical implications, and especially when they can accommodate themselves to the archaic pattern, as Christians later would learn to do, but when they attempt to realize their axial principles or even seem to, particularly in the political sphere, persecution has been severe on more than one occasion.

## TOKUGAWA JAPAN

The Tokugawa shoguns completed what Nobunaga and Hideyoshi had begun: the pacification of the country, the confiscation of weapons from the peasantry, the carrying out of land surveys for purposes of taxation and other measures that guaranteed a degree of central control not evident in Japan since the seventh century. A two-level system of government was established with the center of the main island controlled by the Tokugawa house, its branch lineages or its direct vassals, and with the feudal lords who had submitted only after Ieyasu's final victory in 1600 confined to more distant parts of the country and required to keep their wives and children in Edo (modern-day Tokyo), the Tokugawa capital, and spend alternate years there themselves. The Tokugawa regime also outlawed firearms, which had begun to be used after the Europeans had taught the Japanese how to make them at the end of the sixteenth century, a ban unmatched elsewhere in the world.

The stability of the complex and not very intensive system of Tokugawa rule was due in part to internal pacification, which precluded internal challenges, and to the remoteness and isolation of the country. Japan's isolation has been, until recently, attributed to a policy of national seclusion (*sakoku*), which was believed to have been initiated by Tokugawa edicts in the 1630s restricting Japanese trade to the Dutch and the Chinese at the port of Nagasaki and prohibiting contact with all other foreigners. In fact, however, what the decrees did was to prohibit contact only with the Spanish and Portuguese, and that because of their connection with unwanted missionaries, not because of a desire to restrict trade. Bob Tadashi Wakabayashi has shown conclusively that Japan's isolation from foreign trade in the seventeenth century was due largely to the Dutch control of the seas in East Asian waters and their unwillingness to share Japanese trade with others, not with any actions of the Japanese. He shows that the first serious statement of a general policy of isolation (*sakoku*) came only in 1793 from the hand of Matsudaira Sadanobu, then the effective head of the Tokugawa government, and was not officially promulgated as Tokugawa policy until the Expulsion Edict of 1825.[45] In short, it was rising anxiety about foreign contact at the end of the eighteenth and early nineteenth centuries that led the Japanese to project back to the early years of the Tokugawa regime a previously nonexistent policy of exclusion, instead of realizing that Japan's relative isolation had come about de facto for reasons beyond Japan's control.

It is only worth dwelling on the lateness of the closed-country policy as official doctrine because it is one indication that the Tokugawa period was not stagnant as once assumed, but rather full of vital and creative initiatives in many fields. Peace and stability allowed for continuous economic growth in agriculture and trade, increasing urbanization, and the rise of literacy beyond the level then current in any Western country. The Japanese economy had reached an early modern level of mercantile capitalism comparable to the West before the Industrial Revolution, and through the export of silver and copper (largely to China) played a significant role in the world economy during the seventeenth and eighteenth centuries.[46] Although Japan rejected firearms (until toward the end of the Tokugawa period when self-defense became an issue), it did not reject other Western technological advances. Dutch studies (*Rangaku*) kept the Japanese abreast of developments in the West in science and medicine through the one Western language that was available to them.

How to think of the Tokugawa state in comparative terms has not been easy and has produced no general consensus. "Centralized feudalism," which approaches being a contradiction in terms, nonetheless makes a certain sense, although the government was not completely centralized and feudalism survived in only a very diluted sense: there were feudal lords (daimyo) who held fiefs, but most samurai were not landholders but office-holders. One of the other options sometimes suggested, "absolutism," does not apply to the Tokugawa state in any strong sense. Perhaps the most accurate way of characterizing the Tokugawa polity would be to call it, in Weberian terms, a somewhat decentralized patrimonial bureaucracy. Tokugawa rule was, on the whole, indirect; the shogunate issued instructions for just about every social unit in the country—family, temple, village, guild, feudal domain—but allowed a great deal of autonomy to them, including the responsibility of self-policing.[47] The "social capital" of modern Japan owes more than a little to this Tokugawa pattern of delegated authority, which allowed a great deal of initiative from below.

Given how advanced Japan was in many respects, behind the West in economic development, but certainly not far behind at the moment of the opening of the country, it might seem awkward to insist, as I do, that Japanese culture and society in the Tokugawa period can still be characterized as nonaxial, with a powerful archaic ground bass. The capacity to use the axial against the axial, while continuing to be strongly creative and innovative, is evident in the intellectual and religious life of the period. Again I would like to turn to Herman Ooms's remarkable book *Tokugawa Ideology* to clarify something central about the role of thought in Tokugawa political life. Ooms has shown that the idea that Ieyasu or any of the early Tokugawa shoguns established Neo-Confucianism, as taught by Fujiwara Seika and Hayashi Razan, as an official orthodoxy is simply false and has become the accepted view only because the self-aggrandizing retrospective account of the Hayashi school has been taken as fact. Actually there would not be anything like an official orthodoxy until Matsudaira Sadanobu's (1758–1829) Ban on Heterodoxy of 1790 (the same Matsudaira who first made the *sakoku* policy official).[48] What served to legitimate the new Tokugawa regime, and what was uppermost in the minds of the early shoguns and their closest advisors, was not ideas, but ritual.

Ooms describes a number of ways in which the early Tokugawa shoguns used ritual to give themselves legitimacy, but I will mention only one, the worship of the divinized spirit of Ieyasu at the newly created shrine complex at Nikko, a shrine given the same status as the great shrine of the sun goddess at Ise by imperial decree. The Nikko cult was not intended to appeal to the general populace, though in late Tokugawa times it did attract commoner worshipers. It was above all a political cult for the warrior class, that is, the feudal lords and house retainers of the Tokugawa. But the imperial family was required to send an annual mission to Nikko, while the Tokugawa family sent no comparable mission to Ise. Ooms argues that the intention was to establish a parallel triangle of Nikko, Edo, and the Tokugawa house to the triangle of Ise, Kyoto, and the imperial house. The imperial court was not eliminated, but it was isolated and ignored, while the glories of the shogunate were displayed in Edo and Nikko.[49] Ritual is one of the most basic elements in human culture and is absent in no society. But axial civilizations base themselves above all on the word, the written word, the book, even though they never abandon ritual entirely. That the early Tokugawa shoguns, in creating the structure of their symbolic legitimacy, were much more concerned with ritual than with any verbal orthodoxy is evidence that archaism survived even in the dynamic society that Japan was becoming.

Ooms describes in detail the first comprehensive effort to give a literate defense of the Tokugawa regime, beginning only in the late seventeenth century, that of Yamazaki Ansai (1618–82), with its combination of Neo-Confucianism and Shinto. Ooms believes that Ansai's elaborate system was prototypical of all subsequent Japanese nationalist ideologies, but he points out that Ansai was neither authorized nor encouraged by the political authorities to produce his synthesis, nor did it have any status as an official ideology.[50] Ansai, though he was thoroughly at home in Neo-Confucian texts as few of his contemporary scholars were, "erased," as Ooms puts it, that aspect of Confucianism that would justify replacing an immoral overlord, instead arguing that "rulers, whether virtuous or depraved, had to be served with blind loyalty."[51] The nonaxial presuppositions of the most articulate of early Tokugawa ideologists are thus evident.

Although it could not be said that there was a free market in ideas in the Tokugawa period—there were clear limits to what could be said, and some of them are discussed below in Chapter 5—the range of possibilities was still considerable, and Tokugawa interest in thought control minimal. A wide range of Confucian schools flourished, some of them intensely critical of the supposed Neo-Confucian orthodoxy. The Buddhist establishment, which had been the guardian of intellectual life in pre-Tokugawa times, and out of which all the early Tokugawa thinkers came, including Confucians and Shintoists, soon lost its monopoly on intellectual production and on the whole produced only mediocre thinkers through most of the period. Confucianism and Shinto, by contrast, produced original thinkers with widespread influence.

Perhaps the greatest Confucian scholar of the period, Ogyū Sorai (1666–1728), was anything but orthodox. Stimulated by contemporary Chinese philology, Sorai wanted to return to the original Confucian texts, of which he was a great master, and avoid what were to him the distortions of Neo-Confucianism. His position was historicist, as Tetsuo Najita has emphasized, and practical, taking the existing social order as his starting point and avoiding metaphysics on the one hand or institutions that had no current practical meaning, such as the imperial house, on the other.[52] He took as his model the human creation of social order by the ancient kings, as described in the early Confucian texts, but believed that rulers had to deal with the social reality that they found in existence and not attempt to recreate any preexisting ideal order. In so doing they were to nurture the potentialities of the people so that the variety of social types could realize themselves in a good social order. His iconoclasm and admiration for things Chinese earned him criticism ever after from those who thought like Yamazaki Ansai. He was singled out for attack in Sadanobu's Ban on Heterodoxy, and he was the only major Tokugawa scholar not to receive honors from the Japanese government after the Meiji Restoration, but during his own lifetime he was not bothered and even served as an advisor to the regime.[53] He was the focus of lifelong interest for Maruyama Masao.

Among the popular classes, Ishida Baigan, the founder of the Shingaku movement which I studied in *Tokugawa Religion,* was only one of many who were opening up new possibilities of social and cultural life in the midst of the Tokugawa period. Tetsuo Najita has studied the Kaitokudō Academy, a merchant school in Osaka, that carried on lively debates about all kinds of issues of the day.[54] More recently he has studied the Tekijuku, another Osaka academy, but this one devoted to Dutch studies (*Rangaku*), and has written about one of its leading figures, Ogata Kōan. What Najita found of interest was Kōan's self-confidence in the face of Western learning. His interest was in medicine, and in that field there was much new information to be studied and translations to be made. But on matters of hygiene, exercise, and diet, where the Japanese were already aware of what was necessary, he could ignore his Western sources. In short, Kōan studied Dutch books not in order to become Westernized or even to become modernized, but just because they contained useful information that was relevant in a vital and growing society.[55] Many other examples of creativity from middle and late Tokugawa times could be given. The great printmaker Hokusai lived a long and productive life. Perhaps his most productive period was in his eighties, when, under the sponsorship of a wealthy farmer, he moved to a mountain village in Nagano and painted some of his greatest works, calling himself "the mad old painter."[56]

What these examples illustrate is that in the midst of the period of the closed country (*sakoku*) there was a remarkable spirit of open country (*kaikoku*). What was important was not the source of the ideas—whether they came from India or China or the West—but how they could help in thinking through the problems of the day—scientific, economic, social, or spiritual. We might almost say that although figures such as I have been describing lived under the repressive and closed Tokugawa regime, they were surrounded by the spirit of *kaikokushugi* (openness).

In short, the Tokugawa government, while quite capable of exercising brutal force when it wanted to, relied more on an implicit public acceptance of the social order than on the enforcement of an official ideology. I am not arguing that the lower classes, particularly the peasants, were not oppressed in Tokugawa times. Barrington Moore, in a review of four important books on peasant revolts in the Tokugawa period, holds that "on the basis of the evidence in these books, the peasants under the Tokugawa shogunate appear as the most oppressed and exploited in any agrarian society known to me."[57] Nonetheless the degree and extent of violent rebellion was significantly less than in comparable agrarian societies. Part of the reason was localism: revolts in one area seldom spread to other regions. But a significant factor was the belief in the minds of the peasants that what they wanted was not to overthrow the regime, but to have it act on the principle of "benevolent rule" that it claimed to embody. Indeed, the Bakufu (the term used for the Tokugawa military government), while punishing rebel leaders with death, frequently also punished feudal lords or officials in whose jurisdiction rebellions had occurred, blaming them for the conditions leading to such violence.

Another indication of the unusual nature of Tokugawa rule is the fact that mass pilgrimages to Ise on several occasions during the Tokugawa period occurred with a minimum of social disruption. While in ordinary years some 300,000 to 400,000 pilgrims visited Ise, in the great periodic pilgrimage years called *okage-mairi* many times those numbers were involved. In 1705 as many as 3,620,000 individuals visited Ise, and in 1830 more than 5,000,000 people came. In most agrarian societies the movement of such large numbers of people would have led to serious social disorder and breakdown, yet no such disruption occurred in Japan. We can account for this in part because the government and the wealthier classes, instead of trying to prevent the pilgrimage, supplied aid to the pilgrims in varying degrees, and in part because the thoughts of the pilgrims were devoted either to the idea that worldly blessings would result from making the pilgrimage, or just to the enjoyment of a holiday from ordinary employment. Nonetheless Helen Hardacre notes of the Ise cult that "a connection between the deities enshrined there and the imperial court was generally known," so the Ise pilgrimage kept the existence of the imperial institution alive in popular consciousness.[58] In many respects the *ee-ja-nai-ka* and *yonaoshi* movements at the end of the Tokugawa period expressed more a hope for the fulfillment of the ethical ideals of the people rather than a desire for revolution.[59]

With this background in mind, I think we can understand why a movement such as Shingaku, founded by Ishida Baigan, which in *Tokugawa Religion* I compared to Protestantism in terms of its social function, was neither suppressed nor did it cause great social and ideological conflict. The Bakufu had developed a vigorous religious policy in the seventeenth century, one aimed at outlawing any religious group that explicitly or implicitly questioned Bakufu authority. This policy was aimed mainly at Christians but also at any Buddhist group that attempted to maintain independence of Bakufu authority. One of the Nichiren sects, the Fujufuse, which was particularly recalcitrant to Bakufu authority, was outlawed repeatedly in the seventeenth century, and after the suppression edict of 1663 it was vigorously rooted out.[60] But the suppression of religious groups beyond the pale did not mean that everyone had to accept a single orthodoxy, for the Bakufu favored no particular group, insisting only that people belong to one of the "normal" religious sects, that is, those that accepted Bakufu authority. Thus there was no equivalent to an established Catholic Church with doctrinal orthodoxy that movements such as Shingaku had to confront, and such new movements, though eliciting snide comments from older groups, led to no social conflict.

The decline of Buddhism as a creative force in the Tokugawa period has led some to describe it as a period of secularization. Such a description not only overlooks the religious dimension of the vigorous Confucian schools that were flourishing then but also fails to account for the resurgence of Shinto, especially in the form of Kokugaku, which has been translated literally as National Learning, or more loosely as Nativism. Kokugaku has been seen as an ideology supporting the Bakufu or as one covertly opposing it. I believe, however, that the Kokugaku thinkers, especially Hirata Atsutane and some of his students, were attempting to give a religious interpretation to the Japanese tradition that they were trying to recover. They were offering another version of what they took to be authentically Japanese: the idealized village. Kokugaku's appeal in late Tokugawa times to rich peasants in particular suggests their concern with recovering a communal ethic in a period when economic forces were disrupting the rural village. They were more concerned with the recovery of collective solidarity under the aegis of the Shinto gods than with matters of political authority, although at the end of the period they were drawn into the political disturbance leading to the Meiji Restoration.

Although the Tokugawa state was weak and decentralized, under its aegis something like a modern national consciousness was developing.[61] This was in part the result of the great development of education in the period and the accompanying growth of literacy.[62] The Shinto revival illustrated by the rise of Kokugaku propagated a religio-aesthetic idea of Japanese identity rather than a political one, but one with latent political implications. More obviously political was the kind of fusion of Confucianism and Shinto in the thought of Yamazaki Ansai, but which was more fully worked out toward the end of the period in the writings of the Mito school. The Mito domain was ruled by one of the major collateral houses of the Tokugawa family and the work of the school it sponsored was not conceived of as subversive but rather as supportive to the status quo. Nonetheless, the emphasis of the Mito school on a national polity (*kokutai*) at whose head was an imperial house that had ruled for ages eternal and that gave Japan its uniqueness and superiority to all other nations would in the last years of the shogunate lead to radical political consequences. Thus the openness of the Tokugawa thought world—no other non-Western society had as good a knowledge of the West as Japan in the eighteenth century, even including the Ottoman Empire which was right next door to Europe—was combined with an increasing particularism as Japan became more self-conscious of its difference from the rest of the world.[63]

We have already noted that the increasing unwanted contacts with the West due to the growth of world commerce in late Tokugawa times had caused alarm in high quarters and the formalization for the first time of a policy of *sakoku* (closed country). The defeat of China by the British in the Opium War of 1839–42 and the subsequent infringements on Chinese sovereignty were profoundly alarming to the Japanese as they indicated that the East Asian "world system," with China at its center, which the Japanese had taken for granted, however ambivalently, since the seventh century, was now at an end. Internal difficulties, including widespread peasant unrest, were not lacking in the last years of the Tokugawa regime, but it was the changing impingement of the world on Japan and the struggle over how to respond to it that sparked the regime crisis known as the end of the

Bakufu (*bakumatsu*), beginning with Perry's arrival in 1853 and ending with the Meiji Restoration of 1868. What occurred in this period was the loss of control by the Tokugawa center and the temporary breakup of Japan into its constituent feudal domains.

## THE REVOLUTIONARY RESTORATION

Explaining the Meiji Ishin (literally, Restoration) of 1868 has been a major industry for students of Japanese history at home and abroad. My interpretation is based on a wide, but not universal, consensus nicely summarized by Johann Arnason.[64] The breakdown of the Tokugawa regime in the Bakumatsu period (1853–68) led to a confrontation of three significant sets of actors: the Tokugawa house, including some of its branch lines, the Imperial Court in Kyoto, newly thrust on the scene due to the growing importance of the emperor in late Tokugawa thought, and several powerful "outside" domains whose lords had been defeated by Tokugawa Ieyasu in 1600, but which remained large and prosperous. Chief among the latter were the domains of Satsuma and Chōshū, both in the Southwest, far from Edo. These two domains had, in the Bakumatsu period, been taken over by reforming groups of middle samurai whose efforts to modernize, fiscally and militarily, proved more effective than similar efforts mounted by the Bakufu itself. Pledging allegiance to the emperor and defeating Tokugawa troops in the field, the leaders of these two domains entered Edo, which they renamed Tokyo (the eastern capital), establishing the emperor in the old Tokugawa castle and proclaiming the restoration of central rule under the imperial aegis.[65] What happened was that one group of samurai (from two outer domains, though including a few samurai from other domains and even a couple of court nobles) replaced another group (Tokugawa retainers) at the political center and proclaimed the restoration of an imperial rule that had never in any literal sense existed. This simple description has serious implications. Fundamentally, the restoration involved a shift in power between political actors within the old regime; it did not involve the mobilization of social classes, nor was it the result of popular protest. In the classical Western sense, modeled on the French Revolution, it was not a revolution. Its consequences were, however, revolutionary, more so than many revolutions that more closely conform to the classical model.[66]

In order to escape our temptation to think about revolution primarily with the example of the French Revolution in mind, let us turn to recent efforts to theorize revolutions in a comparative perspective to get a better sense of the extent to which the Meiji Ishin can be considered a revolution.

Randall Collins summarizes recent research in finding three factors that result in the state breakdown now considered to be the precondition for revolution: "(1) state fiscal strain, (2) intra-elite conflict that paralyzes the government, and (3) popular revolt."[67] State fiscal strain had characterized the Tokugawa Bakufu for decades, though it was undoubtedly worsening in the Bakumatsu period. Intraelite conflict was clearly central to the weakening of Tokugawa control. Popular revolt is much more problematic: peasant uprisings were endemic during the Tokugawa period and increased in its final years; there were significant outbreaks of urban disturbances, as well as mass phenomena that suggested signs of widespread unease; yet none of these directly threatened Tokugawa rule, nor were they a major cause of state breakdown. A highly significant causal element in Japan, which Collins notes but recognizes that it lies outside the comparative model, was the real and perceived threat of Western power. It was the slow and inefficient response of the Tokugawa Bakufu to this threat, caused by its decentralized and cumbersome administrative system and its inability to marshal material resources, that opened the door to the intraelite conflict, which eventuated in its fall. It is the lack of a popular revolt, or significant popular participation in the overthrow of the Bakufu, that has led to the notion that the Meiji Ishin was a "revolution from above" and therefore perhaps not radical in its consequences. But if we turn to Collins's definition of a revolution in terms of its results rather than its causes we will see just how revolutionary the Ishin in fact was: "wholesale transformation of the ruling elite accompanied by political and economic restructuring."[68]

With a couple of intermediary steps along the way, in 1871, only three years after the Restoration, the feudal domains were abolished and replaced by prefectures that, like those in postrevolutionary France, did not follow the boundaries of preexisting feudal domains. Also in 1871 the ban on intermarriage between samurai and commoners was lifted, the beginning of several steps that would lead to the abolition of all the old Tokugawa class distinctions. Universal primary education was proclaimed in 1872 and universal conscription in 1873. Thus a centuries-old feudal system was quickly dismantled with only a modicum of opposition, the most serious of which was a rebellion of disgruntled former samurai in Satsuma in 1877.

The remarkable degree of acceptance of the new regime, undoubtedly linked to its legitimation by a restored emperor, and the self-confidence of its leadership are indicated by the absence of most of the top leaders for nearly two years in a round-the-world mission to visit the major countries of the world, particularly the United States and Europe, from 1871 to 1873. Referred to as the Iwakura Embassy because it was headed by the court noble Iwakura Tomomi, the mission was well balanced in its contingents from Satsuma and Chōshū. What the group learned from the West was quickly put to good use on its return as the Meiji leadership embarked on a rapid process of state-building and economic development. But the most significant steps in dismantling the feudal regime were undertaken before the return of the embassy from abroad. The model was surely drawn in major part from the West, but it should be pointed out that educated Japanese long knew of the Chinese model of a centralized empire with no hereditary distinctions in status. There was a not insignificant sense in which the Meiji leadership completed the primary Japanese state-building program of the seventh and eighth centuries, just as it began the new process of creating a modern nation-state. At last a centralized state would be ruled by a bureaucracy based on merit and not on hereditary lineage, even if the examinations that were to determine that merit were based on modern civil service examinations, not the examination system of imperial China. Nonetheless the Meiji state, though primarily modeled on the modern West, had a whiff of T'ang China about it, not least in the imperial ambitions that accompanied it almost from the very beginning.

Thus the military regime came to an end. Or did it? The Tokugawa system was certainly destroyed, but was the regime of military rule that began with the Kamakura shogunate really at an end? Or was the "secondary state" that began then able to reinvent itself in only somewhat attenuated form? When we say "they" destroyed the Tokugawa system, who do we mean by "they"? We mean a remarkably enterprising group of middle-level samurai drawn largely from Satsuma and Chōshū who would monopolize control of the Japanese government for decades to come. Could we not say that what had happened is that two major domains who were on the losing side in 1600 finally managed to oust the Tokugawa house and take control themselves? After all it was the combined forces of Satsuma and Chōshū who won the final battle against the Bakufu. To the victor belongs the spoils. Of course not literally, for the domains of Satsuma and Chōshū were abolished as totally as was the Tokugawa regime, and the feudal lords of those domains were no more in evidence than was the ex-shogun. But what came to be known as the Meiji oligarchs, or, in Japanese, the *genrō*, not only drew quite significantly from their roots in the victorious domains but also on new forms of institutionalization that developed in the Meiji period. Chōshū men dominated the army leadership and Satsuma men dominated the navy leadership. Not only did Chōshū and Satsuma leaders provide all but two of the prime ministers for thirty years after the beginning of the cabinet system in 1885, but they included the Chōshū general Yamagata

Aritomo, the most powerful of the *genrō* over the long run, and the Satsuma admiral Yamamoto Gonnohyōe.[69] In the Meiji Constitution, promulgated in 1890, the army and navy were to report directly to the emperor, on the model of the German constitution, and not to the prime minister or the cabinet. Independent access to the emperor and the sanction of imperial approval, however obtained, gave the Japanese military a capacity to influence government decisions that would prove catastrophic in the 1930s. In an important sense "military rule" did not end in 1868 but only in 1945.[70]

Yet, to the extent that modern institutions based on Western models were massively introduced in the Meiji period—from a modern state bureaucracy, to a modern university system, to modern mass media—can we at last say that axial principles were institutionalized in Japan and that we can no longer refer to it as a nonaxial society? Even our suggestion that the T'ang model had finally been fully implemented would suggest as much. To the extent that axial cultures are based on universalistic principles we can say that in the Meiji period Japan incorporated significant elements of axial culture. But so had it done since the seventh century. The question is, were the basic value premises of Japanese society revolutionized along with so many of its institutions? I will argue, somewhat hesitantly, that nonaxial premises survived, though reformulated and in a complex mixture with axial principles, but with the nonaxial premises still retaining primacy.

First of all, it is important to emphasize just how significantly universalistic principles were institutionalized in modern Japan, beginning in the Meiji period. Universal education and universal conscription were clear indications that the hereditary status system had been abolished. Universalistic criteria of merit became the basis for employment in both public and private organizations of any size. A legal system and an impartial judiciary are primary indications that universalistic criteria had great importance. Religious toleration was promulgated and a small but influential number of Japanese became Christians and asserted the importance of universalistic religious principles. Free publication of newspapers, magazines, and books, with only sporadic censorship, made universalistic philosophical and political principles available to a large literate public. In all these spheres, even in the legal system, we will have to make important qualifications, but the axial principles and institutions that had been present to some degree since the seventh century were enormously enlarged in the Meiji and subsequent periods in modern Japan. How then can we argue that the Meiji Restoration/Revolution, though it led to the creation of a radically new society, still led to one that remained nonaxial in its fundamental premises?

Any form of nationalism that makes the primordial identities of blood and soil its basis will conflict with axial premises. This is obvious in the extreme case of Nazi Germany where all universalistic principles of religion, philosophy, and politics were subordinated to the notion of German racial superiority, but more moderate forms of nationalism also create tensions with universalistic principles. Nationalism in the sense of an effort to create a common consciousness of national identity among all members of Japanese society had already appeared in late Tokugawa times and was a major aspect of state building in the Meiji period. Nationalism is a significant phase in the development of all modern nations, though possibly a transient one, but each such nation differs in the nature of the primordial identities upon which it draws and the degree to which such identities will conflict with axial principles. It is the self-understanding of the Japanese nation and the particular conception of the relation between nation and people that will help us see why axial principles were subordinated to nonaxial ones even in modern Japan.

The Charter Oath of the Meiji Emperor, issued in April 1868, is generally taken to express the progressive side of the new regime. Article One of the oath promised "deliberative assemblies" and that "all matters [will be] decided by public discussion." Article Five said that "knowledge shall be sought throughout the world so as to strengthen the foundations of imperial rule." Article Two, in its inclusiveness, can also be seen as progressive: "All classes, high and low, shall unite in vigorously carrying out the administration of affairs of state."[71] This can be interpreted as an indication of the leveling of social status, of the fact that samurai were now reduced to the status of commoners. Yet this article, and even more clearly later defining statements of the new regime, implied not that samurai had been reduced to the status of commoners but that commoners had been raised to the status of samurai. Already in the Bakumatsu period the Chōshū domain had used commoner troops alongside samurai. Universal conscription meant that the loyalty once expected of samurai, as expressed in the samurai code of *bushidō*, was now expected of all Japanese in the military service. The Imperial Rescript to Soldiers and Sailors of 1882, issued in the name of the emperor but expressing the sentiments of General Yamagata, said, "Soldiers and Sailors, We are your supreme Commander-in-Chief. Our relations with you will be most intimate when We rely upon you as Our limbs and you look up to Us as your head. Whether We are able to guard the Empire, and so prove Ourself worthy of Heaven's blessings and repay the benevolence of Our Ancestors, depends upon the faithful discharge of your duties as soldiers and sailors."[72] Although military service had a central symbolic meaning in the definition of the obligations of subjects to ruler, the Meiji leaders sought to define all Japanese as "loyal followers" of the emperor. The Imperial Rescript on Education issued in 1890, the year the Meiji Constitution came into effect, was read in a solemn ritual in every school in Japan until 1945. It called on "Our subjects . . . should emergency arise, [to] offer yourselves courageously to the State; and thus guard and maintain the prosperity of Our Imperial Throne coeval with heaven and earth."[73]

The process of generalizing the role of the samurai to all Japanese was already well underway in the Tokugawa period. In the eighteenth century Ishida Baigan had argued:

> The samurai, farmers, artisans and merchants are of assistance in governing the empire. . . . The governing of the four classes is the role of the ruler. Assisting the ruler is the role of the four classes. The samurai is the retainer (*shin* [vassal or follower in a lord-follower relationship]) who has rank from of old. The farmer is the retainer of the countryside. The merchant and artisan are the retainers of the town. To assist the ruler, as retainers, is the Way of the retainer.[74]

Although Baigan did not foresee the abolition of the class system, he was concerned to give the nonsamurai classes the dignity and value of samurai in offering service to the ruler. His sentiments were far from unique among spokesmen for the commoner classes in the Tokugawa period.

This line of thinking did not lead to the idea of citizens who rule and are ruled in turn, who elect representatives to govern them and hold them responsible. There were such ideas in Meiji Japan and they attained a wide hearing, but it was precisely the intention of the oligarchs to head off the effective institutionalization of such ideas and to make sure that the Japanese saw themselves as subjects—responsible, active, subjects serving the state, to be sure—but not sovereign citizens in whose hands decisions of state ultimately lie. Here we find the Meiji version of Maruyama's *basso ostinato*: the pattern of thinking of government always from the point of view of those serving from below rather than from the point of view of those ruling from above. In this pattern, since everyone was responsible, no one was, least of all the emperor, who lived "above the clouds" and whose mind was not to be disturbed by those who served him. It was the purpose of the oligarchs in designing the Meiji state to see that those who served best, namely, themselves and those like them, would have the real power, accountable only to the emperor. In this conception there was a fusion of people and state: society was not something different from government, which could hold it accountable. As a result the state encompassed society, but also the other way around, so that the source of initiative and responsibility was never clear. At moments this pattern could produce paralysis, but it could also be dynamic and creative when able people from below took the lead in "serving." By contrast, in a system where no one was ultimately responsible, destructive initiatives by effective leaders could prove extremely difficult to stop, a defect not unique to the Japanese political system.

## EMPEROR AND CONSTITUTION

If state and society were fused in a way not possible in axial civilizations, there was another fusion that was even more indicative of the nonaxial premises of Japanese society: the fusion of deity and ruler, the divine king, the emperor as a living *kami* (Shinto god). Such ideas lie deep in Japanese history, but they were resuscitated and reformulated in quite striking and highly self-conscious ways in the Meiji period. The idea of "inventing tradition" has been applied to Japan. If this is taken to mean the invention of tradition out of whole cloth then it is surely mistaken. If it is taken to mean the radical reformulation of elements of tradition to meet new needs it surely applies to the so-called Meiji emperor system.[75]

Itō Hirobumi, probably the most influential of all the oligarchs with the possible exception of Yamagata, was primarily responsible for drafting the Meiji Constitution. Itō was conscious of the fact that religion provided a firm foundation for civic responsibility in Western nations, but he believed that no comparable religion existed in Japan. It was thus that he turned to the emperor as the foundation of the new regime:

> In Japan the power of religion is slight, and there is none that could serve as the axis [alternatively pivot, foundation, or cornerstone] of the state. Buddhism, when it flourished, was able to unite people of all classes, but it is today in a state of decline. Shinto, though it is based on and perpetuates the teachings of our ancestors, as a religion lacks the power to move the hearts of men. In Japan, it is only the imperial house that can become the axis of the state. It is with this point in mind that we have placed so high a value on imperial authority and endeavored to restrict it as little as possible.[76]

Although the whole idea of a constitution as the basis of a modern nation-state was drawn from Western prototypes, and most of the articles in the Meiji Constitution resemble some Western model or other, the Prussian Constitution of 1850 being the most influential, it was still essential to guard against the idea that the constitution made the people sovereign, or even the idea that it implied, in Itō's words, "the joint rule of the king and the people."[77] The constitution was given by the emperor to the people and the day chosen for its promulgation, February 11, 1889, was the anniversary of the supposed ascension to rule of the Emperor Jimmu, the sun goddess's grandson, in 660 B.C. February 11, *kigensetsu* or National Foundation Day, had already become a national holiday in 1873. The glamour of the ritual occasion, which probably for most Japanese overwhelmed the content of the document, should not let us forget that, in spite of all its limitations, it did create a parliament with the all-important power of controlling the budget. Grudgingly or not, the oligarchs had granted to the people a significant right to participate in their own government. But what they gave with one hand they did their best to take back with the other.

The primary way in which they limited the effectiveness of parliamentary rule was to reserve significant powers to the emperor, to whom they had access and who they could always get to issue a special rescript when parliament resisted their wishes. We will need to consider further the extraordinary measures they took to elevate the emperor to the center of national consciousness. But also significant in limiting parliamentary power was the effort of the oligarchs to discredit, even before the constitution was put into effect, the politicians who would be elected to the new parliament. Agitation for the fulfillment of the Charter Oath's promise of "deliberative assemblies" had already appeared in the 1870s, largely coming from disaffected former samurai, but gradually drawing on broader popular support. This agitation grew into a significant movement in the early 1880s under the banner of Freedom and People's Rights (*jiyu minken*). In response to the growing opposition to the arbitrary rule of the Chōshū -Satsuma oligarchs (the *hanbatsu*, or domain faction) the promise of a constitution by 1890 was forthcoming from the leadership in 1881. But the oligarchs lashed back at their critics by denouncing those who used politics to pursue their own selfish interests. Although the opposition idealized the noble statesman who pursued the good of the people, the example of the members of local assemblies elected in the 1880s was not inspiring. They were described in the popular press as "self-seeking, toadying, and corrupt," and if future Diet members were to resemble them they would not be worthy of respect. The oligarchs could speak in the name of "his Majesty the emperor's government," but politicians were often viewed as merely selfish. The very notion of genuine leaders as those who "serve" rather than as those who "represent" was inimical to respect for politicians. Thus it was not only the calculated scorn of the oligarchs but also popular opinion orchestrated by the press that made the role of politicians difficult. Politicians as such are often suspect in modern societies, but the particularly dark cloud that hung over them in Meiji Japan has not dissipated to the present day. It was the military who exemplified "service," or even the bureaucrats who did so in lesser degree, who had prestige, rather than those who were seen to represent mere partisan interest.[78]

From the very beginning of the Meiji period the new leaders ostentatiously used the emperor to justify the new regime. The "imperial progress" of the emperor from Kyoto to Tokyo in 1868 was unprecedented, since the emperor had not left Kyoto and its environs for centuries. This was only the beginning of many such imperial tours during the first two decades of the period. For many Japanese, more accustomed to think in terms of their own local village or district than of "Japan," this was a powerful symbolic assertion of a larger identity.[79] During these same years the government, carrying out the ideas of a Shinto revival that had long been circulating in the Tokugawa period, began the process of separating Shinto shrines from the Buddhist temples with which they had long been associated, of refurbishing shrines that had suffered neglect, and, above all, of tying Shinto worship directly into national consciousness with the emperor at its center.

It is, however, no accident that the Meiji leadership undertook a new and even more dramatic effort to emphasize the centrality of the emperor in the years leading up to the promulgation of the new constitution. The city of Tokyo as an urban environment and even the living quarters of the emperor had been neglected in the early Meiji years, but in the late 1880s major changes were undertaken. A grand imperial palace, combining Japanese and Western elements, was built in the precincts of the old Tokugawa castle in the center of the city, including an impressive throne room for ceremonial occasions. The plaza in front of the palace was cleared so that large crowds could assemble for major events. The first great ceremony in which all these elements came together was the promulgation of the constitution in 1889. The earlier imperial tours, though novel as such, had used traditional palanquins for transporting the emperor, who remained secluded behind curtains, so that it was his aura rather than his person that was on display. The new ceremonial pattern, inaugurated by the promulgation of the constitution, was directly influenced by the patterns of national celebration that had been created or re-created as part of the state-building process in Europe. Thus for the first time the emperor and empress left the palace grounds in a European-style carriage with clear windows so that the crowd could view them directly.[80] Transportation and communication had advanced to the degree that all Japanese could participate almost simultaneously in the events occurring in the center.

The success of what can only be called the imperial cult was not spontaneous but highly orchestrated, even if the Japanese public seems to have taken to it willingly. Educational and military institutions provided ready resources for mobilization. Thousands of schoolchildren, many of them coming from far away, could be assembled in the imperial plaza for great occasions, and soldiers and sailors could be assembled for impressive military reviews. Although the regime did not neglect verbal articulation, as the several key imperial rescripts and the preamble to the constitution as well as the nationalistic textbooks in the schools indicate, still, just as in the early days of the Tokugawa shogunate, it would seem that ritual had priority over texts in implementing the new vision. And what the ritual affirmed, at the very moment when the people were being given some capacity to participate in their own government, was the fusion of divinity, government, and people, with the emperor symbolizing all three.

Perhaps nowhere was the combination of a strong assertion of that fusion with some acceptance of Western standards of the rights of citizens to be found more clearly than in the policy toward religion as it developed in the 1890s. The Restoration of 1868 had been accompanied by a utopian effort to make Shinto the sole religion of the nation, an effort that involved the persecution of Buddhism and the reaffirmation of the ban on Christianity. This effort was quickly abandoned as intensely unpopular both at home and abroad, but central control of major Shinto shrines and their reorientation toward a focus on the emperor continued. The Meiji Constitution guaranteed the freedom of religion, as all modern constitutions should, but in somewhat equivocal form. According to Article 28, "Japanese subjects shall, within limits not prejudicial to peace and order, and not antagonistic to their duties as subjects, enjoy freedom of religious belief."[81] Interpreters of this article were quick to point out that it was not contradicted by state support for Shinto shrines because "Shinto is not a religion," but rather an expression of patriotic devotion. While this defense was in a sense specious—shrines did carry out functions such as weddings and funerals that would normally be called religious—in another sense it was justified. The word "religion" in Japanese, shūkyō, is a translation of the Western term dating only to the Meiji period. To this day the term "religion" smells of Christianity, or perhaps of Buddhism as well—that is, of religions based on personal and private "belief." Shinto, being an archaic religion, had little in the way of belief—often those worshipping at a shrine had no idea who the deity was, nor did it matter—but largely involved ritual practice as an expression of group belonging. Where religion is fused with people and state the Western category does not work very well. Christianity and Buddhism are religions that are in principle *differentiated* from the state—they involve membership in specifically religious communities—even though not always *separated* from the state. Shinto is in principle not capable even of differentiation, for it has no basis of membership different from the social groups—nation, village, family—in which it is embedded.[82]

As in other modern nation-states, but with its own special twist, the assertion of national identity was directed outward as well as inward. An emperor implies an empire, and modern Japan came of age in the era of high imperialism. Rapid state building was not only defensive, though it was surely that in an age of predatory Western imperialism; it sought not only to resist but also to rival the other empires. It is remarkable how early the urge for overseas expansion appeared, almost from the beginning of the new regime and before major Western influence. The knowledge that China was no longer effectively the "central country" left a vacuum that at least some samurai imaginations found it easy to fill. Indeed the oligarchs had to restrain the zealots from foreign aggression in the early years in order not to precipitate Western intervention to which they could not yet effectively respond. The idea that Japan could become the center of a galactic polity in East Asia, deriving from archaic roots as well as modern stimulus, began to be realized as a result of the acquisitions that followed the war with China in 1894–95 and with Russia in 1904–05. The thought that all Japanese were now the equivalent of samurai and the projection of Japanese power abroad gave the Meiji emperor system a military cast symbolized by the fact that, as Takashi Fujitani puts it, the emperor came down from above the clouds to appear as a human being, one clothed in modern military uniform and riding on a white horse, an appearance, however, that only strengthened his symbolic centrality.[83]

If nonaxial symbolism, the fusion of divinity, state, and society, was characteristic of the most general level of Meiji self-understanding, in spite of the prominence of universalistic criteria in many intermediate institutions, it must also be pointed out that particularism flourished at the base and in the pores of those very institutions as well. The civil code of 1898 enshrined a samurai-like patriarchal conception of the family and injunctions to embody filial piety regularly accompanied injunctions to be loyal to the emperor. Quasi-familial patterns and "small emperor systems" emerged in many sectors of Japanese life, not least in the bureaucracies and schools that were the main carriers of universalistic criteria. The idea of a "family state" was not focused only on the nation as a whole, but permeated all its constituent bodies.

Although relative freedom of publication made it possible to disseminate universalistic conceptions in religion, philosophy, and politics, many who took advantage of this freedom did so to bolster the ideology of imperial

Japan rather than to question it. Official rhetoric was moderate compared to what some of the extreme proponents of Japanism were arguing. In its official form, emperor-system nationalism was usually coupled with support for "civilization" and "progress" as essential elements in the process whereby Japan was to take its rightful place among the nations, whereas extremists were tempted to oppose everything Western root and branch. In short, as in Tokugawa times, "orthodoxy" was less a set of dogmatic beliefs uniformly enforced than a general sense of what is "normal" in Japan. What was abnormal, direct attacks on the emperor system or support for sweeping foreign ideologies like socialism, was severely repressed. But within a vague notion of normality a great variety of ideas, often conflicting, could be found.[84]

## OPENING UP

Using the term resistance in any strong sense, or even the term opposition, when speaking of the Meiji state and society would limit one to rather small and marginal groups, because the Meiji consensus was, though not homogeneous, nevertheless pervasive. But by speaking of "opening up" we can consider not only open hostility to the regime, which was quite rare, but all those tendencies that called into question the fusion of divinity, state, society, and self in the pattern that I am calling "nonaxial." Thus any tendency to assert an ultimate principle higher than the emperor, any effort to affirm the independence of society from the state or the responsibility of the government to the people and not just to the emperor, and any tendency to affirm an autonomous individual self, would be signs of opening up even if involving nothing obviously radical or rebellious. It is a tribute to the relative openness of the Meiji system, whatever the intent of its designers, that criticism of its nonaxial premises could at least marginally be pursued

New religious movements such as those already beginning in late Tokugawa times and spreading during the Meiji period, insofar as they grew outside the bounds of state recognition, would be symptoms of opening up, even though some of the more successful of them, such as Tenrikyō, when they sought and received government recognition and thus willingly accepted a place in the fused totality, showed how easy it often was to reenter the fold. Such an example illustrates not only the readiness of groups to compromise with the state, but the flexibility of the state in not demanding too high a standard of conformity. Compromise and flexibility varied with changing circumstances, both internal and external, and were not constant in the Meiji period or later.

One primary example of opening up that verged on resistance was the effort to make the government accountable to the people. Such an effort was evident in the Movement for Freedom and People's Rights as well as in some party politicians, particularly in the 1920s, but could also be expressed viscerally as in the rice riots of 1918 when economic slowdown combined with rapidly rising food prices led to violent popular protest.

This last example leads naturally to a consideration of the economic sphere as a possible locus for several kinds of opening up. Whereas late Tokugawa Japan was already capitalist in the sense that it had a well-developed market economy, and the Meiji period saw a continuous development of an increasingly industrial market economy, a radical bourgeoisie demanding a share of power in its own name can hardly be located. Merchants and later large-scale capitalists wielded significant influence in both Tokugawa and Meiji Japan, yet I would argue that the dominant value system gave them little legitimacy as independent claimants to power. The oligarchs in the early Meiji years sought to establish Western-style industries under state-sponsorship but, finding that inefficient, turned them over to private ownership by the 1880s. Nonetheless an ethos of service pervaded the economic sphere as it was supposed to do throughout the society. If one manufactured toothpicks it was "for the sake of the emperor," hardly the basis of a self-respecting claim to independence on the part of the capitalist class. Nonetheless the activities of a leading capitalist such as Shibusawa Eiichi, who got his start under the patronage of the oligarchs, displayed significant initiative, such as founding a leading private university.

If the capitalist class showed little independent action beyond defending its own interests, industrial workers and peasant farmers engaged fitfully in significantly more rebellious actions in the face of a watchful Home Ministry that discouraged genuinely independent worker or peasant organization. While unrest and occasional violence as in the case of the rice riots appeared among workers and tenant farmers who bore the brunt of the "uneven development" that characterized Japan before World War II, the chief critics of the economic organization of Japanese society were intellectuals attracted to Marxism as an explanation of Japan's troubles.

But just as significant as the efforts to open up initiated by sectors outside the government, and in some respects even more interesting, was the opening up going on from within the center of the established order itself. Here a prime example is surely the so-called organ theory of Minobe Tatsukichi, a professor in the law faculty of Tokyo Imperial University, the most prestigious locus for the training of high government officials. Minobe, taking the Meiji Constitution at face value rather than as an expression of a mystical "national body" (*kokutai*), argued that the emperor was one "organ" among several established in the constitution, each of which had its autonomous sphere of action. He regarded the establishment of the Diet as the key accomplishment of the constitutional system and saw no reason why its powers should not be significantly broadened. In 1924 he wrote about the "trend of the times" away from feudal subjection and toward individual liberty: "It can be said that the most important ethical imperative of modern constitutional government is that each individual be respected for himself, and that each be permitted as far as possible to give expression to his capacities. The history of modern cultural development is the history of the liberation of the individual."[85] Minobe's theory was widely though not universally taught; it came close to being the established view and the emperor had no objection to it. Although Minobe's views were taken up appreciatively by liberal politicians such as Yoshino Sakuzō, Minobe himself was, as a professor at the Tokyo Imperial University, a state official.

Another law professor at Tokyo Imperial University who shared many of Minobe's views was Nanbara Shigeru, to whom Andrew Barshay has devoted a significant study.[86] Before his call to the university Nanbara had served in the Home Ministry as a reforming district official, trying to root democracy at the village level, and later, in 1919, as the architect of a proposed labor union law that would have legitimated a moderate autonomous labor movement. It is significant that the draft gained the approval of a series of officials including the home minister himself, only to be rejected by the prime minister. Nanbara was a Christian, a follower of Uchimura Kanzō's nonchurch Christianity, and as such, a representative figure, since Christians played a role out of all proportion to their numbers in the cause of social reform in the period before World War II. Sheldon Garon has noted the reliance of the Home Ministry on Christians as "conduits for information on the latest Western programs in the areas of social work, education, and moral uplift."[87] Garon argues that, though the Japanese state and particularly the Home Ministry was more closely involved in organizing "everyday life" than would be normal in the West, many of its interventions were sparked by initiatives from below, not infrequently by Christian but also by Buddhist reformers. The role of the Home Ministry was far from wholly benign, especially after the passage of the Peace Preservation Law of 1925, which accompanied the passage of universal suffrage, because the Peace Preservation Law, enforced by the Home Ministry, suppressed open dissent and created the basis for the thought control that would become even more complete in the 1930s. But at least before the late 1920s, even the Home Ministry provided some space for "opening up," and if "the trend of the times" had not sharply shifted with the Great Depression and the rise of fascism in the West, one can imagine a very different course that prewar Japanese society might have taken.

Among the many symptoms of opening up that could be noted in the early twentieth century is a matter much discussed at the time: individualism. Lacking a tradition of philosophical liberalism, Japanese intellectuals in the Meiji period found the Western ideas of freedom and individualism attractive, frightening, and difficult to understand. The commonest misinterpretation was to see them as invitations to license and self-indulgence, and as such dangerous to the nation. Individualism was the central preoccupation of the greatest early-twentieth-century writer, Natsume Soseki. His novels often focus on the anguish of trying to live a life of individual integrity in a society that does little to support it. Because his heroes are often deeply unhappy he is sometimes considered a critic of individualism, although it has been pointed out that he never opted for the kind of resolution common among other writers: "a passive acceptance of the world or holding out the possibility of a saving union with nature."[88] Soseki spells out his position clearly in his most famous piece of nonfiction, "My Individualism," first delivered as a lecture in 1914. Aware of the frequent misunderstanding of his subject, he speaks of "ethical individualism," and defines it as follows:

> Everything I have said thus far comes down to these three points. First, that if you want to carry out the development of your individuality, you must respect the individuality of others. Second, that if you intend to utilize the power in your possession, you must be fully cognizant of the duty that accompanies it. Third, that if you wish to demonstrate your financial power, you must respect its concomitant responsibilities.[89]

He insists that individualism is not incompatible with a realistic nationalism. If the nation is in danger then all sensible people will give it high priority. But when there is no such danger, then individualism has the higher priority and an obsessive concern with the nation, such as advocated by some proponents of Japanism, is simply ridiculous: "But what a horror if we had to . . . eat for the nation, wash our faces for the nation, go to the toilet for the nation!"[90]

Soseki's individualism was stimulated, as he admits, by English literature and English life, even though he really did not like England (he spent two very unhappy years in London as a student of literature). What he absorbed, however, was a standard independent of the nation in terms of which the individual could decide what priority to give to the nation, a clear example of "opening up," of freeing the individual person from embeddedness in society and state. For many it took a religious standard to justify such independence, as in the example of Uchimura Kanzō. Christians less stalwart than Uchimura, and individualists less stubborn than Soseki would, when collective pressures mounted, as they would in the second quarter of the twentieth century, find it difficult to withstand the pressures for reengulfment in society. But had those pressures never developed, the shoots of ethical individualism evident in the early years of the century might have grown sturdier with time.

## JAPANESE FASCISM

Many students of Japanese history have questioned whether one can use the term "fascism" for Japan in the period 1931–45. Others have held that the Meiji emperor system was itself intrinsically fascist. Properly defined, one can use the term fascism in Japan, but Japanese fascism was neither identical to the Meiji emperor system nor a necessary outgrowth of it, even though the relationship was a close one. Japanese fascism, far from being an inevitable outcome of an earlier period that, after all, showed many signs of liberalization and opening up, required severe outside pressures to bring it about, as I have suggested above in mentioning the world depression beginning in the late 1920s and the rise of fascism in the West. Not least among these pressures was the racism so pervasive in the West and the feeling that no matter how much the Japanese proved their successful modernity they would never be fully admitted to the Western club. The United States, unfortunately, greatly reinforced this view with the passage of the Immigration Act of 1924, which excluded immigration from Japan altogether and reaffirmed the fact that Japanese could not become U.S. citizens, creating widespread indignation in Japan. The rise of anti-imperialist sentiment among the colonial or semicolonial nations of Asia after World War I contributed to the rise of anti-Western feelings among Japanese even of progressive inclination.

With these sentiments as a background, the onset of the Great Depression led to a sense of crisis in Japan and a need to find a new solution if the nation was not to be overwhelmed. Of course the depression was a severe challenge to every nation at the time and only a few became fascist. In order to understand why Japan was attracted to fascism we need to consider more closely what fascism is. Fascism is notoriously difficult to define but almost everyone agrees that it is an exaggerated form of nationalism, or ultranationalism, as Maruyama Masao described it. An important element in modern nationalism cross-culturally is that the nation claimed a kind of sovereignty that in the West was previously reserved for God. Ritual expressions of nationalism were not unique to Japan, and everywhere they came close to claiming the highest loyalty for the nation-state. In most cases, however, the idolatry of the state that is always incipient in strong nationalism was tempered by a recognition of transcendental standards in terms of which the nation can be judged. In the United States, for example, even though there was a strong temptation to believe that "God is on our side" and so to deprive the transcendental reference of real authority, some reference to God was obligatory. The nation itself could not be worshipped. In a more secular society such as France, the transcendent reference might be to reason or civilization, but still the nation-state was conceived as a servant of the highest value, not as the highest value itself. Even in Fascist Italy, though the tendency to make the nation absolute was strong, the Concordat Mussolini negotiated with the Vatican at least formally recognized a higher power. In Hitler's Germany, which has to be the type case for fascism, however, there was no such restraint. The claim of the nation-state and its leader had no rival. But it was not just the state that had become absolute: it was the *Volksgemeinschaft*, the national or folk community, that was divinized. Thus fascism in its most typical form involves a triple regression compared to most modern societies: divinity is reembedded in the state, the state is reembedded in society, and individual autonomy is engulfed in the fused totality. Regression in this case does not imply simply a return to an earlier, less-differentiated historical moment, which would be impossible in any case. Rather, regression at the symbolic level was accompanied by an intense mobilization, involving all the modern technical and organizational capacities of the nation. Only a highly mobilized modern society could attempt the antimodern symbolic and structural de-differentiation that fascism implies.

But why Italy, Germany, and Japan? Undoubtedly part of the reason is geopolitical, as Randall Collins has argued. According to this view any modern nation, given the right set of conditions, could become fascist.[91] Nonetheless, preexisting structural and cultural conditions made fascism a more likely possibility in some nations than in others. I am defining fascism as combining an intense national mobilization with an attempt to collapse significant differentiations—between divinity and state, between state and society, and between society and self—that involves a symbolic regression not only to premodernity, but, with the collapse of the distinction between divinity and the state, even to a preaxial condition. How the society of Kant and Goethe could have regressed so profoundly is a much-discussed question on which I can shed no light here. Nonetheless it seems to me that the very violence of the Nazi regime, the large number of people incarcerated and murdered, suggests how traumatic the regression was and the effort required to enforce it. In Japan, by contrast, the very differentiations that fascism collapsed were only incipient and fragile. The fascist regression of 1931–45, therefore, required only the combination of national economic and military mobilization with the intensification of some preexisting symbolic patterns and the suppression of incipient forms of opening up, but no mass party and no charismatic party leader, the lack of which has led some to argue that there was no fascism in Japan. Let us consider, therefore, how patterns laid down in the Meiji period could be intensified in a fascist direction with concomitant severe repression to be sure, but without the violent intensity of Nazism.

There is a clear relationship between fascism and war: any society involved in a major war will have some of the features of fascism, such as total mobilization for the war effort and reduced tolerance for dissenting opinions. Mobilization characterized the Meiji state from the beginning, with the samurai as the normative definition of the citizen, and the military having the privilege of direct access to the emperor. Preparations for war, actual war, and dealing with the consequences of war characterized the entire period from 1868 to 1931. Thus the precipitate actions of junior officers, although with the tacit consent of the general staff, that led to the takeover of Manchuria in 1931, thus beginning the fascist period, was hardly an unexpected possibility. What ensued displayed the features of a uniquely Japanese fascism. Instead of a fascist dictator claiming to embody ultimate authority, there was the emperor. Harry Harootunian paraphrases Seki Sakayoshi as proposing that the emperor was the whole body, not simply a part, that encompassed all of society.[92] Such a doctrine, if widely embraced, entailed the rejection of Minobe's "organ theory," in which, indeed, the emperor was only a part. In 1935 Minobe was forced to resign his university professorship and his membership in the House of Peers (the very fact that he was a member suggests the degree to which his views had earlier been accepted), and his books were banned.

One of the indicators of the unique features of Japanese fascism is the phenomenon of tenkō, ideological apostasy. In 1933 two leading members of the Central Committee of the Japan Communist Party announced from prison that they were abandoning their opposition to Japan's imperial expansion and to the emperor system and renounced their membership in the party. Within three years 75 percent of those convicted of radical thought or activities followed suit.[93] The treatment of imprisoned leftists was often brutal and some died in prison, yet the effort to obtain a change of heart was without parallel in Western fascist states. Often the prisoners' mothers were encouraged to implore their sons to return to the fold of family and nation. The reason why *tenkō* is better translated "apostasy" than "conversion" is that it involved a giving up of proscribed views rather than the acceptance of new beliefs. One was simply asked to be a "normal" Japanese, to "return to Japan." The remarks of Sano Manabu, former member of the Central Committee of the Japan Communist Party, graduate of Tokyo University, and former economics professor, about Japanese uniqueness after his *tenkō* are indicative of the powerful attraction of a fused identity at the time: "[Whereas in other countries] state and society are in antagonism, and God and the state are not compatible; by contrast, in Japan, God, state, and society form a complete union. To die for one's country is the greatest service to God, the greatest loyalty to the emperor, and also the highest way of life for social man."[94]

There is no space here to consider adequately the widespread attraction of Japanese students and intellectuals to Marxism in the 1920s, covertly in the 1930s, and widely again in the early post–World War II years. Amid the tensions and anxieties of Japan's uneven development, Marxism offered an explanation that was comprehensive, theoretically sophisticated, and offered a clear alternative to the reigning emperor-system nationalism. Like Christianity, it offered a transcendent reference point entirely outside Japan in terms of which to understand the Japanese predicament. But unlike Christianity, Marxism offered a set of theoretical categories in terms of which to explain Japan's problems, a set of categories that were not Japanese in origin, but in terms of which the Japanese case could be understood. It is true that the question of how those categories applied to Japan became the subject of obsessive controversy among Japanese Marxists, and there were temptations to naturalize them in Japanese terms, undercutting their universalistic applicability.[95]

The leading Japanese Marxist economist of the mid-twentieth century, Uno Kōzō, compared his discovery of the key phrase "commodification of labor power" in his reading of *Das Kapital* to the twelfth-century founder of Buddhism Hōnen's discovery of the invocation of Amida Buddha, *Namu Amida Butsu*, as the key to his faith.[96] With that one phrase, Uno was able to unify all his thinking about Japanese social development. The remarkable degree to which Japanese Marxism was text-oriented (the complete works of Marx were published in Japanese even before they were in German) suggests the need to find a reference outside the existing social order in terms of which to take a personal, ethical, and political stand.

The appeal of Marxism in Japan, however, is explicable in part not only because it contains a commitment to universal values that clashed sharply with traditional Japanese culture, but because it too has a tendency to fuse transcendent, social, and personal reality that involves its own form of regression in an effort to transcend modernity. In particular the lodging of ultimate reality in the dialectic of history made possible the attribution of ultimate authority to the bearer of that historical dialectic, the working class, or even worse, to the vanguard party and the leader who claimed to represent it. This structural parallel between Marxism and fascism (after all fascist movements were partly modeled on their earlier left-wing opponents), made apostasy bearable if the leftists could continue to believe that Japan represented a proletariat of oppressed colonial nations relative to the Western imperialist oppressors. A cosmopolitan Marxist/existentialist such as Miki Kiyoshi could entertain such thoughts when he lent his pen to support the war effort late in the 1930s.

Not just extreme leftists underwent apostasy. Andrew Barshay describes the poignant case of the liberal journalist Hasegawa Nyozekan. After a brief interrogation in 1933, Nyozekan dropped the rhetoric of class struggle and within two years was writing about national integration and communitarian harmony. Since he had been a Meiji nationalist in his youth, the "return" seemed natural enough to him, although Barshay heads his sensitive treatment of this event "Return to the Womb."[97] Reengulfment indeed.

Harry Harootunian uses the symposium on "overcoming the modern" (*kindai no chōkoku*) held in Kyoto in 1942 to get at the ideological essence of Japanese fascism. He cites the contribution of Suzuki Shigetaka as proposing that overcoming the modern meant an "overcoming of democracy in politics," an "overcoming of capitalism in economics," and an "overcoming of liberalism in thought."[98] Harootunian points out that although democracy and liberal thought were successfully overcome, the denunciations of capitalism served only to mystify the reality of the Japanese economy. Indeed although capitalism in the abstract could be denounced, no serious questions about property relations could be tolerated, a characteristic that Japan shared with other fascist societies. Nonetheless what these three overcomings represent is an effort to evade the wrenching differentiations of modernity and return to an undifferentiated totality that an allegedly ahistorical Japanese tradition represented.

After a brief euphoria accompanying the great victories in the months after Pearl Harbor, most Japanese intellectuals turned to stoic resignation rather than apocalyptic hope. Few among them, Nanbara Shigeru was one, actually tried to bring the war to an end before the country was completely obliterated.[99] Nanbara never lost his post as professor of law at Tokyo Imperial University, although he was a follower of Minobe's ideas and continued to criticize German Nazism, albeit in obscure journals, even in wartime. Japanese totalitarianism was not absolute, but men like Nanbara were rare.[100]

## POSTWAR

One can ask why it took the Japanese as long as it did to get out of a war that had become a catastrophe well before the atomic bomb was dropped on Hiroshima. One can ask how Japan ever got into such a disastrous war in the first place. John Dower has an interesting comment on the latter issue:

> When Japan attacked Pearl Harbor in 1941, its military and civilian leaders had engaged in no serious long-term projections concerning the industrial potential of the United States or the probable course of the colossal conflict that lay before them. "Sometimes," Prime Minister Tōjō stated at the time, referring to a famous hillside temple in Kyoto, "one simply has to leap off the terrace of Kiyomizu-dera."[101]

It has become common to blame the emperor for getting Japan into the war and not getting it out of the war sooner. But in a polity where all serve (even the emperor was the servant of his ancestors) but no one really rules it is very difficult for anyone to take responsibility once great events have been set in motion.[102] In the end it was indeed the emperor who had to end the war, but only because no one among the many who knew the end had come and who had the power to do so was willing to act decisively. What followed was the Occupation, the first in Japanese history, and a series of changes almost as great as those that followed the Restoration of 1868.

Even in the case of an allegedly homogeneous island country like Japan, it is impossible to understand history within the confines of a single nation-state. I have tried to emphasize that, from its earliest history, Japan is only intelligible in dynamic relation to its neighbors and to powerful cultural influences, some of them originating from far away. Japan's modern history is closely bound up with the development of the system of nation-states that first took form in the nineteenth century. Nationalism, imperialism, capitalism, democracy, and fascism in Japan were all responses to pressures and tendencies that were worldwide in scope. In every case, as with other nations, the Japanese response was unique, formed on the basis of its own earlier experience, but also deeply influenced by what was happening abroad. But the Occupation involved a new level of symbiosis, one that has continued in diluted form even to the present: the history of Japan and the history of the United States became indissolubly linked.[103] Whereas the occupation of Germany was divided into four zones—American, British, French, and Soviet—there was only one zone in Japan, the American zone; and there was a new ruler, General Douglas MacArthur.

Given that in 1868 there was no one man who came close to absolute power, one must go back to 1600, to Tokugawa Ieyasu, to find an analogous figure in Japanese history. MacArthur was the new shogun and he was faced with the same problem that faced Ieyasu, namely, what to do with the emperor; he came to the same conclusion: keep him for the sake of public order. The decision to keep the emperor had been made in Washington before MacArthur arrived, but MacArthur not only accepted that decision; he threw himself into the effort to maintain the inviolability of the emperor in the difficult months and years that lay ahead.[104] The great fear was that American troops could be endangered by a fanatical opposition to the Occupation, and the sanction of the emperor was deemed necessary to avoid that possibility. One wonders whether given MacArthur's—and many other Americans'—view of the Japanese as an exotic, Oriental, underdeveloped people he did not believe the emperor necessary to provide stability even during, or perhaps especially during, the great transition to democracy to which MacArthur was also devoted. Whatever the reason, the survival of the emperor, essentially untouched, after the greatest defeat in Japanese history, provided a singularly important element of symbolic continuity through a period of enormous change.

A structural element of continuity was the result of the American decision not to establish a direct military government, as in Germany, but to govern through the existing Japanese state, particularly the bureaucracy. The military services and the Home Ministry, the locus of the political police, were completely demolished, but the rest of the bureaucracy survived. In particular the state apparatus that had been established for wartime economic mobilization was not dismantled.

Thus the Occupation created three dimensions of continuity between wartime and postwar: military government itself, the emperor, and the bureaucracy. Because the American military government fostered many remarkable democratic reforms it cannot be considered a continuation of the kind of military government that ruled Japan between 1931 and 1945. Nonetheless the fact that it was ever-present, that its orders, even its hints, had to be followed with no appeal within Japan, and the fact that it exercised a far-reaching censorship, less inhibiting than wartime censorship to be sure, but still in certain areas quite absolute, made it clear that a powerful military government was in charge. There could be no discussion, for example, of the consequences of the atomic devastation of Hiroshima and Nagasaki.

The imperial court, conservative political leaders, and the Occupation colluded to change as little as possible with respect to the status of the emperor. In the famous New Year's Day statement of the emperor in 1946, for example, although he renounced the idea that he was a "manifest deity," he did not deny his descent from the sun goddess Amaterasu. Even the Constitution of 1946 drafted by the Americans and clearly making the people sovereign, with the emperor remaining only as a "symbol of the state and the unity of the people," was promulgated in such a way that it could be considered once again as a gift from emperor to people. The prime minister at the time, Yoshida Shigeru, could say in the Diet debate that in the new constitution "there is no distinction between the imperial house and the people. . . . Sovereign and subject are one family. . . . The national polity [*kokutai*] will not be altered in the slightest degree by the new constitution. It is simply that the old spirit and thoughts of Japan are being expressed in different words in the new constitution."[105]

With respect to the emperor, what might have been done differently? Abolishing the imperial institution by fiat of the Occupation could well have mobilized extremist opposition for years to come and made the new constitution illegitimate from the start. But there were other options. A referendum on the continuation of the monarchy, such as that which was held in Italy, could have been required. Polling at the time indicates that the institution would have survived by a strong majority in such a referendum, but it would have been clear that the monarchy survived by the will of the people and the kind of murky interpretation of Prime Minister Yoshida would have been much more difficult to affirm. Or Hirohito could have been encouraged to abdicate, as some leading political figures and even members of the imperial family called for. A new emperor with a new reign period would have indicated a sharp break between the prewar and postwar worlds. MacArthur vigorously opposed both of these options. He had become convinced that Hirohito alone could guarantee a smooth transition to democracy.

Even more clearly than the Restoration of 1868, the Occupation was a "revolution from above," but its achievements were major and lasting: sweeping land reform virtually ending tenant farming, liberal labor legislation, women's suffrage, the legalizing of communist and socialist political parties, the breakup of the family-owned economic conglomerates (the *zaibatsu*), the new constitution that established party government responsible to the Diet with no possibility of interference by imperial edict, and most profoundly and controversially, Article 9 of the new constitution, which renounced war as an instrument of national policy, the so-called pacifist clause.[106] Of all these reforms, the one carried out most vigorously by the Japanese themselves was land reform, a reform that largely, if not completely, solved the long-festering issue of tenancy and rural misery. As a result of all these changes and as an expression of them there developed a feeling of openness and freedom that Maruyama Masao compared to the opening of the country (*kaikoku*) after the Meiji Restoration.

In the heady days following the end of the war not only were many voices long suppressed able to find themselves, but others who had embraced the war effort renounced their former beliefs and declared themselves democrats as well. The newly legalized Communist Party, whose leaders had been released from jail or returned from abroad, joined the clamor for democracy and put on hold the issue of class struggle at least temporarily, although taking advantage of the new labor laws to help organize workers. The structural changes brought about by the Occupation were approved, and efforts to think about the creation of not only democratic institutions but also a democratic culture emerged.

In this effort Maruyama Masao was in the forefront, first with his incisive critique of ultranationalism and Japanese fascism, which he saw as fusing ultimate value and nation leaving little room for individual autonomy, and then with his reflections on the development of a sense of agency among citizens, of citizen subjectivity—expressed in Japanese in the term *shutaisei*, whose literal translation as "subjectivity" hardly contains the meaning of an active citizen consciousness that Maruyama wanted to give to it.[107] His reference point was the modern West, which he took as normative, though he recognized the possibilities of deformation there, as in the cases of Germany and Italy; he did, however, recognize significant Japanese precursors such as Fukuzawa Yukichi and Yoshino Sakuzō. Although accepting the importance of democratic group formation, Maruyama was especially concerned to develop among the masses a sense of conscious membership as citizens in a modern nation-state. Thus when the Occupation began what came to be known as its "reverse course" in the face of the emerging cold war and especially after the beginning of the Korean War, Maruyama took the lead in resistance, particularly to the Japan-U.S. Security Treaty in 1950 when it was first passed and especially in 1960 when it came up for renewal. The hope that a nationwide movement in opposition to the Security Treaty could be translated into a lasting engagement of a politically active citizenry would soon be dashed, but it was the high point of Maruyama's political involvement.

There is some sense that there was a missed opportunity for a democratic revolution in the years after 1945, and that Maruyama's emphasis on citizen consciousness rather than citizen action was somehow in part responsible.[108] Labor unrest in the early years of the Occupation was widespread and the deliberate policy of the early Occupation to help meet only the most pressing needs but not to assist in the rebuilding of the Japanese economy only fueled the dissatisfaction. But Japan in the late 1940s was in no sense ripe for revolution. Thinking of the conditions of a revolution described above, even though there was popular unrest, there was no fiscal crisis of the state. There was inflation and a badly depleted Japanese treasury, but the Americans stood ready to meet any dire need. Nor was there an internal conflict leading to paralysis within the elite. American military power was never in doubt, and the Japanese bureaucratic elite was in full cooperation with the Americans. After the triumph of the Chinese Communists in 1949 and the condemnation of the Japanese Communist Party for its soft line by the Commintern in 1950, there were some on the extreme left who called for revolutionary action, but there was not the slightest chance that it could have been successful. Maruyama's concern to build citizen consciousness was certainly more realistic than revolutionary posturing, although the patient building of democratic organizations might have been higher on Maruyama's agenda.

## REBUILDING JAPAN

The end of the 1940s did see a significant shift in Occupation policy and the Japanese response to it, one that would have major consequences for decades to come. This was the "reverse course" referred to above. It had three major dimensions. One involved the purging of Communist leadership throughout Japanese society. The most serious consequence was the destruction of the most militant wing of the Japanese labor movement and in its place the creation of a relatively tame labor movement that would not challenge the economic mobilization that lay ahead. Purging the far left, though it was a shock to the newly created Japanese democratic consciousness, was justified in cold-war terms, and especially by the dangers of the war in Korea so nearby. Although liberals and leftists opposed these measures, Japanese "realists" among the intellectuals and government bureaucrats had no difficulty in accepting the new direction. The second dimension was the pressure to remilitarize. Public opposition was so great that even the Japanese government resisted American pressure as much as it could. In the event a modest, euphemistically named, "self-defense force" was established, though one that would grow more substantially as time passed. The third dimension, though perhaps least noticed at the time, would have the greatest long-term consequences. It flowed from the decision of the American government to rebuild Japan economically as a bastion in the cold war. Its institutional expression was the creation in 1949, out of remnants of the control apparatus of the economy for war mobilization, of the Ministry of International Trade and Industry (MITI), which would orchestrate perhaps the greatest economic comeback in world history.[109] Concomitant with the changes within the government, the Occupation encouraged the reemergence of Japanese business conglomerates in a new, somewhat more horizontal, form—the *keiretsu* rather than the *zaibatsu*—but the names were often the same, Mitsui, Mitsubishi, Nissan, and so on, with some notable new additions such as Sony.[110]

Although changes in all three of these dimensions were carried out by the Japanese, in every case the prime initiative came from the American government operating through the Occupation. Because of the Security Treaty, American military presence would continue after the end of the Occupation, though in steadily reduced form—it continues today in Okinawa. Even more important than the presence of troops is the fact that the United States and Japan are "allies" in a dangerous world, and that, however independently the Japanese have come to act economically, they are militarily and even politically part of the American system. Thus there can be no understanding of Japan since 1945 without recognizing the continuous presence of American power. In that sense the shogunate is still not over.

Fortuitously, the Korean War proved a boon to the Japanese economy, since Japan was called on to supply the allied forces in Korea and even to make parts for military equipment. During the 1950s economic growth showed continued modest improvement and by 1955 the overall index of production had finally returned to the prewar level.[111] By 1960, with the ending of the last great citizen protests, Prime Minister Ikeda Hayato announced the goal of doubling the national income in ten years. Although greeted by many intellectuals with cynical disdain as an aim unworthy of the "cultural nation" they hoped Japan would become, it was Ikeda and the bureaucratic establishment for which he spoke that set the course for the future.

In fact, the national income tripled in ten years and kept on growing at an extremely high rate for another two decades. In a real sense it looked as if, transcending the disaster of the lost war, the mobilized state that had characterized Japan since the Meiji Restoration, and especially during the fifteen-year war (1931–45), had emerged once again, in some respects stronger than ever, though now the aim was not military and political power but economic growth. Although most Japanese seemed to have been co-opted by rising living standards and pride in the new respect in the world for Japan's economic achievements, critics were still to be found. The revisionist Marxist economist Baba Hiroji, writing in the 1980s, warned that there was a "great likelihood that the Japanese system may collapse." According to him it is "the penchant of affluent societies . . . to gear their institutions—and the domain of social and cultural reproduction generally—to [the] pursuit [of] unchecked and self-justifying" growth. The result could be "an irretrievable internal collapse of 'society.'" Yet Baba held out some hope that though socialism, *shakaishugi*, might never come, *kaishashugi* (companyism), might yet create a more human form of capitalism in Japan.[112] In Japanese the characters for society (*shakai*) when reversed (*kaisha*) mean company, and Japan since 1950 has indeed been a "company" society.

While the formal freedoms and electoral bodies established by the 1946 constitution continue to make Japan one of the freest societies in the world, the democratic upsurge of consciousness in the years immediately after 1945 has subsided, with some notable exceptions, into a much more conformist consensus, symbolized by the revival in somewhat new form of many themes from prewar days. This consensus is expressed in the form of *nihonjinron*, the discourse about the Japanese. The one overriding theme of *nihonjinron*, as expressed in a vast array of book titles, some of which have had very large circulation, is Japanese uniqueness, whether derived from race, climate, or history. Peter Dale has emphasized the continuity of this body of literature with prewar writings, such as those of Watsuji Tetsurō, but also its dependence, whether acknowledged or not, on European, particularly German, sources.[113] The pervasive emphasis on the claim that Japanese culture is "relational" rather than "individualistic" draws from the German preoccupation with *Gemeinschaft*, community, as opposed to *Gesellschaft*, society. The German term *Volksgemeinschaft* (national or folk community) got translated into Japanese as *kokumin kyōdōtai* in the prewar period; and even when the term is not used, the idea continues to pervade this genre of literature.

While surveys of the content of the widespread *nihonjinron* literature, coming to prominence in the 1970s but showing little sign of slackening since, are very helpful, Kosaku Yoshino's empirical study of the genre among educators and businessmen in a middle-sized Japanese city helps us understand its actual function.[114] Even though educators (in Yoshino's sample largely primary and secondary schoolteachers) are normally considered the primary transmitters of culture, they were actually less familiar with *nihonjinron* than were businessmen, though both groups had considerable knowledge. Although many have interpreted *nihonjinron* as a form of indoctrination, it is of interest that most of Yoshino's informants felt they had not learned anything new from it. A businessman said, "They [writers of the *nihonjinron*] discuss what I already know. In this sense, there is nothing new to learn from them. But they are so good at expressing what we normally feel about the Japanese by using carefully selected words that it helps us to organise our thought and express it."[115] And a high school headmistress had this to say:

> Reading such literature is useful in the sense that it helps me to organise my thought on the Japanese. Although they simply write about what we already feel about our society, the fact that they can discuss it so systematically means that they are indeed professional thinkers. We are so busy with school administration and what not that we have no time left to ponder over important issues like these.[116]

The fact that businessmen are more likely than schoolteachers to have to deal with foreigners helps explain why *nihonjinron* is so popular in business circles. It would seem that in dealing with the different, understanding one's own uniqueness becomes more important. Not only do companies promote existing *nihonjin* literature, but also on occasion they produce it on their own. Yoshino notes that the Nippon Steel Corporation produced a handbook called *Nippon: The Land and its People* in 1984 for its own personnel, but then, finding it of general interest, managed to sell 400,000 copies by 1989.[117]

Besides the many continuities between prewar writing on Japanese culture and the *nihonjinron* literature, such as that the Japanese are more community-oriented whereas Westerners are more oriented to the individual, Japanese thought tends to merge subject and object rather than strictly distinguish them as in the West, the Japanese are close to nature, and so on, there are also significant differences from prewar writing. The farmer or the townsman is usually the model representative of the premodern Japanese tradition, rather than the samurai (though the idealization of the peasant was a staple of prewar thought). The absence or diminution of the role of the samurai goes together with a de-emphasis on Japan's military tradition, perhaps the sharpest break with prewar writing. Further, the emperor is largely missing from *nihonjinron*. Some critics of this genre have felt that the emperor is present even in his absence, that *nihonjinron* represents the emperor system without the emperor. Be that as it may, the emperor would seldom have been absent in prewar writing about Japanese culture.

The events surrounding the death of the Shōwa emperor in January 1989 may illustrate the extent to which the emperor today is both present and absent. The death of Hirohito was peculiarly drawn out because he fell gravely ill in September 1988 but did not die until January 7, 1989. The mass media reported daily on his condition, which, among other things, involved blood transfusions that amounted to thirty gallons over the four-month period. From the beginning of the emperor's final illness, the government and the mass media urged the public to exercise "self-restraint," which meant canceling festive events, even postponing weddings, and avoiding excessive public display. Large corporations urged their employees to wear dark clothing and ribbons to express concern over the emperor's condition. While the great majority of Japanese conformed to the pressure to exercise self-restraint, as the days wore on a few questioning voices were raised.

The elderly Liberal Democratic mayor of Nagasaki, Motoshima Hitoshi, in response to a question about the emperor's war guilt, said that, much as he respected the constitutional role of the emperor, he did believe that the emperor had some responsibility for the war and that the tragedies of Hiroshima and Nagasaki as well as the battle of Okinawa could have been avoided if he had decided to end the war sooner. For this statement the mayor was vilified in the national press and expelled from the Liberal Democratic Party. The building where he had his office was surrounded by right-wing trucks blaring denunciatory statements. A year after the emperor's death Motoshima was badly wounded by gunfire from a right-wing extremist. Defense of Motoshima from established intellectuals and media was muted at best. Remarks were heard that Motoshima "wasn't really a Japanese" or "didn't understand Japanese culture." While such statements could have been made about anyone expressing Motoshima's views, it was probably also relevant that he was a descendant of a Japanese family that had converted to Catholicism in the sixteenth century.[118]

Indeed, besides the Communists, it was largely Christians who failed during the emperor's illness to exercise adequate self-restraint. The incident at Meiji Gakuin University, though less dramatic than the one involving the mayor of Nagasaki, was significant in that it involved an entire institution, even if it was the only one. On October 19, more than a month after the emperor had fallen ill, Morii Makoto, president of Meiji Gakuin University, a Christian university founded by Presbyterian missionaries a century earlier, issued a statement that emerged from the Deans' Council that "when the present Emperor passes away, we will not take special action of any kind: for example, classes will not be canceled, students will not be advised to call off the University Festival and the flag will not be flown at half-mast."[119] This statement brought the predictable hysterical response from right-wingers, who called university officials in the middle of the night to rant about their lack of patriotism and to threaten violence against them and their families. After the university held symposia for faculty and students in which a full discussion of the emperor system took place, the *Asahi Shimbun*, one of Japan's largest newspapers, ran a story about the events at Meiji Gakuin University. This story elicited an outpouring of letters to the newspaper and to the university, almost all of them praising the university's stand. This would suggest that apparent conformity to the pressure for self-restraint obscured more than a little private dissent, a not unusual situation in Japan.

Ishida Takeshi in an essay appended to the Occasional Paper concerning the Meiji Gakuin affair, traces the gradual decline of interest in the emperor as indicated by public opinion polls. In June 1988, for example, 47 percent of Japanese expressed indifference to the emperor, 28 percent expressed respect for the emperor, and 22 percent said they had a favorable impression of him.[120] Two weeks after the emperor's death in 1989, 57 percent of Japanese said that the media had artificially created too much of a stir. Ishida warns that the combination of increasing public formality with respect to the emperor on the part of the mass media combined with increasing private indifference is not necessarily a healthy situation, particularly if it leads to public acquiescence to right-wing violence. Perhaps in his own way he is suggesting that the emperor system can continue without the emperor.[121]

## STILL NONAXIAL?

In this all-too-condensed review of the major phases of the development of Japanese civilization I have been focusing on Japanese culture, drawing in part on the work of S. N. Eisenstadt, and on Japanese state formation, drawing in part on the work of Johann Arnason. The interaction between culture and power is central to the story. On the one hand, Japan has shown a remarkable capacity to absorb foreign culture on its own terms in a series of "revolutions from above," for example, the seventh-century appropriation of Chinese culture and the Meiji appropriation of Western culture. The American Occupation imposed a liberal constitution but most of the American-inspired reforms were carried out by Japanese in their own way.

Through all these enormous changes the basic premises of Japanese society, though drastically reformulated, have remained nonaxial. That is, the axial and subsequent differentiations between transcendent reality and the state, between state and society, and between society and self have not been completed.

Although it has become popular to argue that the "emperor system" was invented in the Meiji period and did not exist before, I have tried to show that, through its many vicissitudes, the status of the emperor has provided a kind of litmus test of the extent to which Japanese culture remained non-axial from the earliest historical times. So long as the emperor, however powerless and however personally a nonentity, could provide a conduit through which transcendent reality could fuse with the Japanese social order, a genuine axial break at the highest level of cultural symbolism was thwarted, even though for many individuals and groups such a break clearly occurred.

But given the long and sophisticated exposure to several forms of axial culture and the deep attraction that these forms have had for many Japanese, one cannot argue that the nonaxial ground bass of Japanese culture has continued its hold through sheer cultural momentum, which would be to say that a timeless tradition has triumphed over history, though such a view has had its appeal to some Japanese intellectuals. Rather it has been the deep implication of nonaxial culture with continuously reformulated structures of power determined to prevent the full institutionalization of axial premises that explains the persistence. I am not arguing that the Japanese state in its several incarnations has simply "invented" or "imposed" the nonaxial premises of Japanese culture, which could then be interpreted as "ideology" pure and simple. The existence of nonaxial premises not just in state ideology but in the pores, so to speak, of the whole of Japanese society has greatly eased the role of power in sustaining them. In other words, an axial revolution in Japanese culture could not be accomplished merely by the abolition of the imperial institution, unlikely though that is at present, because an emperor system without an emperor is a distinct possibility.[122] What would need to change is not only the relation of state power to culture, but what Foucault would call the "micro-structures of power" in every sphere of Japanese life, an even more unlikely eventuality at the moment.

Some have thought that the "new social movements" that began to appear in Japan in the 1970s and 1980s might lead to such a transformation, and such may yet be the case. However, Jeffrey Broadbent's careful and incisive study of environmental politics in Japan during those years indicates the ease with which protest can be reabsorbed into the consensus, often not without significant concessions to the protesters, but with the result that no continuing structure of citizen organization and consciousness survives.[123] Nothing that I know about Japanese society gives me the ability to predict the future, but I do think that the enormous vitality and flexibility of the Japanese pattern suggests that it can continue to deal with its many real challenges quite successfully while reformulating, as it has done time and again, but not abandoning, its nonaxial premises.

I am sure that there will be those who will interpret my argument as "Orientalist" and will attribute to me the motive of wishing to exalt the axial West, or even the United States in particular, by using the "backward" Japanese as an invidious case. I might conclude, therefore, by suggesting that in respect to axiality, though for quite different reasons, I would place Japan and the United States in the same boat, and, if there is an implied criticism of Japan in what I have written above, there is a very explicit criticism of America in much that I have written in the last quarter century.[124] I would also argue that in the most important respects Japan is as "modern" as the United States. The problems in both cases lie deeper than modernity.

The United States has from early on operated with the tacit assumption that it has not just fully developed, but actually *transcended* the axial age, that it is a *postaxial* civilization. If America in this understanding is a realized utopia, a version of the Kingdom of God on earth, then its fundamental assumptions cannot be challenged any more than can those of the Japanese. If the Japanese have continuously sought to avoid the introduction of the fundamental tension between ultimate truth and social reality that characterizes axial civilizations, the Americans have collapsed that fundamental tension by believing that it has been resolved in our own society. If the Japanese are in some sense preaxial, the Americans are in some sense postaxial, or at least in both cases they work very hard at believing they are. This accounts for, among other failings, the American unwillingness to see how far behind most other advanced societies we are in dealing justly with our most deprived.

Let us consider what in each case those unassailable premises are. There are remarkable similarities as well as "mirror-image" differences in the two cases.[125] Both Japanese and Americans define nation and people in sacred terms. In Japan this sacredness is primordial: Japan is the divine land, created by the gods and the Japanese people are descended from the gods. While the American identity of chosen people and promised land uses images that could be seen as primordial, it is future-orientation that is stressed. The chosen people is composed of the people who have chosen to become part of it. The promised land is open to all. America is the land not of the past, but of the future: messiah nation or redeemer nation, or in Lincoln's words "the last best hope of earth."

The basic premises of social and political order differ in the two cases relative to the different construction of collective identity. In the Japanese case the individual is seen as embedded in a network of social relations, which is in turn embedded in cosmological reality. The Japanese have been remarkable in the degree to which they have been able to maintain dynamism and openness to change within the framework of embeddedness, which is itself unassailable. In America it is disembeddedness that is sacralized. If America is the new Jerusalem then there is need for neither church nor state: each individual is free to realize him- or herself as he or she sees fit. If the Japanese have a strong version of social realism, the Americans have an ontological individualism. In both cases it is not the fundamental premises that are open to question but only the failure to realize them. In both cases the fundamental premises can be seen as "polluted" by various evil forces, from which they must be defended, but they cannot be attacked.

In recent times the American individual, disencumbered from the responsibilities of citizenship, has been exalted primarily as an entrepreneur in a society of ever increasing economic growth. The widely disseminated idea that there are no limits to economic growth is surely a lie and acting as if it were true is suicidal: the kind of growth that requires the destruction and consumption of the biosphere cannot but stop cultural growth because its biological consequences are terminal.

A major task for Americans, I believe, is to see ourselves as still an axial culture, however much we have been transformed for good and for ill by the great successive waves of modernity. Instead of believing that we are the Kingdom of God on earth, we must recover the idea that we are nothing more than a deeply flawed city of man. We need something like Habermas's notion of a lifeworld in contrast to administrative and market systems, which, when they are not adequately anchored in the lifeworld, can destroy normative community. Our growing understanding that biological and cultural evolution are deeply interconnected could help us see that culture is the living membrane that connects us to the natural world and that institutions are the biosocial organs that allow us to live in this new environment. The Japanese sacralization of embeddedness, of trying to avoid the leap into freedom as far as possible, without, of course, giving up the spoils of capitalism, is not open to us. But our own hypertrophied disembeddedness, our quest for freedom without limit, is endangering the very basis of life on this planet.

In short, Japan and the United States, perhaps the two most dynamic societies in today's world, rest on deeply problematic premises, premises so taken for granted that they can hardly be criticized. Since both societies, however else they differ, have devoted themselves, as their very reason for being, to relentless economic expansion, and that expansion seems destined to lead to global self-destruction unless there is some critical redirection in the not too distant future, they both need to examine the premises that have led to their current predicament. In both cases a rethinking of historic patterns of culture and structures of power have more than academic interest. It might not be too much to say that both societies need to consider the judgments that axial traditions have made concerning self-aggrandizing human action, and whether their own lack of axial reference points are part of their present predicament. Such a rethinking may be an essential step toward avoiding catastrophe.

# 1 The Contemporary Meaning of Kamakura Buddhism

We are gathered together to celebrate the 800th anniversary of the birth of Shinran Shōnin and the great creative phase of Japanese Buddhism in the Kamakura period in which Shinran was a central but by no means a solitary figure. I will have something to say about Shinran and also about Dōgen, whom I will treat as representative figures of Kamakura Buddhism. What I want to concentrate on mainly is the question, How can something that happened 800 years ago mean anything to us? Especially when it is a question of anything so evanescent as religious experience, how can we even understand, much less participate in, something so long ago?

I will try to deal with those problems by adapting some concepts from Miki Kiyoshi's *Philosophy of History.*[1] Following Miki, we can speak of any historical event as involving (1) experience, (2) expression, (3) documents, and (4) reenactment. Experience refers to the immediacy of events as individuals participate in them. Expression refers to the cultural forms that people create out of their experience but which survive beyond the occasion of their creation. There is no absolute boundary line between experience and expression, since cultural forms complete and fulfill experience as well as provide stimulus for new experience. Documents are anything that allow us to know of the experience and expression of the past. Reenactment is the attempt in the present to see what the experience and expression of the past were really like.

When we are dealing with religious experience, there are some particularly difficult problems. Religious experience is, or often claims to be, experience of something transhistorical, eternal, or nontemporal. But religious expression, like all other human expression, is in time and history. The documents, the scriptures and other religious writings that record that experience and expression, reek of the particularities of the place and age in which they were produced. Reenactment, the appropriation of the original experience in the present moment, becomes increasingly difficult as the sacred documents seem ever more strange, remote, and inaccessible. In the case of religion, where a continuous tradition of reenactment is essential for the survival of the religion itself, there is a tendency for the original meanings to become progressively distorted and the function of the reenactment to become magical, social, or even political, rather than to produce an apprehension of transcendence. This situation gives rise to reformations. It is the task of a religious reformation not simply to revive the original historical forms of religious expression, though that is how reformers sometimes see it, but to regain the original experience of the transhistorical. Inevitably, even when the reformer thinks he is merely returning to past forms, a genuine reformation involves the creation of new forms growing out of a new apprehension of religious reality, even though there is still a definite connection with the past.

Viewing Kamakura Buddhism as a reformation, then, raises questions in two directions. To what extent did Kamakura Buddhism recapture in its own forms the fundamental Buddhist experience of the earliest texts and presumably of Gautama the Buddha himself, who lived 1800 years earlier than Shinran and Dōgen? To what extent is it possible for us to apprehend the experience of Shinran, Dōgen, and the other great Kamakura Buddhists without ourselves undergoing a reformation? I will not pretend to answer those questions, especially the second one, but they lie behind all that I will say.

Following Futaba Kenkō I think it is possible to argue that Kamakura Buddhism, especially in the figures of Shinran and Dōgen, not only did involve a reenactment of the fundamental experience of Buddhism, but that it was the first time in Japanese history that a movement based on that fundamental experience reached the masses.[2] Such an argument would imply that Japanese Buddhism in earlier centuries, with many individual exceptions, of course, was essentially a magical-ritual system controlled by the state and used, on the one hand, as a support for existing political power and, on the other, as a means for attaining various utilitarian goals by individuals and groups. Perhaps a brief discussion of original Buddhism will suggest how it differed from early Japanese Buddhism and how Kamakura Buddhism reappropriated it.

Original Buddhism, as far as we can know it, involves the belief that "all conditioned things," that is, all of the aspects of our everyday experience, have three characteristics or "marks."[3] They (1) are transient or impermanent, (2) involve suffering or ill, and (3) are "not-self." To expand slightly on the third mark we can quote the phrase the early texts use to refer to the objects of ordinary experience: "This is not mine, I am not this, this is not myself."[4] Such an understanding of the everyday world that radically deprives it of its meaning and value is not itself simply given in ordinary experience, though there is much in ordinary experience that hints at it. Such an understanding is itself the product of religious experience, and that understanding grows as the religious experience is deepened and disciplined. We should, therefore, be extremely hesitant, lacking that religious perception, to claim that we truly understand what is being asserted, even though we follow the words. Finally, and most paradoxically, original Buddhism asserted that if we truly understand that ordinary existence is transient, involves suffering, and is alien, that is, if we perceive the absolute emptiness of the ordinary world, we will have attained spiritual freedom, nirvana. As Conze says, "In one sense 'emptiness' designates deprivation, in another fulfillment."[5] That which on the one hand is designated as escape, stopping, renunciation, the extinction of craving is also designated as real truth, true being, supreme reality.[6]

However imperfectly we may grasp that original message, let us see whether we can discern in the religious experience of Shinran and Dōgen a reenactment of it. The connections are a bit easier to follow in Dōgen so it is there that we will begin.

Dōgen (1200–53) came from a court family in Kyoto and received an excellent education in Chinese literature and in the many schools of Buddhism. At the age of thirteen he became a monk of the Tendai school, the "mother of Buddhism" where all the great reformers started, and gradually began to master the Buddhist teachings. All that he learned left him dissatisfied until he finally visited Eisai, the monk who first brought the teachings of Zen to Japan. There he formed the intention of following Eisai's footsteps by visiting China and practicing meditation there. Let me recount what happened after he had begun the practice of meditation under the direction of the Chinese monk Ju-ching, as described by Carl Bielefeldt:[7]

> Then in the summer practice period of 1225, one night when the monks were seated in meditation, Ju-ching shouted at the nodding monk next to Dōgen, "Zen is body and mind cast off! How can you sit there sleeping?" Dōgen woke up. He went to Ju-ching's quarters and offered incense. "What does this offering incense mean?" asked Ju-ching. "Body and mind are cast off," said Dōgen. Ju-ching said, "Body and mind cast off! Cast off body and mind!" To which Dōgen responded, "This is just a momentary attainment. Don't give it your seal too quickly." Ju-ching said, "I don't give it my seal too quickly."

Dōgen asked, "What do you mean by that?" The Master answered,
"Cast off body and mind!" Dōgen bowed. Ju-ching said, "Cast off!
Cast off!"

When Dōgen left Ju-ching two years later, the Master advised him
to avoid cities and keep away from the government. "Just live in deep
mountains and dark valleys, and train a disciple-and-a-half: don't let
my teaching be cut off." Dōgen returned to Japan empty-handed, with
nothing to show for his four years in Sung China except knowledge, as
he said, that "my eyes are set side by side and my nose is straight."

The first thing to notice in this account is the sharp break from the past.
Previous monks returning from China, including even Eisai himself, invari-
ably brought with them statues and sutras, charms and spells. Dōgen
returned empty-handed. Previous monks were often sent to China semi-
officially and on their return set up monasteries under government sponsorship. Dōgen was admonished to keep away from government, an admo-
nition he carried out by establishing his monastery, Eiheiji, in the "deep
mountains and dark valleys" of Echizen on the Japan Sea side of north-
central Japan, and by steadfastly refusing all invitations from Kamakura. In
these ways Dōgen asserted a sharp break from the established church and
the established state. He proclaimed a purified and simplified Buddhism
utterly cleansed of utilitarian ends. In his teaching, meditation itself is at
once means and ends and there is no other concern. He said:

> In Buddhism, practice and enlightenment are one and the same.
> Since practice has its basis in enlightenment, the practice even of the
> beginner contains the whole of original enlightenment. Thus while
> giving directions as to the exercise, the Zen master warns him not
> to await enlightenment apart from the exercise, because this exercise
> points directly to the original enlightenment, it has no beginning.[8]

The simultaneity of practice and enlightenment was part of a general sense
of reality for Dōgen. The very mountains and rivers among which he lived
partook of that simultaneity. Bielefeldt summarizes the teaching of the
mountain and river section of Dōgen's greatest work, the Shōbōgenzō, as
follows:

> As for mountains and rivers, then, though we say they are samsâra,
> it is not so easy to say what this means. For samsâra cannot be pinned
> down to this world of birth and death. It is this world of birth and death;
> and yet for that very reason it is completely free from birth and death.
> This is the basic logic of the prajnâ-pâramitâ, the Perfection of Wisdom.
> All dharmas are conditioned being; but a conditioned being has no
> nature of its own; having no own-nature it is empty; being empty

it is free from itself, and free from birth and death. Therefore, these very mountains and rivers of the present are the mountains and rivers of nirvana.[9]

With the same hesitation that I expressed about the message of original Buddhism, namely, that one can hardly claim to understand the words when one does not have the experience out of which they come, I think it can be argued that Dōgen does, in his own unique way, represent a reappropriation of the original message of Buddhism in all its radicalness.

Superficially it might seem that Shinran's message was quite different. As opposed to the *jiriki*, self-power, practice of meditation in Dōgen, Shinran recommends *tariki*, other-power, reliance on Amida Buddha. But, as Futaba Kenkō has pointed out, there may be a deeper structural similarity.[10]

Shinran (1173–1262), twenty-seven years older than Dōgen, came from a similar family background, became a monk at an early age, and, like Dōgen, read restlessly in the vast corpus of Buddhist writings until finding a teacher, in his case Hōnen, who finally helped him find his way. But in Shinran's biography we find a special emphasis on his sense of failure and sin, on his inability to perform the meditations and austerities prescribed to him by his sect. In this situation of doubt and uncertainty Hōnen's teaching that salvation comes through the name of Amida Buddha alone, relying only on Amida's vow to save all sentient beings, was profoundly transforming. Shinran said that he was willing to follow Hōnen's teaching even if it should lead him to hell, for he was headed for hell in any case and Hōnen's message was his only hope.

By taking his place in the little band of followers around Hōnen, Shinran, intentionally or not, involved himself in a break with the established church and state as radical as was Dōgen's. The established sects did not approve of Hōnen's teachings, which they considered subversive of established order, and they brought pressure on the state to suppress them. Eventually two of Hōnen's followers were executed and the rest, including Hōnen and Shinran, were banished to distant provinces. Indeed, it was the separation from Hōnen, whom he never saw again, that brought about Shinran's own independent doctrinal developments. In the isolation of the remote province of Echigo, Shinran faced the hardships of the life of the ordinary peasant. He dropped the last of his monastic disciplines and took a wife, becoming, in his own words, "neither priest nor layman."[11]

In several respects Shinran pushed the implication of the Pure Land tradition further than it had ever been pushed before. While placing all his faith in the name of Amida, he essentially denied that the repetition of the name, even a single time, was itself efficacious for salvation. Salvation is already available in the limitless sea of Amida's vow, and even the faith to accept it comes from Amida. Further, while not denying that the believer will be reborn in the Pure Land after death as the Jōdo tradition maintains, Shinran turned his emphasis to the immediacy of salvation, the simultaneity of faith and salvation in the immediate present.

All of this can be and often has been interpreted along Christian lines in which Amida has been interpreted as analogous to God or Christ. Without denying that there may be something to such interpretations, we must also notice how, at a deeper level, Shinran's teaching resembles Dōgen's and the message of original Buddhism as well. What Shinran is saying about all practices, including the recitation of the name of Amida, as forms of striving, is "this is not mine, I am not this, this is not myself." With Shinran as with Dōgen there is no end to be gained and no self to gain it. Amida is a manifestation of that ultimate reality, which is simultaneously empty and full, as it was for Dōgen. It is in this context that we can understand Shinran's famous passage on Jinen or nature, written near the end of his life. I quote Alfred Bloom's translation:

> When we speak of "Nature" (Jinen), the character Ji mean naturally, by itself (Onozukara). It is not (the result of) an intention (self-assertion—Hakarai) of the devotee. Nen is a word which means "to cause to come about" (Shikarashimu). Shikarashimu (also signifies that it) is not (due to any) effort (Hakarai) of the devotee. Since it is (the result of) the Vow of the Tathagata, we will call it Hōni, i.e., truth. We say of Hōni that it "causes to come about," because it is the Vow of the Tathagata. Since the truth is the Vow of Tathagata, we say generally that it is not (the result) of the effort of the devotee, and therefore the power (virtue) of this Dharma is that it "causes to be." For the first time, there is nothing to be done by man. This is what we should understand as "the reason which is beyond reason" (Mugi no Gi). Originally Jinen was a word meaning "to cause to be." We say Jinen when the devotee does not consider his goodness or evil in accordance with the fact that Amida has vowed originally (that salvation was to be attained) not by the efforts of the devotee, but by being embraced and caused to rely on the Namu Amida Butsu (his name). In the Vow which we hear, it is vowed that he will cause us (to attain) the highest Buddhahood. "Highest Buddhahood" signifies to abide in formlessness. Because we are without form, we say Jinen (nature). When we indicate that there is form, we do not speak of the highest Nirvana. We have heard and learned for the first time that the one who makes known formlessness is called Amida. Amida is the means whereby we are caused to know formlessness.[12]

I hope that enough has been said to indicate that the Buddhist reformation of Shinran and Dōgen was a genuine one, that it did reapprehend the religiously radical message of original Buddhism and make it available to the Japanese masses. The world, including its established social and cultural order, is radically devalued and yet the world as it is is given back in a new way, simultaneously empty and full. I say religiously radical because the message at the outset was not socially radical. None of the Kamakura reformers had a vision of a new social order that they wished to bring about. But the religious awakening of the masses did have political implications. Particularly in the Jōdo Shinshū, but also in the Nichirenshū, the subjective experience of faith made possible a new kind of social organization within the religious collectivity. Indeed, only these religious organizations ever challenged the rising feudal order of medieval Japan. In the end the religious rebellions and movements all failed in their challenge to the feudal order and, more importantly, were themselves permeated by feudal forms. But before we are too quick to judge, particularly in comparison to some alleged ethical-social superiority of Christianity, we should remember that the New Testament, no more than the Buddhist scriptures, contains a blueprint for social order. Faith must always be joined to secular ideologies in order to have political consequences. The political limitations of the Buddhist Reformation are as much the political limitations of the Shinto and Confucian political traditions and the actualities of political power as they are of the Buddhist Reformation itself. This does not mean that there may not be different possibilities today.

Before turning to the modern period in an effort to say something about the meaning of Buddhism generally and the Kamakura reformers in particular for our present-day society in Japan, America, and the world, there is one further period in Japanese history, one further phase in the Japanese internalization of Buddhism, to which I would like to refer, the Tokugawa period.

In the midst of the allegedly secular Tokugawa period, when Buddhism is said to have atrophied and the creativity gone out of it, we can nonetheless speak, if we speak softly, of a second Buddhist Reformation, the Haiku Reformation. Of all the great poets of that period we can single out two who brought the haiku as a poetry of religion or religion of poetry to a kind of fulfillment: Bashō (1644–94) and Issa (1763–1827). In the former we can see a successor of Dōgen, in the latter of Shinran.

Bashō was born of the samurai class, but after the death of the son of his feudal lord, with whom he served as a kind of companion student and of whom he was very fond, he left his fief and settled in Edo as a student and teacher of haiku. He lived very simply, often, during his many travels, experiencing hunger and other sufferings of the poor. Although not strictly a monk he dressed as one and in his own way was also "neither priest nor layman." In all that he did he lived poetry and what his poetry expressed was that simultaneous emptiness and fullness that we have seen in Dōgen. But to suggest the subtle but important difference between the two let us contrast a *waka* of Dōgen with two haiku of Bashō. Dōgen writes:

> Yama no iro tani hibiki mo mina-nagara
> waga shakamuni no koe no ato kana
> The colors of the mountains
> The echoes of the valleys . . .
> All, all are
> Impressions of the voice of
> Our Shakamuni.[13]

Bashō not only shortens the thirty-one-syllable *waka* form to the seventeen-syllable haiku, but he also in a way abbreviates the theology—abbreviates it and makes it more homely, as when he writes:

> Asagao ni ware wa meshi kū otoko kana
> I am one
> Who eats his breakfast
> Gazing at the morning glory.[14]

Here is Buddha's voice imprinted, so to speak, in the almost too pat image of the rapidly fading morning glory, but not only does Bashō not mention anything about the Buddha, he also intrudes his own breakfast, with its aroma of rice and pickles, which also equally well expresses the simultaneous emptiness and fullness of the Buddha nature. In another poem, this time without a trace of humor, once again we find an expression of emptiness, *sunyata*:

> Kono michi ya iku hito nashi ni aki no kure
> Along this road
> Goes no one,
> This autumn eve.[15]

Without that Buddhist depth of meaning that is always hovering just below the surface of Bashō's poetry, this would be merely sentimental, as modern haiku have become after the Buddhist substance has gone. But at that marvelous moment when Buddhist religious perceptiveness has annihilated itself in the world but not yet lost its power stands the figure of Bashō:

> Tabi-sugata shigure no tsuru yo bashōō
> In traveling attire,

A stork in late autumn rain:
The old master Bashō[16]

as Chora describes him.

By contrast with Bashō, Issa, a Jōdo Shinshū believer, is much more involved in the human world. Like Shinran he is acutely aware of the reality of sin and suffering:

Kogarashi ya nijū-yon-mon no yūjo goya
The autumn storm;
A prostitute shack
At 24 cents a time.[17]

Even in the natural world he is alert to suffering:

Nomidomo mo yonaga darō zo sabishi karo
For you fleas too,
The night must be long,
It must be lonely.[18]

But in true Shinshū fashion Issa holds that it is just in the midst of this dirty world that faith is to be found:

Hito no yo ni ta ni tsukuraruru hasu no hana
In the world of men—
In the muddy rice field
The Lotus is fashioned.[19]

At the end of his poetic diary, *Oraga Haru*, Issa gives us a theological reverie that perhaps carries Shinran one step further:

Those who insist on salvation by faith and devote their minds to nothing else are bound all the more firmly by their single-mindedness, and fall into the hell of attachment to their own salvation. Again, those who are passive and stand to one side waiting to be saved, consider that they are already perfect and rely rather on Buddha than on themselves to purify their hearts—these, too, have failed to find the secret of genuine salvation. The question then remains—how do we find it? But the answer, fortunately, is not difficult.

We should do far better to put this vexing problem of salvation out of our minds altogether and place our reliance neither on faith nor on personal virtue, but surrender ourselves completely to the will of Buddha. Let him do as he will with us—be it to carry us to heaven, or to hell. Herein lies the secret.

Once we have determined on this course, we need care nothing for ourselves. We need no longer ape the busy spider by stretching the web of our desire across the earth, nor emulate the greedy farmer by taking extra water into our own fields at the expense of our neighbors.

Moreover, since our minds will be at peace, we need not always be saying our prayers with hollow voice, for we shall be entirely under the benevolent direction of Buddha.

This is the salvation—this the peace of mind we teach in our religion. Blessed be the name of Buddha.

> Tomo-kaku-mo anata makase no toshi no kure
> > In any case
> Leaving all to you
> > Now, at the end of the year.[20]

Issa, the son of a moderately prosperous peasant family, left home and, like Bashō, became a haiku teacher in Edo. Eventually he returned to his native village, where a series of domestic misfortunes overtook him. Like Bashō he stood aside from Tokugawa society, but even more than the earlier poet he expressed quiet contempt for the feudal ruling class, as when returning from a visit to a daimyo that he could not avoid he threw on the dungheap several rolls of cloth the daimyo had given him. Once again, in the case of Bashō and Issa, we see the capacity of profound religious insight to devalue the empirical world, including its established powers, but once again we see no immediate political consequences. These great haiku poets are not easy for us to understand today. But perhaps they are more of our world than the Kamakura Reformers and can provide for us a link to them. But it is a perilous link, for the religious penetration of the world has proceeded so far in Bashō and Issa that it is about to turn into its opposite—the overwhelming of poetry—and religion—by the world itself. But for that it took the influence of the modern world and the modern West.

In the shattering of the traditional Japanese world that occurred after the opening of the country in 1868 there was nothing more profoundly shaken than Japanese Buddhism. Attacked from within by resurgent Shinto nationalists, attacked from without by contemptuous Christian missionaries, and declared irrelevant and obsolete by the purveyors of the new secular and scientific culture of the West, it is no wonder that Buddhists lost self-confidence. This is not to say that the customs and practices of many generations were abruptly abandoned nor that there were no longer many sincere believers among the common people, but only that among the educated elite Buddhism suffered an eclipse in the first decades of the Meiji period, an eclipse that only completed what had begun long before the opening of the country. The fate of Buddhism as a self-conscious religious movement has been, then, that it has had to start again, to find new bases for its appeal, to determine whether and how the message of Buddhism has anything to say to contemporary Japanese. In many respects the circumstances seemed most unpropitious. The social and cultural bases of traditional Buddhism in Japan were all being undermined by the rapid social change brought about by Japan's forced-march industrialization and modernization. A purely conservative effort to continue Buddhism as it had existed in Tokugawa times seemed to have gloomy prospects and has everywhere been more or less unsuccessful. Paradoxically, the emergence of modern Japan provided, itself, new opportunities for religious apprehension. Indeed, does not modern Japan, like the modern West, epitomize a state of mind that Buddhists can only characterize as ignorance and delusion even more than most traditional societies have done? After all, does not modern Japanese society, like modern Western society, worship wealth and power with no sense of their transience, blindly pursue pleasure with no heed to the cost in suffering, and assert in ever louder tones: this is mine, I am this, this is my self? There was the possibility then, even the demand, for a new appropriation of the message of the Kamakura reformers and of the Buddha himself, a new reenactment of the fundamental religious experience of Buddhism, a modern Buddhist Reformation. Has that possibility been fulfilled?

Once again I am diffident about giving any answer that is merely external and descriptive and not based on personal experience itself. There are also grave limitations to my knowledge of modern Japanese Buddhism. Granting those limitations, there are still a few things that I might say.

As a tentative general answer I would say that elements of such a reformation have come into existence, but as yet we cannot say that they have come to fulfillment. An indispensable element in such a reformation, a revival of Buddhist scholarship, was in evidence already in the Meiji period and has become stronger ever since. There is no question but that it is a precondition for the reenactment of religious experience that its earlier expressions, as contained in the scriptures and religious writings, be adequately understood and evaluations of the religious depth of various aspects of the tradition be made possible. There is, however, in the rise of scholarship, and not in the Buddhist tradition alone but just as clearly in the Christian tradition, the danger that knowledge about the tradition will replace immediate religious apprehension. For example, we have learned enormously much about the New Testament from a century of distinguished biblical scholarship, but perhaps Martin Luther King Jr. has taught us more about Christ than all the biblical scholars put together. That is, of course, not entirely fair since Martin Luther King himself had an excellent biblical education, which was undoubtedly a component of his own direct experience, but the general point remains valid. It is true that among the early Japanese Buddhist scholars in the Meiji period there were some who exemplified Buddhism in the whole quality of their lives as well as producing works of scholarship, men like Kiyozawa Manshi and Suzuki Daisetsu, the latter becoming through his scholarship, but even more through his personality, an apostle to the whole modern world. And yet the fact remains that when we go into any bookshop in Japan today and see several shelves of books on Buddhism, we cannot assume that this is an automatic index of widespread profound personal Buddhist religious experience.

To show just a bit more clearly some further signs of an incipient modern Japanese Buddhist Reformation, I would like to mention a few Japanese intellectuals, mainly because I study intellectuals and know more about them, who, not primarily scholars of Buddhism themselves, have incorporated a newly apprehended Buddhist experience into their lives. Perhaps the most influential of all modern Japanese intellectuals, Nishida Kitarō (1870–1945), undertook Zen meditation in his young manhood under the inspiration of Suzuki Daisetsu, and the Zen experience profoundly marked his entire philosophical enterprise. Nishida's interests ranged through all the problems of Western philosophy and involved him in a deep encounter with both Classical Greek philosophy and German Idealism. Nevertheless, in developing his own metaphysics he arrived finally at a point unmistakably Buddhist in inspiration. He argued that the notion of the "intelligible Universal" was the highest mode of being known to Western philosophy. But then he goes on to say: "Whenever a Universal finds its place in another enveloping Universal, and is 'lined' with it, the last 'being' which had its place in the enveloped Universal, becomes self-contradictory. According to this, the intelligible Universal can not be the last Universal; there must be a Universal which envelops even the intelligible Universal; it may be called the place of absolute nothingness." If I may interject, the place of absolute nothingness is that place where all places have their place but which does not itself have a place in anything else; it is thus a no place. But to continue: "The place of absolute nothingness. That is the religious consciousness. In the religious consciousness, body and soul disappear, and we unite ourselves with absolute Nothingness."[21]

That is clearly an echo of Dōgen, but a little further on he sounds more like Shinran:

> The sinner who has lost his way is nearest to God, nearer than the angels.
>
>   As content of the intelligible self, there is noematically no higher value visible than truth, beauty, and the good. In so far, however, as the intelligible Universal is "lined" with the Universal of absolute Nothingness, the "lost Self" becomes visible, and there remains only

the proceeding in the direction of noesis. In transcending in that direction the highest value of negation of values becomes visible: it is the religious value. The religious value, therefore, means absolute negation of the Self. The religious ideal consists in becoming a being which denies itself. There is a seeing without a seeing one, and a hearing without a hearing one. This is salvation.[22]

Finally, back to the mood of Zen again, Nishida writes, "If one is really overwhelmed by the consciousness of absolute Nothingness, there is neither 'Me' nor 'God'; but just because there is absolute Nothingness, the mountain is mountain, and the water is water, and the being is as it is."[23] What this kind of thing actually meant during the period between the First and Second World Wars when Nishida was most popular has been much debated. Certainly he was no radical social critic. Certainly some of his close students became apologists for the war and the totalitarian state. And yet, it seems to me that Nishida's teachings did deprive the state of its ultimacy and did provide a context of sanity for many educated Japanese who lived through those troubled times. But to his critics Nishida perhaps suffered from a tendency endemic in the Zen tradition. The mountains too quickly become the mountains again and, in spite of all the talk of *zettai-teki mu*, absolute Nothingness, the full depth of Buddhist negation with all its suffering and tragedy was not experienced.

One such critic who looked for that depth of negation in the tradition of Shinran rather than Zen is Ienaga Saburō (1913– ). For Ienaga, suffering acutely during the conditions of the dark valley in the late 1930s and early 1940s, the reality of human existence is sin and misery. In a remarkable little book he published in 1940 called *The Logic of Negation in the Development of Japanese Thought*, Ienaga criticized most of the Japanese cultural tradition for its simple this-worldliness and its inability to take seriously enough the true human condition.[24] For Ienaga, Shōtoku Taishi's saying, "The world is a lie; only the Buddha is true," has been profoundly meaningful, though more in its first negation than in its second affirmation. As a result of his deep sense of human suffering, Ienaga has in the postwar years engaged in many social and political activities to improve Japanese society. But he has not found a way in which his religious faith as such could be effectively affirmed.

There are many more figures who have contributed to making Japanese Buddhism available in contemporary form if there were time to discuss them: men like Hatano Seiichi and Tanabe Hajime, who mutually illuminated the Buddhist and Christian traditions; men like Watsuji Tetsurō, who wrote brilliantly in the tradition of absolute nothingness and who introduced Dōgen to modern readers; men like Miki Kiyoshi, for whom through all the vicissitudes and troubles of his intellectual and political life Shinran's *Tannishō* was a constant companion and whose last unfinished book, written during the final years of the war and itself interrupted by the author's imprisonment and death, was on Shinran. It would also be helpful to speak of the way in which Futaba Kenkō and others in the postwar situation have tried to relate the fundamental religious message of Buddhism to social action and social concern, and the criticism of the past links of established Buddhism to political power and Japanese particularism that that effort entailed. What all these efforts add up to, even when not dramatic or even very evident on the surface of cultural life, is the making accessible once again of the Buddhist message for contemporary Japanese. Only out of the actual religious experience itself will we be able to find the eventual fruits.

Finally, let me say just a word about the meaning of Buddhism, especially Japanese Buddhism, in contemporary America and, by implication, the world. We have already pointed out how modern society exemplifies so typically the ignorance and illusion that Buddhism has shown to be the human condition, and in this respect America is the most typical modern society. A society whose economy is based on the deliberate stimulation of insatiable human desire, whose politics revolves around anger and violence, and whose stance in the world is one of blind self-adulation so that it could in Vietnam undertake one of the most brutal wars that a powerful nation has ever inflicted on a small and weak one, would seem to be the perfect exemplification of the Buddhist assertion that this world is a burning house, a literal hell. Of course it is also a part of the Buddhist teaching that most people are ignorant of the truth of their condition, and perhaps most Americans would not recognize the description I have just given of them. But increasingly since the Second World War and especially since the decade of the 1960s some Americans have begun to recognize this description. Perhaps even more significantly some sober people who have probably little or no knowledge of Buddhism have begun to say that the self-destructiveness of our way of life is so great that it cannot long continue. Our drive to satisfy ever more insatiable desires is destroying our natural environment, causing us to oppress weaker nations and our own minorities, and destroying our own social viability and mental health.

In such a situation it is not surprising that Buddhism, which radically criticizes all the basic assumptions of modern society, should seem attractive to some Americans. The availability of inexpensive, reasonably accurate, reasonably attractive books about Buddhism, and particularly Zen Buddhism, has made many young, educated Americans familiar with the Buddhist message. More important than knowledge about is experience of, and that is very hard to gauge. The establishment in California and other parts of the country of monastic and semimonastic communities, often of Zen inspiration, at least signifies a serious desire to move beyond concepts to realities. The danger that such communities may become simply hermetically sealed centers for self-salvation, with little to say to the general population or to the society as a whole, is perhaps even greater in America than in Japan, though the value of a witnessing community, even though relatively closed to the outside world, should not be underestimated. Those few who have tried to relate Buddhism to the cultural and social needs of contemporary American society—Alan Watts, Gary Snyder, Norman O. Brown, Theodore Roszak—have as yet had only ambiguous results. It is easy to condemn them but the way in which America consumes, seduces, and destroys its own prophets is indeed frightening. Perhaps they deserve a careful, critical hearing more than adulation or dismissal.

The last thing I would want to be interpreted as saying is that Buddhism is the total answer for the problems of modern Japan, America, or the world. Our problems are so grave that only the full range of our moral and scientific intelligence can begin to meet them. I do believe, however, that beyond morality and science, religious insight is also needed. It seems to me that, in view of the profundity of the Buddhist past, the religious depth of the Kamakura reformers for example, it is possible that a reenactment of Buddhist religious experience in the present may still have much to teach us.

# 2 Ienaga Saburō and the Search for Meaning in Modern Japan

Modernization is usually discussed in economic or political terms. Certainly the major "impact" of the West on Asian countries has been economic and political, and the "response" has had to deal centrally with economic and political problems. Yet it is generally recognized that cultural problems are also involved and that attempts at modernization, successful or not, involve a cultural dimension, even though this dimension has as yet been much less carefully studied than the political and economic dimensions. Central to what I am calling the cultural dimension of modernization is the problem of meaning. How do the people and more especially how do the intellectuals, those especially responsible for interpreting the meaning of the world, make sense out of what is happening? The situation in which modernizing nations find themselves is often interpreted in sloganlike phrases: "imperialism," "national essence," "socialism," "capitalism." Behind these phrases lie more or less coherent political ideologies, formulated out of traditional, Western, and newly created elements by the intellectuals. For most people, including most intellectuals, the problems of meaning raised by the Western impact and the consequent attempts at modernization are answered by one or other of the popular ideologies of the day, ideologies that are heavily political in vocabulary and explicit concern.

But behind the popular ideologies, implicit or in some cases explicit in them, lie deeper problems of meaning, problems of a historical, philosophical, and even religious nature. The traditional culture had its own view of the world and of man; the modern West has quite a different view. Can the two be reconciled? If so how? What must be given up, what changed? The problem of how to act in a given historical situation leads to the deeper problems of what is true, what is good. Conscious concern with such problems has not been widespread or typical, though the degree to which unconscious concern with them has goaded leaders or even large groups remains an open question. But in most of the modernizing nations there have been a few men who have grappled with such problems in more than a superficial way. For one who is interested in cultural change, and who believes that although it operates on a longer time scale than economic and political change, it is even more profoundly important in human history, such men are of the greatest significance. An interest in this sort of problem has led me to study the work of Ienaga Saburō.

Ienaga is a specialist in the history of Japanese thought, and in recent years he has become widely known as a political ideologist. Yet it is not as an ideologist that I wish to study him; rather, I wish to deal with his deep concern with the moral, philosophical, and religious issues underlying Japanese modernization. The relation between the two sides of Ienaga's work cannot be neglected, but this study claims to be relatively complete only with respect to Ienaga's more philosophical thought. This means that his work before 1952 will receive the most attention even though the popular image of him both in Japan and the West is largely based on his post–1952 activities.

Although I have said Ienaga has been concerned with the moral, philosophical, and religious issues of Japanese modernization (a concern that makes him relatively unique among modern Japanese intellectuals—I am not at all claiming that he is typical), he is not a philosopher or theologian, but rather he is a historian of thought. His approach then is always through history. In his search for answers to what are clearly existential questions for him he has been led to peruse the whole course of Japanese history and subject it—ancient, medieval, and modern—to a series of stimulating reevaluations. It is with these reevaluations that I am concerned, and I will bring in only so much biography as is necessary to understand them. I am chiefly interested in the ideas, representing as I think they do, cultural mutations. Therefore I have relied on Ienaga's own work for my data. The biographical details are derived mainly from his own reminiscences and have not been checked with other sources. They represent therefore largely Ienaga's own view of himself. As for the thought, that exists in his writings; it is against those writings that my interpretations must ultimately be checked.

## THE YOUNG IENAGA AND HIS WORLD (1913–35)

Born in 1913, Ienaga spans three major periods of modern Japanese history: Taishō Democracy; the Nationalist period from the Manchurian Incident of 1931 to the end of the Second World War; and the new Japan that has emerged subsequently. Known primarily as a student of ancient and medieval Buddhism who after the Second World War became "progressive" and took up the study of modern intellectual history, Ienaga's early grounding in the Taishō spirit is sometimes overlooked or forgotten. But the events and influences of those early years were in many respects decisive, and it is there that we must look first if we are to understand him.

The "prehistoric period" in his intellectual life begins with his enjoyment of historical stories told by his mother and read in grammar school.[1] It takes on more serious significance in middle school, where he first read Natsume Sōseki's *Botchan* and became a partisan of his.[2] At the same time he noticed among his elder brother's college textbooks a copy of Minobe Tatsukichi's (1873–1948) *Kempō satsuyō* (Constitutional outlines) and read it.[3] This book made a great impression on him and remained a favorite for many years. Because of its "clear logic" Ienaga was attracted to the study of law and at this time read such abstruse things as a book on the Japanese penal code and the *Collected Statutes* (Roppō zensho). Also while in middle school he was introduced to the scientific study of Japan's ancient history through Nishimura Shinji's *Yamato jidaishi* (The history of the Yamato period).[4]

In First Higher School Ienaga underwent a decisive experience that is best described in his own words:

> When I entered Higher School in the spring of 1931, just before the Manchurian incident, Marxism was still at its zenith. In the year I entered school there were two strikes arising from questions of student thought. Facing that atmosphere for the first time in my life and seeing that the nationalist morality [*kokka dōtoku*] which had been poured into me at home and at school was without authority, I felt that the ground on which I stood had crumbled. Seeking for something on which my spirit could rely I took hold of philosophy. After the orthodox morality which had no basis outside of the historical tradition of the past had slipped from the seat of my heart, philosophy, which speaks of "what one ought to do" had for me a fresh fascination. Throwing away many years of educational precepts I was spiritually reborn. This is an incident which can be called the Copernican Revolution [*tenkai*] in my spiritual life.[5]

The book in which he discovered his solution was Tanabe Hajime's *Kagaku gairon*.[6] In it he was introduced to the "value philosophy" of the Southwest German school of Neo-Kantian thought, of which Windelband and Rickert were the leading figures. For him the idea of "value" that is not "existence" or "value which ought to be" independent of "existence" offered the only way out when the notion of *kokutai*, namely, that "Japan is a country blessed with a single line of emperors for ten thousand generations from most ancient times" had collapsed.[7] While in higher school, besides German Neo-Kantian and Japanese Kyoto school philosophy, Ienaga was also reading books on Marxism and Christianity, as well as Buddhism.[8] Among the latter was the early biography of Shotoku Taishi, *Jōgū Shōtoku Hōō teisetsu*," and Shinran's *Tannishō*.[9] Ienaga relates his reactions to the changing situation in Japan at this time in a passage that directly follows the one quoted above:

> After I had begun to think in this way in my own mind, the Japanese thought world gradually underwent a drastic change in the direction of fanaticism. After I had tasted the forbidden fruit called liberty, an unbearable atmosphere became pervasive. Not yet having a place of discussion in the body of students, I sought an outlet for my unexpressed indignation in the magazine *Dai ichi* put out by the alumni association of my Middle School. In the November 1935 issue of *Dai ichi* I published an article concerning the problem of the "organ theory" of the emperor which I concluded with the following sentence: "Doesn't one feel that the whole Japanese thought world generally has gone mad since the Manchurian incident? The most important admonition for our people is exhausted in the one sentence 'Keep your feet on the ground.'"[10]

Most of the major themes of Ienaga's later work were foreshadowed in interests of his middle and higher school years. The rest of this chapter will involve a working out of these themes. But here we must pause to consider some of the implications of his "Copernican Revolution." This is an example of the kind of experience that many Japanese have been going through ever since the opening of the country (and in a sense some Japanese went through long before that). It involves the replacement of the traditional social system, defined in narrower or broader terms, by a set of universal principles, as the ultimate locus of value. In the traditional view there is a harmony between the natural order, the moral order, and the actual social order. Maruyama Masao, in the second chapter of his *Studies in the History of Japanese Political Thought* (Nihon seiji shisōshi kenkyū), has described this undifferentiated conception of order as it existed in orthodox Confucian thought in the Tokugawa period. Ishida Takeshi in the first part of his *Studies in the History of Meiji Political Thought* (Meiji seiji shisōshi kenkyū) has described the formation of the "family state" concept in the late Meiji period, which may be seen as the adaptation to new circumstances of virtually the same tradition of thought that Maruyama described for the earlier period. It was this new orthodoxy centering around the concept of *kokutai* (national body) with the imperial line at its heart, against which Ienaga was reacting.[11]

The set of universal principles that for many has broken through the "inherited conglomerate" (to borrow Gilbert Murray's phrase from another context) has probably in most cases in modern Japan been provided by Christianity or Marxism, but secular Western philosophy has also played its part. But in the latter case it has perhaps usually been the more radical French or British philosophies as in the case of early Meiji utilitarians (for example, Fukuzawa Yukichi) or the non-Christian *Jiyū minken undō* (Freedom and Peoples' Rights Movement) leaders (for example, Nakae Chōmin). In the case of Ienaga, although Marxism clearly played a role destructive to his traditional ideas, and Christianity may have been in the background, it was German Neo-Kantianism that provided the basis for a new way of thought.[12] At any rate what is important is that henceforth for Ienaga "what is" could not automatically be identified with "what ought to be." His adoption of a transcendental morality put him in critical relation with his environment and must have, especially in the circumstances of those days, increased the tension between himself and his world. But at the same time, that philosophy of value provided him with the basis for a "spiritual rebirth." In it he found meaning when the "ground on which I stood" had crumbled and he was threatened with meaninglessness.

It is interesting that out of his spiritual crisis and his confrontation with the sharp change occurring in the intellectual world came an impulse to social action. The specific instance that we know about involved the constitutional theories of Minobe Tatsukichi (who was attacked for believing that the emperor was an organ of the state) whose work Ienaga had admired before his higher school days.[13] His recent concern with constitutional and other social problems may appear strange to those who know only his writings on Buddhist thought before the end of the war. But it does not seem so once one knows of his early history. Although his attention soon turned rather exclusively to religious history, this can be considered as a temporary shift in emphasis for both inner and outer reasons, rather than a radical shift in ideology (*tenkō*). There is no evidence in any of his writings before 1945 for any support for statism or ultranationalism or the *kokutai* or "Imperial Way" ideologies. Indeed, even when not being specifically political Ienaga was sufficiently out of step with the spirit of the times to have his first scholarly article, arguing for Buddhist influence on an important passage of the *Nihon shoki*, pulled at the last minute by the editors of *Rekishi chiri* on grounds that the sale of the issue might be banned if it contained such an article.[14] At any rate it should be clear that Ienaga, while still in his student years, participated in the major trends of thought associated with the period of "Taishō Democracy" (even though in these early Shōwa years it was in its twilight stage) and was profoundly shaped by them. This is the indispensable precondition for understanding his later work.

In his first year in Tokyo Imperial University (1934) Ienaga underwent a new spiritual crisis, this time of a religious nature. "At that time for various reasons I was beaten in mind and body [*shin-shin tomo ni uchinome-sarete ita*]," he wrote of this experience in 1961. He had great anxieties about his own abilities in facing the choice of a special field that would determine his whole life. "The dry and lifeless university lectures without any real thought in them" could not save him from a feeling of despair. On top of that Ienaga who had never from childhood been physically strong was afflicted by a turn for the worse in his physical condition. In this situation he understood existentially for the first time the meaning of Shōtoku Taishi's words "The world is empty and false; only the Buddha is true," which he had already read in higher school.[15] In this statement he found support in the midst of despair, and partly through reflecting on it, he kept his balance in the "dark valley" of the years of frenzied nationalism that lay immediately ahead. It seems likely that a deeper knowledge of Shinran's thought also contributed to his emergence from this spiritual crisis.[16] It is certainly around Shinran that his subsequent studies of Buddhism revolve.

In a sense the university crisis and its solution involve a deepening of the problems of the earlier crisis in higher school: the shift is from the realm of morality to that of religion. This implies a further differentiation. Whereas the earlier crisis had led to the differentiation of social system and morality in his thought, this second one led to the differentiation of morality and religion. A concern for the moral nature of man continues to be very important for Ienaga and is deepened by his religious experience. But during the period of greatest concern with religious problems there is an almost complete withdrawal from concern with social and political action. This withdrawal must be explained in terms both of inner preoccupations and outer pressures of the period. There is a further shift involved in the university experience worth noting. This is a shift from primary concern with modern thought (constitutionalism, German Idealism), which is Western in origin, to ancient (Shōtoku Taishi) and medieval (Shinran) thought, which is Japanese.[17] Thus at the same time that he has moved to the level of the ultimate problems of meaning (religion) he has moved to a consideration of his own historical heritage. The choice then of ancient and medieval Japanese Buddhist thought as his field of scholarly specialization was not fortuitous but came directly out of his own experience and as he would say "practical" concerns. This is a characteristic of Ienaga in all his work.[18]

## THE "LOGIC OF NEGATION" AND THE HISTORY OF JAPANESE THOUGHT (1934–45)

After his graduation from the university in 1937 Ienaga was affiliated with the Tokyo University Shiryō Hensanjo (Institute for the Compilation of Historical Materials), taught for a while at the Niigata Higher School, and eventually became a professor at the Tokyo University of Education. From his university days until the end of the war his research was almost exclusively directed to the history of Buddhist thought. He published a series of important books on this subject from 1940 to 1947.[19] In his first book Ienaga lays out his general interpretation of Japanese thought, focusing around the problem of the development of the "logic of negation" in Japanese Buddhism. All of the other studies are developments of various parts of the schema of the first book.

*The Development of the Logic of Negation in the History of Japanese Thought* is a small but remarkable book. It shows Ienaga at the age of twenty-seven already at the height of his powers as a scholar. Although the terminology of the book, beginning with the notion of the "logic of negation" itself, certainly smacks of the Kyoto school, the terms take on a special meaning in the context of Ienaga's analysis, which is always historical rather than abstract.[20] The distinctiveness of Ienaga's position relative to the Kyoto school and the basis for the difference will perhaps appear most clearly after the contents of the book are summarized.

1. The first chapter traces the development of the logic of negation (*hitei* can also be translated as "denial") in the West as a background for the clarification of the Japanese material. Ancient Greek philosophy, says Ienaga, had no category of negation. It was based on a theory of being (*u*) rather than nonbeing (*mu*). From this point of view the ideal is a fulfillment of the real, not a negation of it, and the ideal god is a fulfillment of the human. Plato proceeds in an unbroken line from this-worldly goods to the Good. Only in their tragic drama did the Greeks express the logic of negation. In the tragedies men must submit to fate—their free will is crushed when they struggle with divine authority. In this relation of opposition and contradiction between gods and men, "god" is not an idea or *eidos*. So among the Greeks the logic of negation can be recognized, but it is not expressed as such in philosophy.

In Hebrew and Christian thought, however, the logic of negation is openly expressed. Value resides in God, not in man. God is not an ideal man. Salvation comes from God alone and not by human effort. Christian *agape* comes first from God and differs from the *eros* of Greek philosophy.

2. As in the West the most ancient Japanese thought did not know of the logic of negation. Just as Christianity brought this logic to the West so Buddhism brought it to Japan. However, at first it was only an imported idea. The present book is an attempt to describe the process whereby the Japanese people only gradually and through their own experience grasped the meaning of the logic of negation.

Pre-Buddhist thought in Japan was entirely affirmative (*kōteiteki*, the opposite of *hiteiteki*). Its optimistic view of man emphasized purity from contamination rather than salvation from sin. Its notion of "other worlds" (*takamagahara, yomi no kuni*, and so on) was simply one of other places not essentially different from this world and even at certain points spatially connected. For the early Japanese these "other worlds" are much like this one, for, since they did not deny this world, they had no wish for an ideal other world.

3. Shōtoku Taishi was the first Japanese to understand Buddhism. Buddhism's basic dialectical movement is the absolute denial of the actual (*genjitsu*) and as a result of that denial the return to an absolute affirmation on another plane. This Buddhist "logic of negation" Shōtoku Taishi clearly understood when he said, "The world is empty and false; only the Buddha is true."

In the Seventeen-Article Constitution Shōtoku criticized the individual and social evils of the Japanese society of his day—for example, party spirit, flattery, envy, covetousness, bribery, oppressing peasants, disorder between ruler and people, lack of loyalty to ruler, and lack of benevolence to people on the basis of Confucian ethics. But he says ethics is not enough: we cannot expect the final solution by human effort alone, but must rely on the three treasures of Buddhism.[21] There is only one way to escape from this world and that is by thoroughly denying it. For evil and suffering are not discrete phenomena but the essence of the human world; this is a world of fire and there is no one who does not suffer. But through the experience of absolute denial of this world one can attain the other shore, the Pure Land, which as the denial of the denial is the Buddha world of absolute affirmation. The core of Shōtoku's teaching is the idea of turning (*ten*), that is, turning from illusion to truth.

Shōtoku of course transcended his time. In the general consciousness the

Buddhist logic of negation was not grasped but Buddhism was used instead as a magical power for obtaining recovery from illness or protection of the state. But even there the absoluteness of Buddhism was recognized and there was at least not the simple optimism of earlier days. The *Manyōshū* reflects a quite new feeling of human limitation, transience, and consciousness of death. But on the whole, social conditions in this ancient period had not yet mediated the consciousness of the logic of negation. Shōtoku's understanding may have been partly motivated by anxiety aroused by the collapse of the old clan (*uji*) system, but this was not enough to bring about his consciousness of the need for absolute negation. This consciousness was rather mediated by his extraordinary soul.

4. The Nara court was not particularly conducive to the development of *hitei* thought and the early Heian court was even less so. The latter saw a reversal of the earlier pro-Buddhist policy and its replacement by an emphasis on Confucian morality with its reliance on human this-worldly effort. Buddhism was rigidly controlled and the court favored Hinayana legalism. Saichō's life and work were a protest against these new policies but later Tendai thought and Kūkai's Shingon sect compromised with the *kōtei* tendencies of the court. The esoteric sects propagated the idea that everything is a Buddha and that denial of the world is not necessary. In practice the esoteric sects simply catered to the satisfaction of worldly desires through magical means.

But in the disturbed conditions of the late Heian period a situation arose in which the essence of human life and the logic of negation could be more deeply grasped. Although they lived in the midst of pleasure, the aristocrats had begun to grasp its limits. But they were not ready for the absolute denial of this world: they preferred to place the Pure Land or its artistic illusion in the midst of this world (for example, the Byōdōin) and enjoy it. By encouraging self-power methods (such as contemplating statues and pictures of Amida) they retained the tie between this and the other world, which existed from of old in Japan and hindered the full realization of *hitei* thought.

5. The late Heian aristocrats wanted to pray for an afterworld so that they could continue to enjoy their pleasures in it, not in order to make a basic turn (*ten*) away from actuality. In order to break out of this superficial and primitive optimism to a deeper and more concrete worldview there had to be an absolutely negative experience that could mediate the consciousness of the logic of negation. The collapse of Heian life in the Heike and Genji wars

provided just such an experience. The fall of the aristocracy was a great moment in the history of Japanese thought, because it provided the basis for the thorough grasping of the logic of negation.

6. But probably the contradictions of suffering could not be felt in their deepest sense by the aristocrats. The latter at their best sought for a real, sudden enlightenment. However, suffering that can be solved by one sudden enlightenment is not real suffering and consequently a turn toward salvation whose aim is such an overcoming of suffering cannot be a truly dialectical absolute turn. Only in facing a truly impossible antinomy is absolute negativity realized. Consequently it was not the nobles but those whose very way of life necessarily bound them to the wheel of Karma and who had no hope of salvation, such as warriors, hunters, monks who had broken their vows, prostitutes, and the like, who felt the extreme of suffering and who became conscious of their inescapably evil nature.

7. Already in Genshin there was a tendency to equate this world with hell, but the tendency was not yet complete. By Kamakura times the recognition that this world is hell was fully expressed. The conditions for the fulfillment of the development of the logic of negation were complete. Shinran's doctrine is its fullest expression.

In Shinran with his deep sense of sin the recognition of the inescapable nature of human evil becomes dialectically the positive basis for salvation. On these grounds Shinran could say, "If the good are saved, how much more the wicked." For in the recognition of his own inescapable sinfulness the sinner casts away all self-power and so it is possible for him to attain salvation through absolute other-power. In connection with the exegesis of Shinran's views Ienaga quotes Romans 3.10: "None is righteous, no, not one," and refers to Karl Barth's discussion in his *Commentary on Romans.*[22]

Zen Buddhism attacked the main premises of the Pure Land view and reasserted self-power, yet it still participated in the currents of the age (for example, Dōgen's rejection of the world).

8. The absolute denial of Kamakura Buddhism also contained an absolute affirmation. After the Kamakura experience in the Muromachi age the affirmation could be more freely expressed, but it was not the naive affirmation of ancient times. It had the quality of "not having to deny all human life as a dream but viewing this dream as a dream and expressing the feeling of living quietly alongside it."[23] This was the ideal of "*wabi,*" not to avoid suffering but to live quietly in its midst. What would be denied by most people is

affirmed as it is by the man of *wabi* (*wabibito*). Just because the world has no fixity it is splendid. Is this not perhaps the highest stage of the logic of denial? The Muromachi period was also a time of great disturbances and turmoil for which this was an appropriate way of thinking. A free heaven and earth could be maintained in spite of external travail.

But this absolute affirmation of the Muromachi age cannot be traced back simply to the earlier absolute denial of the Kamakura age alone. There is an element of fusion with the old Japanese idea of a limitlessly amiable world. Deep suffering dissolves into sentiment and so deep thought gradually is made shallow. The resurgence of the ancient affirmative feeling and amiable view of the world destroys the dialectical opposition that existed in Kamakura Buddhism. This tendency is related to the fact that Zen thought replaced Pure Land thought in the center of cultural life. Zen denies the opposition and asserts a simple unity, though it has a latent dialectic within it.

But the element of negation is still at the base of Muromachi culture, for example, in Seami's conception of *yūgen* (mystery) as the essence of the Nō drama. In the tea ceremony the starting point is absolute negation as is also the case in the arts of garden building and flower arrangement. All these arts start from the dialectical basis of seeing the greatest by making themselves into the least. We cannot deny that these arts had a negative character partly as a result of external pressures arising from the disorders of the day. But we must remember their paradoxical structure in that in an important sense this external defeat meant an inner victory. In the smallest things the Muromachi artists saw the largest, and through one stick or one stone they saw the whole world. Without saying that these Muromachi arts had no connection with the ancient Japanese spirit we can say that they are chiefly understandable as having arisen in a world of high affirmation that had just passed through the depths of denial.

However, from late Muromachi times things changed greatly. The dictators beginning with Oda Nobunaga destroyed medieval feudalism and established absolutism. The dictators relied on military and economic power and placed no reliance on anything metaphysical. Their position drove them to self-deification and both Nobunaga and Hideyoshi planned to have themselves worshipped as gods.

In subsequent years Bashō and a few others kept the tradition of *hitei* alive but most people lost it. The common people became swallowed up in commercial interests and the rulers were absorbed in a this-worldly Confucianism. However, to the extent that the realism (*genjitsushugi*) of the Tokugawa period is a product of the Middle Ages it differs from ancient realism. In Tokugawa literature there is expressed a thorough respect for the actual, which sees as absolute the wealth and pleasure of "today." But such respect for the actual is premised unconsciously on a bottomless uneasiness about the limitations of "today" because of the limitless darkness between today and tomorrow. Everywhere in Tokugawa culture the logic of negation is vanquished, yet everywhere it shows unquenchable remnants even though these do not eventuate in a positive view of humankind, but are rather controlled by quite other elements.

For 300 years there has been a loss of connection with the logic of negation. In this respect the modern period is continuous with the Tokugawa period. The Enlightenment philosophy and later Neo-Kantianism just continued, though outwardly different in form, the Tokugawa respect for this world. But now partly due to Western influence there is a chance to create a new philosophy of negation, which will require a new logic of negation, as Nishida Kitarō has indicated.[24]

Even from this inadequate summary I think it will be recognized that Ienaga's *The Development of the Logic of Negation* is from a number of points of view a remarkable construction. It is very clear that Ienaga's turn to religion did not mean the renunciation of his critical intelligence. He was able "dialectically" to utilize his own partly externally forced withdrawal from more immediate problems for the purpose of a deeply critical analysis of some of the most basic problems of his own and Western culture. Just how critical the book is (even to the point of political implications) will become clear when we reflect that it was published in 1940 when the Japanese market was being deluged with eulogistic histories of the "Japanese spirit." In the face of this flood Ienaga published a book that was almost a complete denial of the Japanese tradition, or at least it was a denial of every element in the tradition that was not itself premised on denial. In it Shinto and the ancient Yamato spirit are dismissed as "primitive and superficial," Confucianism is rejected as "shallow and this-worldly," and the *kokutai* and the emperor are not even mentioned. Of course it can be argued that Ienaga was not writing a general history of Japanese thought but only trying to follow up one strand, but it is nonetheless true that by implication this is the strand he considered to be really valuable, which had real universality and could contribute to a positive solution of present and future problems.[25] Such a position could only imply an intensely negative evaluation of the prevailing intellectual currents.

Ienaga's essential structure is simple, even somewhat somber, but it only gains in suggestive power on those accounts. At the beginning stands

Shōtoku Taishi, the first hero, who foreshadows in his own person what is to come, but remains an isolated figure, rising above the limitations of his time. Then through a process of ever more drastic experiences with social disruption the logic of negation, which was grasped already by Shōtoku Taishi, is gradually borne in on the Japanese people. Out of the recognition in the Kamakura period that "the world is hell" the Japanese people finally came to understand Buddhism themselves and their experience was most rigorously expressed in Shinran, the second hero, who stands at the climax of the story. The apparent fruits of the great age of denial in the Zen-inspired Muromachi culture, however, turn to an early decay and the process from there on is a steady falling away mitigated only by an occasional Bashō and by the knowledge that the experience of negation has only been repressed and remains hauntingly in the unconscious. At the end there is no third hero and the reader is left alone to face himself.[26]

It is interesting that in this first book the notion of "modern" (*kindai*), which will later play such an important part in his thought, receives only a negative evaluation. Modern thought like that of Tokugawa Japan suffers from an unbroken this-worldliness. It may seem natural in this period when in Japan "modern" was a bad word and something to be "overcome" that Ienaga would not evaluate it highly. Yet this judgment seems to come from other roots. It certainly has no relation to the prevailing judgment that what is "Japanese" is good as against what is Western, for his criticism of the modern spirit is in precisely the same terms that he criticizes the characteristic Japanese affirmativeness. And it is especially noteworthy that while "modern" is negatively evaluated "Western" is not. It is worth taking a closer look at the place of Western references in *The Development of the Logic of Negation*.

References to the West enter at three points in the book, at the beginning, at the climax, and at the end. Ienaga actually sets his case by discussing the relations of Greek and Christian thought and posits the same relation between Japanese and Buddhist thought. For all the concern for what is specifically Japanese in the book, the comparative setting gives the discussion a strong note of universalism. This note is again reinforced by the introduction of references to the New Testament and to Karl Barth during the climactic discussion of Shinran, where again there is the strong sense of similarity between something central in the Christian tradition and the product of Japan's most creative religious mind. Finally at the end there is the suggestion that Western influences may help in the solution of the problem of reviving the logic of denial.

The position of the Kyoto school of philosophy was similar, and yet there is a certain difference in Ienaga. Tatsuo Arima has recently argued that Nishida Kitarō was trying to find a logical (Western) structure for Japanese thought rather than to synthesize East and West.[27] Ienaga is trying to do neither. He finds a profound point of linkage in the fundamentally similar experience of Paul and Shinran, but this involves neither synthesis nor the assertion of essential difference, nor the superiority of either side. It is a ground from which problems can be commonly viewed. The difference from Nishida probably resides mainly in what they took to be basic in the Japanese tradition. For Nishida it was Zen, which must always perhaps remain mysterious from the point of view of Western thought and transcend its categories. Thus Nishida's philosophy has the quality of "capping" or "completing" or adding a missing quality to Western thought. But Ienaga has always been profoundly mistrustful of Zen and unconvinced of its claims. Because he bases himself on Shinran's sense of sin and proclamation of salvation through faith alone, coming to terms with Christian categories almost ceases to be a problem for him. Perhaps this difference is also related to Ienaga's deeper concern with social problems than has been characteristic of the Kyoto school. Zen tends to go "beyond good and evil" to a realm of "pure experience" in which the individual and the absolute are united. But Shinran could not forget evil and sin any more than could Luther. Perhaps this helped provide Ienaga with a greater moral realism than Zen did for Nishida. But of course the Lutheran analogy indicates all too clearly the weaknesses of Shinran's position as a basis for social action. Other things obviously had to enter Ienaga's thought in order to produce his later social concern.

In two subsequent books, *Studies in Ancient Buddhist Thought* and *Studies in Medieval Buddhist Thought* (both of these refer exclusively to Japanese Buddhism), Ienaga spelled out in much greater detail some of the essential ideas contained in *The Development of the Logic of Negation*.[28] But in his long essay "The Development of the Religious View of Nature in the History of Japanese Thought" he expands and supplements the overall scheme of *The Development of the Logic of Negation*, and he suggests that the two be read together.[29] In intrinsic interest this essay rivals Ienaga's first book, but within the confines of this chapter it must receive briefer treatment. The concern for nature has been a pervasive one in much modern Japanese thought.[30] The idea that there is something specifically Japanese about finding an ultimate answer in or through nature is not original with Ienaga. But given his urge in these years to come to terms critically with the whole of his tradition, it was natural that he would attempt a systematic analysis of a position that is in some ways similar to "the logic of negation" but also differs significantly from it. Probably the book remains the most ambitious attempt to develop a critical analysis of this strand in Japanese thought and as such is another of Ienaga's major scholarly contributions.

The "dialectical" element in Ienaga's approach is illustrated throughout, but we must confine ourselves here to only a few examples. From the outset Ienaga draws a sharp distinction between what he is calling the religious view of nature and primitive animism.[31] The religious view of nature in Ienaga's sense develops only after the influence of continental culture when nature is seen as something *different from* human life, something with which one can aesthetically and consciously commune. Animism is precisely a state of primitive undifferentiation of consciousness in which nature as nature is not known. He quotes Motoori Norinaga on the indiscrimination with which the ancients worshipped natural objects. It was their inherent power alone that mattered and considerations of good or bad, respectworthy or despicable, and even beautiful or ugly were quite beside the point. The earliest Japanese poetry is about love, war, and hunting, not nature, and when nature does emerge as an important theme, as in the *Manyōshū*, the treatment of it betrays continental cultural influences. It seems to me that this initial point serves two functions besides that of being an empirical generalization. It indicates that Ienaga is not talking about the mysterious Japanese folk-soul that goes back for ages. And it brings in right at the beginning an element of brokenness, of tension and negation, which must be present if the religious view of nature is to interest Ienaga. If he felt that the religious view of nature were simply the celebration of the harmonious union of the Japanese with nature it seems to me unlikely that the subject would have ever received his consideration.

The treatment of the development of the religious view of nature is quite parallel to the treatment of the logic of negation. Both depend on contact with foreign culture for their initiation, but both develop and deepen only through becoming part of the actual experience of the Japanese people themselves.[32] From being a temporary consolation nature gradually becomes an absolute savior. This realization is made apparent through the same process of deepening social disruption that was described in the earlier book. Similarly it is the Kamakura period that sees the fulfillment of this tendency. It was gradually realized that temporary visits to natural sites were not enough and so the ideal of the *yamazato* (mountain retreat) as a permanent dwelling place developed.[33] This *yamazato* ideal reached its fulfillment in Saigyō and Kamo no Chōmei in Kamakura times. In this ideal there is the sharpest antagonism between the world of men and the world of nature. Only by fleeing to the bosom of nature can one escape the contaminations and sufferings of human troubles. Thus there is involved here too a type of logic of negation.

However, and this Ienaga believes to be specifically Japanese, the *yamazato*, which was supposed to be a realm of escape from suffering, turns out to have its own kind of suffering, the suffering of loneliness, which he illustrates with a wealth of poetic citations.[34] Japanese being people of strong human feelings and close human ties cannot easily give up human companionship and in fact can be miserably unhappy in its absence. Consequently the *yamazato* hermit longs to see a human face and may even wistfully dream of the happy bustle of city life. But of course a return to the city and its complexities could only make things worse. In this situation the *yamazato* hermit has reached an absolute impasse analogous to that of Shinran's sinner.

> At this point he reaches an insoluble difficulty. However, this contradiction is broken not by neutralizing it but rather by a seemingly paradoxical acceptance of the contradiction as a contradiction in a higher frame of mind. That is to say, an absolute contradiction causes the self to open up through absolute negation. To explain more concretely, a special frame of mind opens up in which the loneliness [*sabishisa*] of the *yamazato* in its loneliness itself is conversely the highest joy and becomes the salvation of the spirit. After all, the sadness and misery [*kanashisa, wabishisa*] which nature contains differ from the suffering arising from human difficulties and are linked to a quality which one feels as a difficult to define consolation within the sadness and misery.[35]

Ienaga discusses another strand of the *yamazato* tradition represented first clearly by Fujiwara Teika and some of his fellow *Shinkokinshū* poets. Unlike Saigyō and Chōmei these court nobles did not actually go themselves to dwell in nature, and so to that extent were not as thorough. But in their poetry they developed a symbolic nature that, though different from real nature, had the same function as a savior. Ienaga sees this symbolic *yamazato* tradition as one of the ingredients (besides the Zen cultural influences from China) that went into the highly symbolic Muromachi culture in which nature (in the tea house [*chashitsu*] with its accompanying arts of flower arrangement, gardening, ink painting, and so on) plays a central role.[36]

In Bashō the *yamazato* tradition finds a late embodiment: "So finally the decisive reason that Bashō is the true heir of the *yamazato* spirit is that he experiences an unlimited religious ecstasy in the loneliness [*sabishisa*] of loneliness as loneliness itself and that sphere of paradoxical salvation of the *yamazato* actually finds in him its most typical, even its most thorough expression."[37]

On the whole the Edo period was not conducive to this kind of experience, but after all the religious view of nature has never died out and remains alive in modern Japan, as quotations from Nagai Kafū and Natsume Sōseki indicate. Ienaga argues that the history of Japanese religion is not fully encompassed by the categories of "Shinto," "Buddhism," and "Christianity." "Did not Saigyō and Bashō, who could not be saved by Buddhism, experience tranquility for the first time when they were embraced in nature's bosom?"[38] Thus any history of Japanese religion that leaves out the religious view of nature will be distorted.

In this book written in the midst of the war (1944) and more concerned with the Japaneseness of the Japanese than are any other of Ienaga's writings, he even toys (in quotations from others, not directly in his own words) with the idea that the religious view of nature is an element of superiority that the Japanese have over the West.[39] But this mood is quickly dispelled in the question that opens the penultimate section of the essay: Was this salvation after all an absolute salvation? "Nature has certainly come to be a great salvation for the spiritual sufferings of the Japanese. But was this salvation after all an absolute salvation? Does the *yamazato* ambiance have the capacity to dispel all human illusion? Here I think there is in this special Japanese religious sphere an insurmountable limitation."[40]

Ienaga cites the long tradition of criticism of the *yamazato* tradition that also existed in Japan, especially the criticism from the Pure Land point of view, namely that the *yamazato* is not a real "other shore" but a part of this transient world and subject to its contaminations. "If we press this far an entirely new road opens up. If the *yamazato* is after all part of this sad world and is not therefore a place of absolute repose, is it necessary to seek salvation by fleeing from men into the mountains and hating the world? Rather salvation comes not through fleeing from the troubles of this dirty world, but by facing them head on and seeking it in committing oneself in the midst of them."[41] Here Ienaga returns to the theme of *The Logic of Negation*. One enters the dirty world as it is. One does not flee from sin but uses it as an opportunity for salvation. Indeed, for Shinran, man's finitude is a positive precondition for salvation and this is why he spoke of the "remembrance of sin." This way of salvation is entirely different from that of Saigyō and Chōmei.[42] But the essay closes by attacking those who criticize the religious view of nature as escapist from a purely this-worldly point of view, whether in Tokugawa or modern times. He argues that this experience is apt to be permanently meaningful to the Japanese people.[43]

Before summarizing the religious position that Ienaga had reached by 1945, we must consider one more important essay: "Natsume Sōseki as a

Thinker and His Historical Position."[44] This, it might be noted, is the only study in all of Ienaga's work before the end of the war that is primarily concerned with a modern figure. He chooses to treat Sōseki as a "thinker" because of the deep moral and religious concern that pervaded the whole of his work. But in interpreting Sōseki's thought Ienaga opposes two current conceptions of it, which might be called the historical materialist and the religious pantheist. He recognizes that there is in Sōseki's work, especially the early work, an element of social criticism, both of feudalism and feudal remnants and of the excesses of capitalism. At the same time his criticism lacked any clear theoretical basis or guiding principle so that while "liberating from the fetters of the old morality" his work contains no new positive morality to take its place and often ends up simply in indignation.[45] While recognizing that Sōseki's later work turns away from direct social criticism, Ienaga refuses to see in this a religious escapism or simply an expression of "the agony of 'egoistic liberals at the end of Meiji,' " as a powerful current of interpretation among Japanese intellectuals who make the "social viewpoint" primary would have it.[46] On the contrary, according to Ienaga it is not that Sōseki's moral and ethical concern did not continue to the end—it did strongly—but that in the early work he was concerned with discerning good and bad people whereas later he was concerned with the basic human structure. All men, he came to see, are untrustworthy sinners. Having come to understand the fundamental evil of the human condition he could no longer simply judge the relative good and evil in social life. But this does not mean a rejection of the moral problem; rather, it led to a profounder understanding of it.[47]

If Ienaga rejects the historical materialist interpretation of Sōseki and positively evaluates the later religious preoccupations, he also opposes a common interpretation of Sōseki's religious position, one which would assert that he found final consolation in the spirit of Zen and haiku. Here Ienaga is on more delicate ground, for Sōseki was all his life devoted to Zen and haiku. But Ienaga believes that through a careful analysis of Sōseki's novels it can be discerned that he actually attained a somewhat different position. Ienaga interprets the Zen-inspired euphoric pantheism of such early novels as *Kusamakura* and the poetry that he wrote throughout his life as merely the starting point of Sōseki's spiritual quest, one that would eventually be found wanting. Similarly he interprets the ecstatic religious experience of 1910 as stemming from primarily physical conditions brought on by illness and exhaustion.[48] So he turns to a step-by-step analysis of the later novels in order to discover Sōseki's final religious position.

According to Ienaga, around 1909, with *Sore kara* as the watershed,

Sōseki's style underwent a great change. From the elegant optimism of the *Kusamakura* period Sōseki's mood becomes more somber and his style more direct. The shift is something like that from late Heian aristocratic Buddhism to Kamakura Buddhism, says Ienaga. The sufferings and limitations of the petit bourgeois life, which had not previously occupied Sōseki's attention, come increasingly into the subject matter of the later novels— first notably in *Mon*. But the thing that chiefly attracts Ienaga's attention in *Mon* is the failure of the hero to attain any solution to his problems through Zen meditation. For the hero, Sōsuke, the "gate" of Zen is closed. The situation reminds Ienaga of Hōnen in tears because he had failed at the practices of the Shōdō (Holy Way, with the implication of salvation through works).[49]

In the next three novels, *Higan sugi made*, *Kōjin*, and *Kokoro*, the gloomy mood in which *Mon* ended is successively deepened. The scholar hero of *Kōjin* fails in the attempt at Zen meditation as completely as the petit bourgeois hero of *Mon* had before him. He finds himself with but three choices: to die, to go mad, or to enter religion. The novel closes without a solution. *Kokoro* represents a kind of end of the road for Sōseki. In it "Sensei" has arrived at a completely negative view of human life and has no alternative but to commit suicide. Ienaga's account of Sōseki's religious development as seen through the novels now reaches its climax:

> The thunder roars and the lightning falls. As the effort of the whole
> life of a human being is not worth a hair before God, all human sin
> is buried beneath the avalanche in the valley. But isn't it just at the
> moment when the sin which it is so hard to rise above is buried at the
> bottom of the abyss of death that one meets anew the call of the "God
> of love"? The little human soul which died with the death of the hero
> of *Kokoro* was completely buried in absolute negation, but a great self-
> less love is resurrected from the blood of the cross. The new life thus
> arisen from the depths of death became concretized in the novel *Michi-
> gusa* of 1915.[50]

For Ienaga it is only in *Michigusa* and *Meian* that Sōseki indicates that he has attained his early aim of "overcoming life and death." And that he sees as happening not through any cosmic euphoria or sudden enlightenment, but only through a profound confrontation of the fundamental sinfulness of human life.

According to Ienaga, Sōseki virtually identified religion with Zen. He implies that this was natural for an intellectual of his day. Thus whenever Sōseki speaks of religion objectively in his essays he is using Zen categories. His philosophy of *sokuten kyoshi* (to model oneself on heaven and depart from the self) Sōseki defined as *kenshō jōbutsu* (attaining enlightenment and becoming a Buddha), using Zen terminology.[51] But Ienaga feels that Sōseki's actual religious experience as expressed in the novels transcended his conscious categories. He stresses the limited knowledge that Sōseki had of the Japanese tradition in contrast with his thorough knowledge of the West, with the implication that Sōseki was not aware of the full meaning of the Japanese Pure Land tradition. But for Ienaga, of course, the important thing is that he attained the insight, not the words he used to express it.

At the end of the essay Ienaga returns to the first point and to those who would interpret Sōseki entirely in terms of the "crisis of the age." He says, "To me Sōseki's deeper historic meaning lies in the fact that he was a great religious thinker who pointed out the way to understand and overcome the permanent human crisis which is mediated to men by the 'agony of the age' but always transcends it."[52]

We have now completed a review of the major writings of Ienaga before 1945 that bear on the problem of meaning. It seems evident that in the years 1935 to 1945 he worked out a religious position of great cogency that not only allowed him to maintain his own stability in those years, which were indeed a "dark valley" for any sensitive Japanese intellectual, but also from which he was able to develop a critical interpretation of the Japanese tradition in its religious aspects. Rejecting completely those parts of the tradition (Shinto, Confucianism) that were too simply affirmations of a traditional social system, Ienaga turned to Buddhism with its more complex dialectic. Here he found a correspondence between his own experience and the "logic of negation" of Shōtoku Taishi and Shinran. Salvation comes not through fleeing from the world but through "facing it head on" and recognizing its sinful and suffering nature. This position, as he wrote of Sōseki's, does not reject the problem of morality but treats it from a deeper level. For Ienaga religion does not dissolve the tension between the real and the ideal—it offers no resolution at all on this level—but insists on remaining acutely conscious of it. Salvation comes not through any kind of "solution" but "through accepting the contradiction as a contradiction." This is about as antimagical as a religious position can get. This highly critical, realistic character of the position, together with the seriousness with which it takes human suffering and sin, perhaps help us to understand its relation to the more directly socially conscious earlier and later Ienaga.

From this position it is easy to understand his evaluation of Zen Buddhism and the religious view of nature. Both are attractive to him for both have something of the dialectical quality of the "logic of negation." But both are in the last analysis unsatisfactory for they tend easily either toward a retreat from the merciless nature of reality into the mountains or the meditation hall, or they offer too easy a salvation that ends in an unbroken acceptance of the given. Christianity, by contrast, while it is to be criticized for its retention of mythical forms and for its theism, is nevertheless deeply congenial in its symbolism as the almost unconscious use of it in the passage describing Sōseki's attainment of religious insight ("God of love," "blood of the cross," and so on) indicates.[53]

Ienaga's religious position gave him a place to stand in relation to his world, his cultural tradition, and that of the West. Perhaps it is not unrelated, in a paradoxical sort of way, to the fact that it was precisely during the midst of the war itself that Ienaga began to turn away from the problems of ancient Japanese religion and to face "head on" the problem of modernization.

## THE MODERN SPIRIT
## AND ITS LIMITATIONS (1942−52)

It would perhaps be best to let Ienaga describe the next major phase of his development in his own words:

> I don't remember today exactly when I first put my hand to the study of the history of modern thought. But since my first essay concerning this area, "Opposition to Tendencies Favoring the Revival of the Past in the Tokugawa Period," was published in the magazine *Rekishi chiri* in March of 1943 it was probably around the beginning of the Pacific War. In that atmosphere which was like being in an oppressive prison I began to study the ABC's of the history of Meiji thought. I still remember vividly my feelings at that time—when one had to read currently only material which lacked any sane meaning—how moving were many of the passages in [Meiji magazines such as] *Kokumin no tomo* and *Rikugo zasshi* which I was perusing in the Meiji Newspaper and Magazine Library.
>
> Until the end of the Pacific War I was concerned only to preserve my own conscience; I lacked the leeway to reflect upon others. Also, until that time, because my responsibilities were light, I thought that to get through with that would be doing well enough. But, from the time of the war's final debacle I became unable to continue indefinitely with that attitude. I had, in my family, in my place of work, and finally in regard to society to grapple with the problem of modernization. The question of modern thought was not simply an object of scholastic concern, rather it became an urgent problem pressing in on me, one that I could not refuse. [Therefore] I, who until then had taken ancient or at best medieval Japanese intellectual history as my field of study, was forced, completely by the above spiritual considerations, to throw myself into the study of modern intellectual history.[54]

It is important to keep in mind how long the shift described above actually took. Ienaga first turned to the study of modern thought around 1942. It was not until ten years later, in July 1952, that he first became involved publicly in political action. The changes are with respect to fields of study and types of political and social action, not with respect to basic political thought itself, which we have reason to believe remained fairly stable ever since his higher school days.[55] Nevertheless the shift from the "old liberal" position of constitutional monarchy to the more "progressive" position of principled rejection of the emperor system, the most dramatic aspect of his change of political views, is, in the Japanese context, of considerable symbolic significance.

The thing that recalled Ienaga from his preoccupation with religious studies to research on more contemporary problems was the "strengthening of Fascism" that occurred with Japan's entry into the war. Although he did not cooperate at all with Fascism and so had a clean conscience on that score, the fact that he did not openly oppose the war became a matter of later self-reproach.[56] He was actually at that time trying to get a clearer picture of the beginnings of Japanese modernization, the reception of modern Western culture, and what this has meant for Japanese society. For these purposes the Meiji period is particularly strategic and it is to this period that his empirical researches have been largely confined almost until the present time.[57] The loss of the war and the beginning of the American occupation, which precipitated a rush to the standard of "democracy" in the Japanese intellectual world, had no such effect on Ienaga. He "felt a certain inability to trust in the sudden popularity of 'democracy' " and held aloof from the nearly uniform propaganda in its favor that appeared to him something like the reverse side of Fascism.[58] This attitude earned for Ienaga the sobriquet of "reactionary" in the years just after the war. It was the threat to the constitution arising from the "reverse course" (*gyaku-kōsu*) policy of the occupation in the last years of the decade of the 1940s that precipitated Ienaga's move into the political arena in defense, as he believed, of liberty and democracy in Japan. But, as is indicated in the quotation at the beginning of this section, this was the result of his experiences in home and place of work with the concrete problems of modernization in Japanese society, even before the political currents changed, and so was not merely a change in ideology.[59]

It should be evident from this review that Ienaga's shift to concern with contemporary problems and political activism, while of course related to changes going on in Japanese society, proceeded gradually. When we come to consider the book that stands at the end of this period of transition and summarizes eight years of reflection on the problems of Japanese modernization, namely, *The Modern Spirit and its Limitations* (1950), the essential continuity in his development should become even more clear. But first we must consider some of the problems of theory and method that occupied Ienaga more in the years 1945–50 than before or after.

Methodological problems must have come to a head for Ienaga in these years partly because of the great currency of the Marxist approach to history, in relation to which he must have had to define his own position, but also because of the need to secure a firmer theoretical grounding in his approach to the understanding of modernization. In an article on the "New Conception of Intellectual History"[60] he says that intellectual history understands thought "above history" and at the same time historically. Proper method starts with the first task, that is, to understand the thought as it is in itself in its own inner meaning, and is completed by a consideration of the thought in relation to other thought and to non-ideational historical elements. Further, since all thought is conditioned by society in its historical development, it is ultimately necessary to understand the whole course of Japanese society from primitive times to the present day if one is to understand a single Japanese thinker.

In another longer essay of the same year he amplifies these ideas while reflecting on "The Past and Present of Japanese Intellectual Historiography."[61] Here he asserts that Japanese intellectual history was virtually founded by two men: Muraoka Tsunetsugu (1884–1946), and Tsuda Sōkichi (1873–1961). These men, he asserts, "complete" tendencies already discernible in the work of two men in the Tokugawa period who foreshadowed the scientific study of intellectual history: Motoori Norinaga (1730–1801), to whom he links Muraoka, and Tominaga Nakamoto (1715–46), to whom he links Tsuda. The strong point of the former pair is that they grasp the inner meaning of the thought as it is. Motoori was the first to penetrate deeply into the worldview of the ancient Japanese classics. Muraoka, of course, lacks the nonscientific overtones of Motoori and so fulfills the possibilities of this approach. Muraoka's weakness, however, is that, while dealing sensitively with particular works and writers, he does not relate them to the social context or see them in the sweep of historical development. The strong point of the latter pair is precisely that they do see the social context and the historical development. Ienaga considers Tsuda's *A Study of Our National Thought as it Was Expressed in Literature* (Bungaku ni arawaretaru waga kokumin shisō no kenkyū, 4 vols., 1916–21) to be the greatest single work in the field and the starting point for future work. Nevertheless he feels that Tsuda fails to appreciate certain writers and movements and sometimes makes value judgments from present concerns that distort the original thought. These are defects even though critical appraisal of past thought from the point of view of present needs is not in principle bad.

In an essay published in 1949 Ienaga takes the issues sketched out above to the philosophical level.[62] Here he faces the Marxist position head on. Basing himself on the general position of Nicolai Hartmann, he argues that "while the substructure conditions the superstructure there are elements in the superstructure which cannot be understood in terms of the substructure."[63] For example Shinran's thought may have been conditioned by the society and economy of thirteenth-century Japan, but it is not explained by it. It is not a necessary product of that society and economy nor is its meaning exhausted only by considering its function in that society. According to Ienaga the self-conscious subject has an essential, if conditioned, freedom. Consequently his thought can never be reduced simply to a reflection of the substructure. In the case of Shinran it was his "meticulous reflection on human reality and thorough criticism of previous Jōdō thought arising from his highly developed consciousness" that allowed him to arrive at his radical religious conclusions. These conclusions were not "necessary" or "externally determined" consequences of any social process.[64]

Ienaga admits that in the historical process thought is, compared to substructural elements, "weak." But this is from the point of view of cause and effect relations. From the point of view of value what is weak, that is, thought, has high value and what is strong has low value.[65] Finally he turns to the problem of the categories to be used in intellectual history. He notes that they can be drawn from the conditioning social structure (for example, the thought of slave society, feudal society, capitalist society) or from the structure of the thought itself (for example, Shinto thought, Buddhist thought, Confucian thought). He notes that either of these alone is inadequate and that what is needed is a way of putting together meaningful categories that will take account of both types of factors.[66]

As recently as 1957 Ienaga has reiterated his position on the point of the relative independence and value of culture in relation to social structure. We may quote from an essay first published in that year: "Finally and most importantly is the fact that there is sometimes in culture accompanying its character as the product of its age and its class character, something which may be called its pan-human character which transcends its period and class character, or may there not even be something which transcends its pan-human character?" He suggests that Jesus's Sermon on the Mount or the faith of Shinran as expressed in the *Tannishō* may be recognized as having this sort of character.[67]

In these writings we can discern the same basic Neo-Kantian position, with its distinction between "existence" and "value," which Ienaga adopted in his higher school days. Since Ienaga's primary concern is with value there is always a strong practical (in the Kantian sense) element in his work. This has led to the evaluation of his work as "subjective." He says that relative to the academic empiricists, the historical materialists, and the students of Max Weber—each in their own way "objective"—there is indeed a "subjective" character to his work that makes him somewhat isolated in the scholarly world.[68] It is of course this "practical" character in all his work from beginning to end that allows us to treat him as a thinker as well as a historian of thought.

We must now turn to the first book in which Ienaga's general approach to modernization becomes clearly discernible. The book is entitled, significantly, *The Modern Spirit and its Limitations* (1950). The work consists of four separate but not unrelated studies: "The Modern Bourgeois Spirit in Kitamura Tōkoku," "The Modern Spirit and its Limitations—An Intellectual Historical Examination of Uchimura Kanzō," "The Class Consciousness of Fukuzawa Yukichi," and "The 'Sociology' of Taguchi Ukichi."

The figure of Fukuzawa Yukichi (1835–1901) broods over the whole book. From the outset it is stated that whereas many figures represent various aspects of the modern spirit in Japan, Fukuzawa does so completely.[69] References to Fukuzawa form a kind of counterpoint in the essays on the other men who are constantly being compared to and measured against him. Fukuzawa was the great stalwart in the struggle against feudalism. He was the champion of independence for the individual, freedom and equality in human relationships, a democratic family ideal, and so on. But at the same time that he provides an ideal type of the modern spirit he also provides an ideal type of its limitations. The essay on Fukuzawa's class consciousness is largely concerned with pointing these out.

Fukuzawa's basic limitation is that for him "modernization" meant "establishing capitalism." Consequently when he was for freedom and equality it meant basically the freedom of enterprise and the equality of the middle classes. It did not mean a thoroughly free and equal society. Though his opposition to feudalism may have been based on universal human feelings originally, from the time he first came into contact with the capitalist spirit of Europe and America in Bakumatsu times it was indissolubly linked to the advancement of capitalism.[70] It was because of this basic limitation that Fukuzawa was never able to sympathize with the poor or the working classes. He attributed poverty and bad living conditions to the lack of energy or even the criminality of the people concerned, and he did not feel there was any social responsibility to remedy the situation. Nevertheless the fact that Fukuzawa favored capitalism does not mean that his thought is of low value, for that was "an extremely progressive attitude" for that time.[71] But this does not mean we should overlook its limitations.

Finally Ienaga asks the question of why Fukuzawa, who had such a sharp social understanding, could never be a friend of the proletariat. He does not feel satisfied with an explanation purely in terms of Fukuzawa's own class identity. He was not after all himself a capitalist. Ienaga suggests that the reason is bound up with the utilitarianism and pragmatism that formed the essence of his thought. Consequently, says Ienaga, Fukuzawa lacked the Kantian principle of "act so as to treat every man as an end, never merely as a means." Since for Fukuzawa a strong economy is a necessary means for an independent nation and the concentration of capital is a necessary means for a strong economy both the capitalist class and the working class are means. Consequently, it is hard to see how the poor as ends in themselves could have much meaning for him. But Uchimura Kanzō, who was similar to Fukuzawa in that he fought feudalism and could not espouse socialism, was quite different from him in his idealistic spirit.[72]

Since it is Uchimura who emerges in the final paragraph of the essay on Fukuzawa as a possible alternative to the latter's limitations, let us turn to the essay on Uchimura, by far the longest in the book. In a sustained passage of about twenty-six pages Ienaga builds up a picture of Uchimura as struggling for many of the values that Fukuzawa espoused.[73] First there is his openness to the world, his bitter attack on the "closed country" (*sakoku*) idea. He opposed a parochial "Japanese" point of view and insisted on viewing matters from a worldwide perspective. His position was based on his Christian universalism. Men are basically citizens of the kingdom of heaven and this comes before their being Japanese or Western. Unlike the bureaucrats who favored "Europeanization," Uchimura stood for a universal position that was above "Europeanism" as well as "Japanese purism."[74]

Secondly, Uchimura favored the development of public spirit and a public morality against the purely private nature of traditional Japanese morality as he viewed it. According to Uchimura, loyalty and filial piety (*chū* and *kō*) are based on personal relations and so are personal obligations. As opposed to personal obligation (*giri*) he supported duty (*gimu*), which he defined as having a universal moral character. In sociological terms Uchimura advocated a universalistic ethic in place of a particularistic one.[75]

Thirdly, Uchimura opposes the respect for empty forms that characterizes traditional Japanese feudal society and advocates a greater degree of naturalness and directness. Fourthly, he opposes the negative retrogressive side of feudalism that revered tradition above change. As against the feudal dislike of the new and untraditional, Uchimura argues for advance, progress, change. Nothing in the society is sacred to him because it is old. As against the feudal "negative morality" of abstaining from doing evil he urges a positive morality that tries to fulfill its ideals in practice.[76]

Fifthly, Uchimura, like Fukuzawa, vigorously attacked the traditional family system. He favored monogamy, opposing the traditional double standard and degradation of women. He opposed the patriarchal family and argued that love, not authority, should be the basis of family relations. While remaining traditional to the extent of stressing obligations of children to parents, he nonetheless argued for the small nuclear family as the ideal type of family structure.[77]

Sixthly, Uchimura opposed the feudal status system and its survival in Meiji times. Like Fukuzawa he favored a system of formal equality for all citizens, but unlike him his ultimate reason was that in Christ all distinctions of class between men are overcome. And seventhly, Uchimura was a stalwart fighter for freedom, democracy, and peoples' rights. In fact his position on questions of political democracy was more thorough than most of the leaders of the Movement for Freedom and Peoples' Rights.[78]

In conclusion, then, Ienaga argues, contrary to the opinion of Masamune Hakucho (that Uchimura's thought was not as "advanced" as Fukuzawa's), that Uchimura was actually more advanced and thorough than Fukuzawa even on the issues where Fukuzawa himself made his main contribution. And on a number of other issues where Fukuzawa was not so clear Uchimura was far beyond him. For example, he criticized as false a civilization (*bummei*) that has more respect for battleships than for human beings, and as empty a democracy that exists in names and forms only. Although, like Fukuzawa, he favored capitalism, he wanted free productive enterprise and opposed monopoly. Unlike Fukuzawa he wanted some controls on absolutely free competition when this competition had destructive social consequences. He argued for respect for labor and the laborer, as against Fukuzawa's contempt for the lower classes. Again, unlike Fukuzawa, he bitterly opposed the "rich nation, strong army" idea. He was patriotic and a nationalist, but he always held the nation to be the instrument of higher ideals, never an end in itself. One of the duties of the patriot, he felt, was to criticize his country vigorously when it required criticism. He never apologized for an oppressive statism, as Fukuzawa on occasion did. He was one of the first to speak out against imperialism in Japan, even before Kōtoku Shūsui.[79] If Uchimura opposed his epoch, it was not because he was behind it, but because he was ahead of it. "It cannot be doubted that he was the most splendid embodiment of the Meiji modern spirit," says Ienaga.[80]

But the thing that makes Ienaga evaluate Uchimura so highly is more than his stand on particular issues. It is the special kind of individualism for which he stood. Of course this special individualism is based on Uchimura's Christianity. Uchimura wrote, "The individual is the basis of church and the foundation of the state. God dwells in the spirit of the individual before he dwells in the church, he faces the spirit of the individual before he faces the nation." Individual conscience should be beyond any coercion, according to Uchimura. Not only should pressure from ruling powers above be resisted, but pressure from the power of the masses below should also be resisted. "However good a principle, it cannot fail to be a bad principle if it is enforced from without," he said.[81] Christ alone is the basis from which the individual can fight all the powers of the world.

In summing up Ienaga says:

> Individualism is an essential element in the modern spirit, an ines-capable component of it. But the Meiji enlightenment thinkers [*keimō-shisōka*] were apt to run in the direction of a utilitarianism which makes the individual's pleasure his highest value. They were unable to establish an ethical individualism which makes individual moral duty its absolutely highest thing. So even after modernization advanced successively in the Taishō and Shōwa periods, as before there did not appear a firm individual selfconsciousness but only a vacillating tendency to follow blindly whatever opinion was current. If we reflect on this situation, the intellectual historical meaning of Uchimura's unique individualism is that it showed for a Japanese a remarkably rare height.[82]

It was from his position of ethical individualism with its ultimately religious basis that Uchimura could make his profound criticism of not only the traditional Japanese society but the modern spirit itself. He criticized the false modern individualism that would deify the self, just as he criticized any tendency to deify progress, or the state, or socialism.[83] "How many people besides Uchimura," says Ienaga, "would we find among all the Japanese thinkers since Meiji who truly reached the foundation of the modern spirit, stood there and broke through its limitations?"[84]

Finally Ienaga turns to the problem of the latter years of Uchimura and his apparent turn to conservatism. He points out that to some degree Uchimura's progressive attitudes continued to the end and quotes some sharp critical comments from the early and late 1920s. Further, some of his antiprogressive tendencies are only seemingly so. For example, his praise of *bushidō* is not to be taken literally. It is not *bushidō* as it actually was but an idealized Kantian *bushidō* in which the element of selfless duty has been extricated from the particular nexus of feudal relationships. Even when all this has been said Ienaga admits that there really was a retrogressive tendency and proceeds relentlessly to document it. What most of all Ienaga finds difficult to forgive is Uchimura's backtracking on the family ethic, which he takes as a kind of touchstone of modernization.[85] But, finally, Ienaga denies that the later retrogression can detract from the "high historical meaning carried by his early thought."[86] (Any more than the conservatism of the aging Luther can dim the achievements of his early years.) And even in his "betrayal" of his own progressive past Uchimura maintained his integrity, says Ienaga. Such betrayal has been common enough in Japan, but usually it has been carried out in a group and under some kind of group pressure. Not so with Uchimura. Even his "betrayal" manifested the quality of his individualism, for he carried it out at his own time, for his own reasons, in his own way.[87]

Since the essays on Taguchi and Kitamura only supplement themes already sketched out in the Fukuzawa and Uchimura essays, we may turn to a general estimate of the significance of *The Modern Spirit and its Limitations* as a work that summarizes a nearly ten-year period in Ienaga's development.[88] The most impressive thing to me about this book of 1950 is its essential continuity with his earlier work on religious history, a continuity considerably greater than one might have expected from reading the quotation with which we began this section. There is in this book a shift in basic interest from religion to what I shall call the "moral level." But there is no indication of a rejection of earlier positions, most of which are directly or indirectly reaffirmed. Of course the shift in primary concern is itself of the highest significance. In the earlier work on religion it is remarkable that the moral problem is almost completely ignored. It was salvation through the logic of denial that had interested Ienaga, not any implications about human moral action. But Ienaga had never denied the possibility of moral implications, and indeed by insisting on keeping the religious man so firmly in this world and resisting any tendency to escape from the actualities of human existence, he seemed actually to be setting the stage for a working out of those implications.

Ienaga's attitude to the modern (*kindai*) is itself a test case of what I call his continuity. We saw at the end of *The Development of the Logic of Negation* a basically negative evaluation of the modern, whereas by 1950 he was a firm supporter of modernization. But this is no mere reversal. The essential grounds on which he had criticized the modern spirit in 1940, namely, its utilitarian and nontranscendent aspect, are reaffirmed in 1950 and indeed again in 1960.[89] It is not that Ienaga has become a utilitarian or a materialist. While remaining faithful to his own basic religious and philosophical commitments, he has nonetheless changed his evaluation of the possibility of realizing those commitments in modern society. The modern is good precisely because it more fully expresses the values that Ienaga had long held. Relative to traditional "feudal" society the modern society and culture have greater "universality" (*fuhensei*) and give a fuller and more adequate expression of human capacities. This is the constant theme of Ienaga's evaluation of "progressive" tendencies. In this respect it is clear that, within the realm of the modern, Ienaga feels that socialism is a fuller expression of human universality than capitalism, and consequently though it is good to favor capitalism relative to feudalism it is even more progressive to favor socialism relative to capitalism. But there is nothing in the sphere of the modern, including socialism, that is not subject to criticism from a value position. Ienaga never collapses his early distinction between what is and what ought to be. He never deifies history or idolizes the modern. In this connection it might be well to consider another statement by Ienaga that shows his attitude toward the relation of Western culture and modernization and what this means for Japan:

> It is already clear that Western culture is not the only human culture. Besides Europe and America there are various different societies and cultures and consequently besides Western history there exist the histories of a number of peoples and regions. But, since the West's modern culture has a world universality and its power of diffusion has swept the globe, it has come to be thought that the Western culture which is the womb of that culture is a model form for world history.
>
> Formerly some people of narrow thought have supposed that Western culture is materialistic and Eastern culture is spiritual and much superior to Western culture and such like. That is not to be believed. Modern culture which had its source in Europe and America does not simply belong to Westerners only; now it is the world's culture and no one can overlook that. Pre-modern oriental classical culture does not have the power to replace this modern culture. However, if you say that modern culture is complete and has no lacks that is not at all so. It must not be forgotten that it contains not a few contradictions and lacks deriving from its womb. . . .
>
> It cannot be that Japan can fail to feel the suffering coming from the contradictions and lacks mentioned above. Now the Japanese together with the other peoples of the world are facing the great task of overcoming the contradictions and lacks of modern culture. Today may be said to be the age of the labor pains of giving birth to a new future.[90]

The essentially new element in the period under discussion is the working out of Ienaga's moral position, bringing with it a heightened sense of moral responsibility, as indicated in the opening quotation in this section. The core of his ethical position is an ethical individualism of which Uchimura is the paradigm. (Ienaga indicated to me in 1961 that Uchimura remains for him the most significant modern Japanese.) This is an individualism that accepts the duty to be oneself, which refuses to renounce that responsibility through dependence on any group, but which avoids self-deification and finds its highest realization in an unshakable loyalty to values that transcend the self. It is in this context of working out his moral position that I think we can understand Ienaga's refusal to plunge into the political struggle right after the end of the war. He had genuinely to appropriate a position that would really be his own, and that took time and could not be rushed. As was his habit, he worked these problems through by defining himself in relation to paradigmatic figures in the past. By 1950 he had added Uchimura Kanzō to the figures of Shōtoku Taishi and Shinran as the third hero. Having moved back from the religious sphere to the moral, not through renouncing the religious but through working out its implications in relation to human actuality, he was now in a position to answer the call to social responsibility.

## FACING HISTORICAL CRISIS (1950– )

If we can characterize the preceding period as one in which Ienaga moved from primarily religious to primarily moral concern, this most recent phase of his development can be seen as still a further shift in emphasis from the moral to the social institutional level, but of course with the same proviso as above, that the shift did not mean abandonment of earlier positions. In addition to the conditions in family and place of work that aroused his social concern it was the "reverse course" policy of the late 1940s, which seemed to involve a recession from the democratic reforms of the early occupation years, and threatened to make the constitution "empty words," which stimulated Ienaga to become involved in political matters. A very strong motive was the desire not to have to repent a second time for having failed openly to oppose the reactionary elements in Japanese society.[91]

From March 1952 Ienaga has been a regular contributor to popular newspapers and magazines on topical political matters. The first paragraph of the first of these articles, "University Self-government" (*Asahi Shimbun*, March 4, 1952), gives an example of the motives that prompted him to take this step:

It is said that very recently the idea that university presidents be chosen by the government is being talked about, but this is a matter which ought to surprise us. The supporters of this idea say that even in the case of the university there is no freedom to cause social anxiety. But is it after all the university which is causing social anxiety? Or is it indeed the policy of those people who, overlooking the clear wording of the constitution, want to strengthen "war power" and reduce "the freedom of assembly, association, speech, publication and all other forms of expression"? A wise nation will not make a mistake in judging [the answer to these questions].[92]

His topical articles have been collected in three volumes so far, *Facing Historical Crisis* (1954), *History and Education* (1956), and *History and Today* (1959). They contain articles dealing with a wide variety of subjects but mainly centering around questions of educational and political policy and above all the defense of the constitution. Another volume that should perhaps be mentioned at this point is his *Criticism of the Courts* (Saiban hihan) (1959), which is an independent essay discussing the legitimacy and appropriate limits to public criticism of the judicial process. The legal emphasis in this most recent period should not surprise us when we remember Ienaga's fascination with constitutional and legal matters from middle school days. Also we must remember the 1935 article published in his middle school alumni magazine on the question of the "organ theory" of the emperor.

In addition to vigorous journalistic activity Ienaga has also been active in a number of movements in defense of the constitution and liberal causes. He was very active in the opposition to the security treaty of 1960. In response to criticisms that say that the scholar's duty is to scholarship and, besides voting, he ought not to bother with politics, Ienaga made this defense in the preface to *History and Education:*

> Firstly, a scholar must be a member of society before he is a scholar. Is it permissible for him, while fulfilling his occupation as a scholar, to renounce his duty as a member of society? Just as it is natural that the scholar, being a member of a family should fulfill his moral obligations to the family, is it not also natural that he, as a member of larger social groups, should positively cooperate in the running of those social groups to which he belongs? Since in a democratic country all the people bear a responsibility for the management of the country, it is not a matter of asking about occupation. It cannot be said that the scholar alone is exempted from that responsibility.

At any rate it is clear that Ienaga has not allowed his concern for social and political issues to divert him from his professional activities for he has continued to publish with amazing frequency during this most recent period. Here we can only review briefly the major categories of his recent work.

During the decade of the 1950s Ienaga wrote several historical surveys of which the most important are *A History of Japanese Moral Thought* (through Meiji) (1954) and *A History of Japanese Culture* (through the Tokugawa period) (1959).[93] In these books Ienaga returns to an overview of the development of Japanese thought and culture such as he had not undertaken since *The Development of the Logic of Negation* and *The Development of the Religious View of Nature,* but they are very different in character from the earlier books. Unlike the earlier books, which drew their categories from the sphere of thought itself, these utilize categories that are drawn mainly from the "substructure," such as, for example, the moral thought of the nobility, of the warriors, of the townsmen, of the peasants, and of the bourgeois.[94] One of the most interesting chapters in the *History of Japanese Moral Thought* is on the moral thought of the monks, which is not exactly a "substructural" category though it is in a sense a social category. Since Ienaga's work always has its "practical" aspect, it is probably not illegitimate to ask what is the function of these books in the context of Ienaga's most recent concerns. Here it seems to me that they serve the function of providing a historical grounding in the Japanese tradition for a modern democratic Japan. Given the almost complete lack of an explicit democratic tradition, this means that a great deal of weight has to be given to the relatively inarticulate "peoples' struggles" down through the centuries and the occasional unorthodox thinker, like Andō Shōeki (who receives more pages of discussion in the *History of Japanese Culture* than any other figure in all Japanese history).

While the treatment is always rich in illustration and often subtle in analysis, I cannot help but entertain a certain feeling of dissatisfaction with these books compared with the rest of Ienaga's work. Although in no orthodox sense Marxist, they do at times seem to have a mechanical quality. This is especially evident it seems to me in the case of the treatment of feudal society. In the *History of Japanese Moral Thought,* for example, while the treatment of the aristocrats and monks, on the one hand, and of the Meiji bourgeois, on the other, seems to be insightful, the discussion of the warriors (*bushi*), townsmen (*chōnin*) and peasants seems to be one-sided. For example, it is hard for me to accept the characterization of the warrior ethic as "utilitarian" (chapter 7) or the townsmen and peasants as quite as progressive as Ienaga would seem to have it (chapters 8 and 9). Ienaga's treatment is perhaps understandable. The Japanese tradition of "feudalism" is still too strongly alive, not only in the massive weight of reactionary survivals, but within the soul of even progressive individuals, for most Japanese intellectuals yet to be able to assess it entirely objectively. Yet I cannot help but feel that here is one of the few points at which Ienaga's "practical" primacy has distorted his objective analysis. Part of the difficulty, however, is the inevitable schematization that arises from a brief treatment of a very large subject. In this respect the hundred-page treatment of Meiji thought in the first volume of *A Symposium on Modern Japanese Intellectual History* (1959), since it involves a smaller time span on a broader canvas, is a more richly suggestive discussion.

Perhaps even more closely related to the constitutional and political concerns of the decade of the 1950s is Ienaga's preoccupation with the figure of Ueki Emori (1857–92).[95] Ueki is important for Ienaga as a leading thinker in the Movement for Freedom and Peoples' Rights and as an early constitutionalist. In attempting to establish the Japanese democratic tradition in modern times Ueki is a key figure. These interests are continuing in his most recent as yet unpublished work where he is turning to Minobe Tatsukichi (1873–1948) and Taishō democratic thought, coming back in a sense to the point where his own intellectual development began.

In this most recent period Ienaga's problem is not primarily religious or moral. It is the problem of how to institutionalize democracy securely in Japan. It is natural, therefore, that legal and constitutional matters should figure prominently in his concerns. Much of Ienaga's political writing seems Marxist, at least to an American, but this reflects mainly the current political vocabulary in Japan.[96] In the case of Ienaga the reader soon discovers the basically liberal and democratic values beneath the vocabulary.

But if political concerns have had primacy in this most recent period, Ienaga's moral and religious concerns have not gone unexpressed. A small book on Taoka Reiun (1870–1912)[97] seems to represent what we have called Ienaga's moral concern, for Taoka was not a political leader but a somewhat "contradictory" literary critic whom Ienaga appreciates chiefly because of his "sense of justice and his love of humanity."[98] On the religious side, in 1961 Ienaga published a brief article in *Shūkan dokushojin* reaffirming the significance to him of Shōtoku Taishi's statement, "The world is empty and false; only the Buddha is true," though stating that it is the first phrase that continues to have meaning for him. Perhaps even more interesting is Ienaga's criticism in 1960 of Ueki for the latter's tendency to self-deification, which he finds responsible for his singular lack of self-criticism.[99] In the course of this discussion he raises again his old objections to utilitarianism, the philosophy of "limitless progress," and the idea of making the human being ultimate (*ningenshijōshugi*). Finally in answer to the question as to what was lacking in Ueki's philosophy of human ultimacy and limitless progress he answers, "the logic of negation" (*hitei no ronri*).[100]

## EPILOGUE

Ienaga Saburō, like all men, is the product of his age. But unlike most he has been acutely sensitive to its pressures and has made its problems his own. The three main phases in his thought broadly conform to three main phases of modern Japanese history: Taishō Democracy, the Nationalist period, and the postwar period. But though always in dialogue with his epoch he has been capable of saying no to it as well as yes. In fact in spite of the clearly definable stages in his thought reflecting different sorts of external pressure, there is an equally clear continuity and cumulativeness. In dealing with the cultural problems of his day he has made his own synthesis, drawing from such diverse sources as Buddhism and Christianity, Liberalism and Marxism. It is not that Ienaga has or claims to have solved the problems of Japan's cultural modernization. But he has clearly discerned what some of them are and uncovered some of the cultural resources that may be used in their solution.

Ienaga notes that in all his reading of Ueki's writings, including his journals, he never came across a single instance of self-doubt. This, he says, is not unique to Ueki but is a characteristic of his generation. Fukuzawa Yukichi (1835–1901), Nakamura Keiu (1832–91), Katō Hiroyuki (1836–1916), and we could probably add Nishimura Shigeki (1828–1902) were the same. How different, he notes is the next generation of people like Kitamura Tōkoku (1869–94) and Uchimura Kanzō (1861–1930), with their deep inner conflicts and doubts. It is interesting that the generation of the great enlighteners grew up in Tokugawa times. Those men all came to know who they were when the traditional order was intact. This provided the fundamental personality stability that carried them through all the vicissitudes of later years. They became heroes of Japan's social, political, economic, and scientific modernization. But the next generation, already growing up in a broken world, never knew the personality security of their elders. For them modernization implied the "spiritual breakdown" which Natsume Sōseki spoke of as following the impact of Western culture.[101] But nevertheless that generation produced the first heroes of the "modernization of the soul" if such a phrase is permissible. Kitamura, who committed suicide, and Uchimura, who retrogressed in his later years, are nonetheless heroes for Ienaga. The strain on them of their own inner revolution was too great to be borne and they were unable to actualize all of its possibilities. But, in a sense, what they have done does not need to be done again in quite the same way. They do not save succeeding generations from working out their own solutions, as the life of Ienaga itself shows. But they make it more likely that that working through will be successful. And of course Ienaga and men like him become examples for those who follow in the task of gradually creating a new cultural tradition for Japan.

# 3 Japan's Cultural Identity

*Some Reflections on the Work
of Watsuji Tetsurō*

It has become customary among many Western scholars to consider Japan
as part of an East Asian cultural area, or as a participant in Chinese or Sinic
civilization. In a general conception of Asian culture viewed as consisting of
East Asian, South Asian, and Middle Eastern cultural areas dominated by
Chinese, Indian, and Islamic civilizations respectively, it seems obvious that
Japan belongs in the first category. Yet most Japanese scholars use another
classification that would divide Asian culture into four areas: Islamic, Indian,
Chinese, and—as a separate category on the same level as the other three—
Japanese. Without denying the close relation to China, the Japanese scholar
is apt to emphasize the unique configuration of Japanese culture that makes
it in some sense sui generis. This is only one among many manifestations
of the widespread feeling in Japan that Japanese culture is "unique" and
"different." This sense of Japan's uniqueness may give rise to pride, sorrow,
or a feeling of loneliness; but that it is shared by Japanese with otherwise
quite varying views is itself a significant fact.

Correlative with the sense of uniqueness is a strong feeling of personal
identification that Japanese feel with their culture. A Japanese abroad seldom forgets that he is Japanese, just as a foreigner in Japan is seldom
allowed to forget that he is not Japanese. (The overtones of the Japanese
word *gaijin* are scarcely captured in the translation "foreigner.") Perhaps it
would even be possible to stretch the concept of role narcissism, which
George DeVos has developed, to apply to the representative role of being
Japanese.[1] Such a "national narcissism" is, of course, found to some degree
in any country. To apply the term especially to Japan is not to say that Japan
is in this respect pathological, but to emphasize that Japan is, comparatively
speaking, extreme.

Given the salience of Japanese self-consciousness, it follows that Japanese would be likely to show great concern about the national self-image or cultural identity. This in fact seems to be the case. Not only has there been a long and continuing concern with what is Japanese, but often studies of other societies seem more interested in placing Japan relative to them than in understanding them for their own sake. Again, the Japanese are not alone in this, but the preoccupation seems greater than elsewhere. Some effort will be made to explain this special Japanese preoccupation in the final section of this chapter after illustrative material on particular Japanese self-conceptions has been presented. The main body of evidence will come from the work of Watsuji Tetsurō, one of the leading interpreters of Japanese culture in this century. But first I turn to a brief sketch of some of the conceptions of Japan's cultural identity that have appeared in the last century.

Few Japanese in late Tokugawa times had any very sophisticated conception of the world and Japan's place in it. Hirata Atsutane (1776–1843) knew more than most about the West, but he was capable of bizarre views as to the physiological peculiarities of Westerners and seems to have believed that Japan's superiority over other nations is proved by the fact that the sun first shines on it each morning.[2] As an example of the sort of thing that was current in early-nineteenth-century Japan, we may cite a passage from the influential thinker of the Mito school, Aizawa Seishisai:

> The earth in the firmament appears to be perfectly round, without edges or corners. However, everything exists in its natural bodily form, and our Divine Land is situated at the top of the earth. Thus, although it is not an extensive country spatially, it reigns over all quarters of the world, for it has never once changed its dynasty or its form of sovereignty. The various countries of the West correspond to the feet and legs of the body. That is why their ships come from afar to visit Japan. As for the land amidst the seas which the Western barbarians call America, it occupies the hindmost region of the earth; thus, its people are stupid and simple, and are incapable of doing things.[3]

The cruder aspects of these comfortable assumptions were soon to be exploded, but the habits of thought that lay behind them were not so easily dispelled. A tacit assumption that Japan itself provides a standard for all values goes far back in Japanese history. This cannot be called nationalism as there was no concept of nation, certainly no notion of a sovereign people so indestructibly bound up with modern nationalism. If there was any structural reference at all, it was not to the nation but rather, as in the case of Aizawa, to the imperial dynasty. Shinto, on the whole lacking an explicit theological structure, gave ritual expression to the largely inarticulate union of land and people. It is true that Buddhism in the case of Shinran and Dōgen and Confucianism in the case of Ogyū Sorai produced thinkers oriented to transcendent or universalistic values for whom Japan itself had no ultimate meaning; but it was generally the fate of Buddhism and Confucianism to become subsumed in and subordinated to Japanese particularism. Since loyalty was primarily to what Nakamura Hajime speaks of as a "social nexus,"[4] however broadly or narrowly defined, and not to a set of abstract ideas, there was not, in the Japanese tradition, a strong philosophical or religious orthodoxy such as existed in China, the Islamic world, or the West.[5]

The opening of the country in the early Meiji period gave a severe blow to Japanese cultural particularism and provided the possibility for the growth of certain tendencies counter to it. But from middle and late Meiji times Japanese particularism, never seriously menaced as an unconscious assumption, was able vigorously to reassert itself. As examples of the countertrends, two of the most important thinkers of the Meiji period may be mentioned, Fukuzawa Yukichi (1834–1901) and Uchimura Kanzō (1861–1930).[6] Both of them were Japanese nationalists, but neither of them was a Japanese particularist. Both of them based themselves on values that could not be derived from or reduced to the Japanese social nexus.

Fukuzawa, who seemed to embody the rather untheoretical pragmatism of Tokugawa culture, found theoretical expression for it in English individualism and utilitarianism. For him personal independence and national independence were inseparably related. But the independent nation made sense for him only as a framework for the independent individual, not subordinate to any ultimate social nexus. As a tactical measure Fukuzawa could support the suppression of political freedoms for the sake of national unity in the dangerous international climate of the late nineteenth century, for loss of national independence would destroy any hope of independence for the individual. But it was to liberal individualism that he gave his ultimate loyalty.

Uchimura was linked more to the idealistic current in Japanese tradition, to the great religious thinkers and the men of action who died happily for lost causes. He found in Christianity an absolute religious reference for his idealism. Japan would become great to the extent that it embodied the commands of Jesus. The individual, because he is ultimately a citizen of the kingdom of heaven, can never find final meaning in an earthly social nexus.

Both liberalism and Christianity were important currents in Meiji thought, but they by no means went unchallenged. Rather, Japanese particularism found a new degree of theoretical explicitness in the thought of what the Japanese call the "emperor system," which began to crystallize from about 1890.[7] The problem was raised sharply by the beginning of con-

stitutionalism in Japan. Western constitutionalism rests ultimately on a nat-
ural-law basis with strongly theistic presuppositions. If the Japanese constitution was not to rest on a notion of God that was neither indigenous nor
well understood, what would be the locus of ultimate authority and value?
The answer as embodied in the imperial rescript on education and the constitution itself is: the imperial line, unbroken for ages eternal. No clearer
assertion of Japanese particularism was possible.

Though sometimes referred to as an "orthodoxy," it should be evident
that emperor-system thought was not an abstract philosophical or religious
system. It was rather an assertion about ultimate authority and value that
for many proximate purposes need not be invoked at all. A wide variety of
types of thought could operate under its mandate, rousing no strong objections unless certain sensitive areas were touched upon. The difficulty was
that what was considered sensitive could not be predicted but varied in
accord with the general state of Japanese society. What might be said with
hardly a mutter of protest in 1914 could be condemned as un-Japanese and
treasonable in 1935. What had changed was not the idea expressed but the
sensitivity of Japanese society, or rather of its established guardians.

Although emperor-system thought was securely established from the
1890s, antiparticularistic tendencies were also present in Taishō and early
Shōwa times. Chief among these were liberalism and socialism. It is true
that liberalism, or at least populism, and some aspects of Marxism, could be
harmonized with the emperor system and indeed did provide strands in the
"emperor-system fascism," which developed in the 1930s and early 1940s.[8]
But to the degree that liberals or Marxists maintained a loyalty to universalistic principles that transcended Japan, there was always the possibility of
direct confrontation. The liberal Kawai Eijirō (1891–1944) and the Marxist
Kawakami Hajime (1879–1946) provide cases where the confrontation
became irreconcilable.

Having briefly outlined the development of Japanese particularism and
its countertendencies in modern Japan, we now turn to the conceptions of
Japanese history and culture developed in association with these various
trends. The old praise and blame historiography of largely Confucian inspiration that took loyalty to the emperor as its highest criterion was seriously
undercut in the rush of new learning that entered early Meiji Japan.[9] Both
Christians and liberals taught a conception of history dominated by the idea
of progress in terms of which Japanese history could be understood but
which endowed it with no special meaning. Although social Darwinism
could be appropriated, like almost everything else, by the emperor system,
and indeed was as a justification for imperialism (as elsewhere), nineteenth-

century positivistic history could not solve all the needs of revivified Japanese particularism.

Inoue Tetsujiro (1856–1944), author of the official commentary on the imperial rescript on education, was perhaps the closest approximation to an "official" philosopher of the emperor system.[10] Inoue, whose chief claim to scholarly standing rested on surveys of Tokugawa Confucianism, ransacked the Japanese tradition for suitable materials.[11] He came to focus on three concepts that became the heart of Japanese ethics as taught by the Ministry of Education: *kokutai, chū,* and *kō. Kokutai* is the almost untranslatable term for the quintessence of Japanese particularity; *chū* and *kō* are loyalty and filial piety, respectively. Inoue and others like him asserted the ultimate value of the harmony of Japanese emperor and people (*kokutai*) and the obligations to emperor and ancestors that flow from it (*chū* and *kō*).

But even as Inoue was arguing with the liberals and Christians, other sensitive and educated Japanese were finding commitment to simpleminded "national ethics" or to doctrinaire Western ideologies unacceptable. The writer Natsume Sōseki (1867–1916) and the philosopher Nishida Kitarō (1870–1945) were representative of this latter group. Feeling a deep nostalgia for Japanese culture and values, yet unable to turn away from the intellectual achievements of the West, they hoped for a reconciling position to which they could devote themselves. It was Nishida, more than anyone else, who, with the help of Zen Buddhism and German Idealism, contributed to the formation of the new position that strongly influenced all Japanese literature, thought, and culture from the period of the First World War.

The new basis that Nishida found rested on aesthetic experience and mystical insight, neatly skirting the issue of ultimate value and authority, for the personal experience that he valued so highly had no immediate relevance to social and ethical reality. Nonetheless from his positions there were certain social implications. Although never engaging in vulgar nationalistic propaganda, he nonetheless spoke of the individual and the whole mutually negating themselves with the imperial household as the center.[12] Absolute negativity that was so central to his philosophy provided in actuality no alternative to the human nexus as a locus of authority and value. It is not surprising then that though Nishida himself withdrew into obscure privacy as the Second World War approached, some of his leading disciples were ardent, though sophisticated, propagandists for Greater East Asia.

Finally, before turning to Watsuji, we must mention several cultural historians who took positions in varying degrees outside the established view and who produced conceptions of Japanese culture quite different from that of the Nishida school. Tsuda Sōkichi, a great scholar of China as well as of

Japan, represents the liberal and pragmatic position applied to the history of Japanese culture. For example, he interpreted the Taika Reform in terms of power politics rather than lofty ethical idealism, and he viewed *bushidō* as a cover for the essentially self-interested land grabbing of the feudal warriors.[13] In a book published in 1939 and suppressed during the war Tsuda argued that Japan is essentially modern and has little in common with "oriental" culture as found in China.[14] He held that the old Japanese pattern of an emperor who reigns but does not rule is appropriate in modern society. In all these respects Tsuda's work tended to explain Japanese cultural history with the categories of liberal utilitarian social thought leaving little basis for a mystical Japanese particularism.

Hani Gorō is one of the best known of the Marxist writers who from the late 1920s began to give their version of Japanese cultural history. Hani interpreted certain Tokugawa thinkers such as Arai Hakuseki and especially the Kokugaku movement as representing middle-class thought in opposition to feudal thinking.[15] The Marxists interpreted Japanese culture in terms of general categories rather than particularism.

Still another antiparticularist interpretation was that of Ienaga Saburō who, in his prewar writing, developed a view of Japanese culture that might be seen as consonant with the position of Uchimura Kanzō.[16] In Ienaga's view the greatness of Japanese thought rests in those few men who were able to transcend Japanese particularity and attain to universal value, especially Shōtoku Taishi (in his rather special interpretation of him), Shinran, and in the modern period Uchimura.

It should be remembered that these men, who were either persecuted or led very retired lives during the war, were representative of a small minority. Most writing during the 1930s and early 1940s dealt with the Japanese spirit in mystical and absolute terms, based either on fairly straightforward translations of classical Confucian and Shinto texts or utilizing more or less elaborate theoretical structures like those of the Nishida school. A few, of whom Muraoka Tsunetsugu is perhaps the outstanding example, were neither particularist nor antiparticularist, but devoted themselves to the highest standards of scholarly research.[17]

Watsuji Tetsurō (1889–1960), born the son of a small-town doctor, received the best education available in the Japan of his day.[18] Graduating from the First Higher School in Tokyo, where he had been profoundly impressed by its recently appointed principal Nitobe Inazō and the great novelist Natsume Sōseki, he entered the Philosophy Department of Tokyo University in 1909. After seriously considering a literary career—he had translated Byron and Shaw, written a number of stories and plays, and col-

laborated on a literary magazine with his friend Tanizaki Junichirō—
Watsuji decided to devote himself seriously to the study of philosophy.
Although responding negatively to the pedantry and self-importance of his
teacher Inoue Tetsujirō, he found spiritual sustenance and encouragement
in the teaching of Okakura Tenshin and especially the famous Koeber Sensei
(Raphael Koeber, 1848–1923), the Russian-born philosophy professor who
influenced a whole generation of Japanese thinkers.

After this auspicious beginning Watsuji's career unfolded with ever more
brilliant success. Having been one of the first to introduce existentialist
thought in Japan with his book on Nietzsche in 1913 and his book on
Kierkegaard in 1915, Watsuji turned to the study of ancient Japanese culture
and comparative culture in general.[19] During the 1920s he published epoch-
making studies on early Japanese art and literature, early Indian Buddhism,
the Buddhist cultural influence in Japan, Greek culture, and primitive
Christianity.[20] In 1938 he rounded out his series of original researches on
ancient cultures with a book on Confucius.[21] He was very close to the dominant literary and philosophical movements of the day, namely, the Shira-
kaba literary circle and the Kyoto school of philosophy centering on Nishida
Kitarō. In 1927–28 he visited Europe where he studied with Heidegger in
Berlin and traveled extensively in Italy and Greece. In 1925 he was appointed to a professorship at Kyoto University and in 1934 became professor of ethics at Tokyo University.

But it is with an event of 1944 that I wish to begin my consideration of
the thought of Watsuji Tetsurō. On July 10, 1944, the first pamphlet in the
"Wartime National Library" was published, and two million copies were
distributed by the Ministry of Education. It was composed of two short
pieces entitled "The Way of the Subject in Japan" and "America's National
Character," whose purpose was to indicate the superiority of Japanese culture to American and the necessary collapse of the latter when confronted
by the former.[22] The author was Watsuji Tetsurō.

It is not unusual to find a scholar writing what is in effect war propaganda, but these pieces have more than usual interest. In these pages we can
see one of Japan's most widely educated minds reflecting on the meaning of
the war. Here is not to be found the hysterical rhetoric characteristic of
much Japanese wartime writing, but the clarity of expression and the fine
use of Western methods of scholarly analysis for which Watsuji is so
famous. The essay on American national character can even be compared to
its American counterpart—Ruth Benedict's *The Chrysanthemum and the
Sword*—though it is much briefer and less ambitious.[23] The Pacific War
posed for Japan the profoundest problems of its cultural identity—the rela-

tion of Eastern to Western culture and the relation of the Japanese past to the modern era. It is instructive to see how Watsuji dealt with those problems at that critical juncture.

"The Way of the Subject in Japan" was first delivered in 1943 as a lecture at the Naval College, and this fact helps to explain some of its content and intention. Watsuji begins by quoting a naval officer who defined the Japanese military spirit as involving two stages. The first is "to die happily for the sake of one's lord." But an even higher stage is expressed in the injunction, "Do not die until the enemy is defeated." Watsuji explains that the first statement is good but still contains a strong consciousness of self and of the importance of one's self-sacrifice. But the second statement, which puts one's duty above everything else, is truly to throw away the "I" and attain a standpoint beyond life and death. In this essay Watsuji reflects on the "Way of the Subject" throughout Japanese history in order to distinguish the true ethical realization of that way from limited and partly selfish expressions of it. There is little doubt that these historical reflections are aimed in part at the immediately contemporary situation and in the context of the Naval College even represent a veiled criticism of the dictatorial army leadership of the day.[24]

But the point of interest to us is not so much that immediate problem, but the fact that the pamphlet brings up the general issue of universal ethical value in the Japanese tradition and the special nature of that tradition when compared to other traditions. For Watsuji the core of ethical value in the Japanese tradition and the reason for its superiority to other traditions lies in the Way of Reverence for the Emperor. The ancient Japanese, he says, grasped the absolute in reverence for the emperor. That method was fundamentally different from the so-called world religions of Christianity, Buddhism, and Islam. To them the absolute was limited to their particular religious forms; that is, Jehovah, Buddha, or Allah. Holding these to be absolute, they had to oppose all other gods and deny their existence. This led to intolerance, persecution, and religious wars against peoples of other religions. Christianity and Islam are equally belligerent in these regards, but Buddhism seems to be more tolerant. Actually it is only Japanese Buddhism, says Watsuji, that is really tolerant; Indian Buddhists undertook cruel persecutions of heretics. Besides their hostility to other gods, Christianity, Buddhism, and Islam all attempt to express the absolute in dogma, which is to turn the absolute into something limited and use that dogma in order to attack every other dogma.

According to Watsuji, the early Japanese, however, grasped the realm of the absolute without limiting it as an absolute god and without constructing a dogma. Among the several gods of early Japan, Amaterasu the sun goddess was most revered. But Amaterasu was not the first of the gods, nor was any claim made that she was an absolute god. Rather the absolute was mediated through Amaterasu as an intermediate god, and so the absolute could be truly expressed without having to attack the gods and beliefs of others. The emperor, who, as the descendant of Amaterasu, bears some of her sacredness, has an analogous function. Sacredness is absolute but as manifested in Amaterasu and the emperor it is not exclusive. Through relying on the emperor, one could rely on the absolute. Thus the absolute was concretized in the early Japanese state in a more specific way than in the world religions and in not making the absolute into a fixed god, the Japanese had a higher, potentially more inclusive, standpoint than the world religions. From this higher standpoint any religion can be placed under the influence of the emperor and be accepted in Japan. From this there developed the broad ideal of taking the best from all countries.

Thus Watsuji turns the tables on those who would hold Shinto to be inferior to the world religions and who would stigmatize early Japanese culture as inferior because primitive. Watsuji was fully aware that early Japan was primitive, but he believed that Japan's primitiveness was the seed of its vitality, its sense of living community, and of the emperor system that provided the legitimation for the acceptance of foreign culture. He did not at all believe literally in the myths of early Shinto, but held that they could be reinterpreted in terms of the more sophisticated higher culture later introduced from outside without thereby losing their true significance.[25]

Returning to the pamphlet, let us consider the decisive theoretical justification Watsuji gives for his position. That which relates men to their deepest and most basic absolute is only actualized truly and concretely in a human relational structure, most fully in the state. The claim of the world religions that they relate men directly to the absolute is only a pretense. They actually develop human relational structures like the *sangha* and the church as substitutes for the state. For the sake of the power of those substitutes they try to destroy the sacredness of the state.

This position can be understood better if we take into consideration Watsuji's more extended analysis of these problems in his *Ethics*.[26] There he argues that there is no such thing as a universal religion or a religion that relates the individual to the absolute without any social context. He holds that the so-called world religions only became extensive in the context of "world empires." Thus the Roman Empire was a necessary precondition of Christianity. Further, Christianity is only widespread in the modern world because of the power of Western imperialism. All religions are necessarily the religions of particular peoples and cannot be truly universal. Watsuji points out that Yahweh in origin is nothing but the national god of Israel and remains to the present in some sense a "tribal deity."

For Watsuji religious organization is valid and makes an ethical contribution when it gives up any claim to being an organization superior to the state and accepts its place as an organization *included in* the state. For Watsuji the state is the highest ethical structure. It is the "relational organization of relational organizations." Only in the state are selfishness and factionalism overcome and every private relation transmuted into a selfless public relation. For Watsuji the state is the expression of the absolute whole that is the same as absolute negativity or absolute emptiness. He views human nature as composed of two mutually negating aspects, the individual and the social, which by denying each other give rise dialectically to the absolute negativity that is their ultimate source. All human groups—the family, kinship groups, local groups, economic groups, cultural groups—have this quality of self-negation, but each tends to express selfishness and partiality anew at the group level even when overcoming it at the individual level. Only in the state is selfishness overcome absolutely and the truth of man's nature and the nature of the absolute realized. Reverence for the emperor, which is the heart of Watsuji's ethics, is precisely the particular Japanese expression of this universal truth.[27]

In the second essay in the 1944 pamphlet Watsuji portrays the Anglo-Saxon character, especially as it was developed in America. Here Watsuji finds the almost perfect negative image both to his conception of human ethics in general and of Japanese ethics in particular. He opens with a quote from George Bernard Shaw's *Man of Destiny* in which Napoleon describes the English character as motivated solely by self-interest, but always justifying its acts in the name of religion and morality.[28] He finds the chief Anglo-Saxon traits to be individualism, utilitarianism, and a legalistic moralism, and he traces these back to their classical expression in the seventeenth-century thinkers Bacon and Hobbes.

Watsuji relies on a distinction that developed in Germany, especially in the work of Spengler, between civilization and culture, to express the essence of Anglo-Saxon character.[29] Bacon, says Watsuji, believed only in civilization, meaning the mechanical utilitarian control of nature. He was totally uninterested in culture, that is, the realm of the spirit as expressed in ethics, religion, and art. The Anglo-Saxon respects culture only when it is useful, when it has immediate practical results, and places his chief emphasis on mechanical inductive natural sciences. Watsuji recognizes the contribution that this attitude made to the development of modern science but holds it to be very one-sided.

Hobbes developed a theory of society that is consonant with the Baconian view of civilization, says Watsuji. It is to Hobbes that Anglo-Saxon individualism is to be traced. The essential truth, for Hobbes, is the war of all against all. Individuals only agree to abide by moral rules out of self-interest and are bound to obey them only so long as they accord with self-interest. Thus the Anglo-Saxon emphasis on equality is only the equality of the struggle of nature, and Hobbesian theory can be used to justify any kind of imperialism.

Watsuji then traces the development of Hobbesian characteristics in America. Unlike the Spanish, who wanted to conquer the Indians for the sake of religion, the Anglo-Saxons wanted to conquer them only for the sake of their land. Using the slogan "the only good Indian is a dead Indian," the Americans justified their aggression on the grounds that they were a more "civilized" people, that is, more mechanically advanced. Getting the Indians drunk with rum, they induced them to sign contracts selling their land for a pittance and then found them "lacking in morality" and "failing to understand the sacredness of contract" when they failed to clear out of the vast forests that had been thus extracted from them. Such immoral people could be justly slaughtered, according to Anglo-Saxon morality. Without any pangs of conscience the Anglo-Saxons adopted precisely the same attitude toward the Negroes whom they enslaved and brought to work for them. The phrase "all men are created equal" that occurs at the beginning of the Declaration of Independence does not mean what it seems to, for Indians, Negroes, and, later, Asiatics are not included. Rather what it really means, according to Watsuji, is that "all Anglo-Saxons are created equal" and that Anglo-Saxon Americans are as good as Anglo-Saxon Englishmen. The "Treaty of Friendship" that Perry concluded with the Japanese under threat of naval bombardment has the same character as the "treaties" the Americans had concluded with the Indians. Similarly at the Washington Disarmament Conference the Americans as usual in the name of "peace" and "righteousness" forced the Japanese into a treaty whose only aim was the furtherance of American national interest.

The development of Baconian characteristics in America is expressed in the great stress on mechanical invention and on respecting learning only for the sake of utilitarian results. Benjamin Franklin is the true American representative of the Baconian tradition. Franklin was greatly interested in practical invention and experiment and made a great contribution to the development of journalism, which is the characteristic American form of cultural expression, much more than religion, art, or politics. The Americans have since reached the extreme point in the development of machine civilization. Themselves lacking in morality and art, they judge all other peoples in terms of machines. Those lacking machines are "uncivilized" and so justly to be regarded as inferior. But the American has become helpless without his machines.

American democracy means that every man is his own boss and there are no followers. Everyone has slaves: cars, radios, refrigerators, and so forth, and lives better than ancient kings. But at the same time the Americans have become enslaved to the machine and have lost all feeling for anything but comfort. Such a world in the control of machines is everywhere quantified. The Americans conform the qualitative human spirit to quantitative machines rather than the reverse. Number is the demon of American civilization. Number is the highest expression of this civilization, which is the extreme development of the Baconian spirit.

Watsuji sums up his assessment of the Americans as having the character of colonizers (*kaitakusha*). In the face of a difficult environment the Americans have performed a great task in opening up a new continent and subduing it mechanically. But in the course of this enterprise the original calm, patient, and stolid Anglo-Saxon character has been undermined. The American "pursuit of happiness" has become a craving for strong stimulation and the discharge of energy. It is expressed in a love of action and tension, as indicated in the American fanaticism about sports. The Americans have come to need a constant succession of explosions. They want success for the stimulation it gives—not for any moral reason. In this they are like gamblers. Only in this context can we understand America's scheme of world domination, says Watsuji. There is no reason or necessity for them to invade and conquer others—they do it only out of the gambler's desire for stimulation. Thus they invade Asia out of no high ideal and use "peace and righteousness" only as cloaks for their misdeeds. Filled with irrational self-righteousness they rely solely on machine power. However, before they have met only helpless natives whereas now they meet those whose mastery of machine power is superior to theirs. They rely on quantity and numbers to crush their enemies, but they are heading for a nervous breakdown. A people's basic strength is moral, spiritual power, not quantitative power. A gambler who bets everything will collapse when he least expects it.

Thus Watsuji concludes his 1944 pamphlet. In it we see the vivid contrast between the particularistic Japanese *Gemeinschaft* community (*kyōdōtai*) in which all persons and groups are taken up and both included and negated in reverence for the emperor as the expression of the absolute whole, and the American *Gesellschaft* society (Watsuji's Japanese term is literally "profit society," *rieki shakai*) based only on naked utilitarian self-interest; between Japanese culture (*bunka*) and American civilization (*bummei*). Although this is perhaps a starker statement of the basic confrontation in terms of which Watsuji interpreted contemporary world history than is to be found elsewhere in his work, it is in almost every element foreshadowed in his writings dating from well before the war, in some cases even from the early 1920s. It is not a conception produced to order for wartime consumption. It has roots deep in some of the main currents of Japanese thought, and that is what interests us here.

The civilization/culture contrast is found in the first chapter of Watsuji's *The Significance of Primitive Christianity in the History of Culture* published in 1926. There he compares the Roman world at the time of the origin of Christianity to the world of the twentieth century. The Romans represented civilization overcoming the early Greek culture, just as today the Anglo-Saxon civilization is replacing the earlier European culture (to which English and Americans contributed at an earlier stage). Americans of today, he says, bear a surprising resemblance to Roman portrait busts, not so much in their physical form as in the expression of their inner life. Like the Romans, the Americans give the impression of being uncultured, realistic, and practical. Roman achievements are chiefly measured in terms of size and technical ingenuity as are the skyscrapers and machines of the Americans. The Roman love of bloody sports in the coliseum is matched by the American passion for insane automobile races. The Romans were masters at the creation of artificial social structures through law, and the Americans are equally adept at the conscious creation of groups through legal devices. And just as the Romans ruled the world of their day with weapons and Roman know-how, so the Anglo-Saxons after the First World War have come to rule the world with weapons and the power of modern science. Roman wealth at the expense of the conquered nations is matched by the unheard-of concentration of wealth in the Anglo-Saxon countries and the extreme impoverishment of the rest of the world.[30] Here indeed we see what can almost be considered a preliminary sketch for his later essay on American national character.

Watsuji's notion of the special nature of the Japanese *Gemeinschaft* community and the role of reverence for the emperor in it is foreshadowed in *Ancient Japanese Culture* published in 1920. This is the first of several rather idealized treatments of early Japanese society and culture. An interesting article contained in *Studies in Japanese Spiritual History* of 1926 on

"Political Ideals in the Asuka and Nara Periods" is an answer to Tsuda Sokichi's critical evaluation of the Taika Reform of 645. Contrary to Tsuda who viewed the reform as having little real meaning and impugned its ideals as hypocritical, Watsuji sees the Taika Reform as a very model of Japanese political action and refers to it as an attempt to establish state socialism under the harmonious influence of the emperor.[31] In *The Practical Philosophy of Primitive Buddhism* of 1927 Watsuji developed his ideas of absolute negativity and absolute emptiness as the basis for ethical action. These notions are quite close to Nishida's conception of absolute nothingness and serve to give a deep historical grounding in the basic philosophy of Buddhism to the general position of Nishida philosophy. In *Ethics as the Science of Man* (1931) and the first volume of *Ethics* (1937) Watsuji developed in detail the dialectical negation of individual and group in the absolute whole, which is then related to an essentially Buddhist metaphysical underpinning, on the one hand, and the specifically Japanese *Gemeinschaft* community and its emperor, on the other.[32] So by 1937 virtually every element in "The Way of the Subject in Japan" had been worked out.

The dramatic confrontation of two closed systems in the wartime pamphlet is not only stark, it is also static. But it is interesting to note that Watsuji viewed the same confrontation as actually going on inside Japan. This is especially clear in two essays in the second volume of *Studies in Japanese Spiritual History*, one on the "Japanese Spirit" and the other on "Contemporary Japan and the *Chōnin* Character." In the latter of these essays we discover that most of the character traits of the Anglo-Saxons—individualism, utilitarianism, and a self-serving moralism—are also found in Japan, even before the modern period, in the *chōnin*, or townsman class. It is precisely the character of the *chōnin* to make profit take primacy over all other considerations and to adopt only such morality as will be practically useful. The only specifically Japanese aspect of the *chōnin* is that perhaps unlike the Western bourgeois, his concern is with family profit rather than with the profit of the isolated individual. However, the *chōnin* character was not very well rationalized in theoretical terms, depending mostly on the hackneyed moralizing of the Shingakusha. But after the Meiji Ishin all the advanced philosophical and political theories of Western *Gesellschaft* society came into Japan to make up for this lack. Utilitarianism as a philosophical theory was widely espoused and the notion of the state as existing just for the interests of individuals got established through the Popular Rights Movement. The chief agents of this propaganda were the enlightenment publicists like Fukuzawa Yukichi for whom Watsuji felt very little affection.[33] It is true that Watsuji accepted the advancement of *Gesellschaft* society to some extent as dialectically necessary, but he argues that it is only progressive if it leads to the emergence of a new *Gemeinschaft* community at a higher level. In the essay on the Japanese spirit this general problem receives more extensive treatment. Watsuji's main problem in this essay is that intellectuals seem to feel that talk about the Japanese spirit is somehow reactionary or even fascist. Watsuji argues that the Japanese spirit is simply the Japanese expression of modern nationalism and is reactionary or progressive depending on the context and the uses to which it is put. He argues that on the whole such notions as those of Yamatogokoro, Yamatodamashii, and Nihon Seishin have been more progressive than reactionary.[34] Kokugaku, for example, contributed to the destruction of the feudal system in the Tokugawa period by stimulating a feeling of national consciousness. The Yamatodamashii spirit of the Sino- and Russo-Japanese wars, he argues, was not reactionary, for those were anti-imperialist wars and in fact the consciousness of national community expressed then was the harbinger of a general turn in world history away from *Gesellschaft* to a new form of *Gemeinschaft*. It was precisely Japan's role as an Asian nation, oppressed by all the Western nations, which made it become conscious of this new need before other nations and gave Japan a special world historical mission. Watsuji argues that socialism is basically a form of *chōnin* ideology. It accepts the bourgeois premises of materialism and utilitarianism. It is merely a family quarrel within the confines of *Gesellschaft* society and it is not really progressive. Watsuji pays tribute to the spirit of idealism and self-sacrifice of the young Marxist students, but says they are unconsciously expressing the basic Japanese traits of practical idealism and absolute obedience to authority (in this case the authority of the Communist Party). It is the role of the Japanese spirit today, said Watsuji in 1935, not to oppose the bourgeois society and socialism in a reactionary way by wishing to go back to something earlier, but to oppose them by overcoming them and going beyond them so as to build a new, more adequate *Gemeinschaft* society.[35]

Finally, in clarifying Watsuji's analysis of the cultural situation, let me refer to an eloquent article of 1937 on "The Standpoint of Persons Responsible for Cultural Creation."[36] In this article he excoriates those who argue that cultural pursuits are meaningless in a time of crisis. He argues that Japan's historical position is precisely to be understood in terms of culture. Japan's isolation in the world is caused by the combined hostility of the imperialist powers to Japan, who stands as the sole protector of Asia's millions from complete enslavement. Japan is the champion against racism and imperialism. Furthermore, Japan is the champion of culture against civilization. Watsuji says that not only must Japan accept and protect the high culture of India and China, which have been reduced to such a miserable condition in their homelands, but Japan must accept and protect the high culture of the West against the perversions of modern Western civilization. Japan must be a beacon for all world culture, and it is precisely here that Japan's world historical mission lies. Thus there are no grounds to disparage cultural activity on grounds of military urgency.

In Watsuji's position as I have developed it there are obviously links to the general trends of thought that dominated the intellectuals during the war, especially to the movement associated with the phrase "overcoming the modern" (*kindai no chōkoku*) and the "philosophy of world history" developed by several members of the Kyoto school.[37] But for present purposes I would like to concentrate on Watsuji himself in an effort to understand what it meant for one of Japan's most intelligent, creative, and best educated modern thinkers to have held such a position.

Watsuji's *Autobiography* was unfortunately far from completion at the time of his death.[38] It carries his story only halfway through his years at the First Higher School. If he could have finished it, or even if he had been able to carry the story up to 1920, it might have been one of the most interesting personal documents to have been written in modern Japan. Still, materials are not entirely lacking for reconstructing his spiritual development. He tells of being a rebel in his youth, of disliking received convention and authority.[39] In his middle school years he was an avid reader of the Heimin Shimbun, which espoused universal suffrage, socialism, and pacifism.[40] He was early attracted to English literature and published a translation of Byron's "The Prisoner of Chillon" in his middle school magazine. In higher school he wrote essays on Shaw and Ibsen, translated Shaw's *Mrs. Warren's Profession*, and wrote original stories and plays of his own. Steeped in Western culture in these years, he had relatively little interest in things Japanese. In his autobiography he tells how he loathed the required ethics lessons, and it was not until he heard Nitobe Inazō speak in higher school that he developed any interest in such things as *bushidō*. Even then the students were chiefly impressed with the fact that Nitobe's *Bushidō* was originally written in English. Watsuji's later very negative reaction to Inoue Tetsujiro, the fount of "national morality," fits in with this general picture. In all of this Watsuji is very much a child of his time and place. He was one of the fortunate few able to participate in the rich new world of Western culture, which the best schools and universities were opening up. Cut off culturally from most of his countrymen by a thorough-going exposure to Western culture, and cut off from his family and hometown background by his life as a student in Tokyo, it is natural that Watsuji, like so many others in similar circumstances, should become concerned with the problems of individualism and self-realization.

These concerns were undoubtedly the chief motivations for his work on Nietzsche and Kierkegaard. In the preface to his *A Study of Nietzsche,* he says, "The Nietzsche who appears in this study is strictly my Nietzsche. I have tried to express myself through Nietzsche."[41] In these studies we can detect Watsuji's aspiration to construct an ideal self and his struggles with egoistic desires. In his preface to *Soren Kierkegaard* he says, "My intention is to struggle resolutely and construct a life for the self (*jiko no seikatsu*). My mind does not rest night or day. I recognize in myself many ugly, weak and bad things. I must completely burn these up through self-discipline."[42] But the resolute self-assertion of Nietzsche and the personal faith of Kierkegaard were not able to provide an adequate solution for Watsuji. Isolated individualism did not in itself provide him with any answers— instead, as he said, it "led him to an abyss of emptiness."[43] These years of crisis for Watsuji coincided with the last years of Natsume Sōseki, who died in 1916. The grim last novels of Sōseki, which portray the dead end of pure individualism, apparently moved Watsuji greatly, and Sōseki's philosophy of *sokuten kyoshi* ("identify with heaven and throw away the self") as expressed in his Chinese poems may have contributed to Watsuji's own solution, as his later interest in Nishida philosophy and Buddhism would suggest.

Watsuji's book of 1918, *Resurrection of Idols,* indicates the main direction in which Watsuji turned after finding individualism inadequate. This book documents a "change of thought" (*tenkō;* Watsuji uses the word as the title of the first essay). It is God through such men as Paul who destroyed the idols. But now, as Nietzsche has said, God is dead, and God, too, was an idol. Yet men still need idols and it is now possible to resurrect the idols. Idols, says Watsuji, never die. It is only man's understanding of them that become lifeless. If we can understand the idols properly, then they can be alive for us again. What the idols were concretely is perhaps indicated in Watsuji's next book, *Pilgrimages to Ancient Temples,* which describes in vivid prose the early Buddhist temples and sculptures of the Nara region. But more generally the idols stand for a return to, Japanese society and culture. In an essay in *Resurrection of Idols* entitled "The Roots of the Tree," he tells of climbing in the mountains and finding an ancient pine tree with its roots extending deep into the cracks in rocky surface of the mountainside. He "felt ashamed of his own shallowness of roots" as he stood looking at the tree.[44]

From all we know about Japanese personality and group structure, it is not, perhaps, going too far to interpret Watsuji's youthful experiences as examples of what seem to be general tendencies.[45] Japanese group experiences are both very constricting and very rewarding. Watsuji seems to have been more than usually rebellious and to have had more opportunity than most young Japanese to indulge that rebelliousness and let it lead him where it would. But the anxiety brought on by isolation, acute for any Japanese, was too much to be borne. He certainly did not capitulate entirely to that which he had earlier rejected, but he did turn his back on individualism and return in his own way to the warm *Gemeinschaft* community of Japanese life. Indeed, the 1920 volume on ancient Japanese culture is a celebration of that harmonious life in which the individual is perfectly blended in the group, which is such an important aspect of the traditional Japanese ideal.[46]

Of course Watsuji did not turn his back on the West. His interests continued to be global and he was dependent on Western scholars almost exclusively in the development of his distinctive methodology.[47] Indeed, it is the method of hermeneutics (*kaishakugaku*) that allowed Watsuji to resurrect the idols in the first place. That is, the methods of cultural research developed largely in Germany and transmitted to Watsuji by Koeber and others (Nietzsche's work on ancient Greece may have been part of the influence) gave him the possibility of understanding the cultural forms that had become dead to him before and thus bring them to life. All of Watsuji's scholarly work is closely influenced by the approach of the German culture historians and phenomenologists.

But the West is a threat as well as a source of light. The West threatens not only the political integrity but also the cultural identity of the East. Watsuji's immersion in Western studies had, as in so many cases, raised a problem of cultural identity and cultural self-respect. So already in *Pilgrimages to Ancient Temples* (1920) we see a continual comparative interest. Watsuji is not just interested in exalting things Japanese, he wishes to define the special nature of what is Japanese over against comparable phenomena from the West and other cultural spheres. From this concern developed Watsuji's profound sense of climate and place, which gave rise to one of his most influential books, *Climate and Culture*.[48] In the preface he tells how he came first to reflect on this problem. It was in the summer of 1927 when he was in Berlin reading Heidegger's *Sein und Zeit*. Intrigued with Heidegger's insistence on the importance of time in the structure of human existence, he was dissatisfied that space was not given an equally important consideration. In *Climate and Culture* he develops a theory of three main types of climate and their cultural meaning: monsoon, desert, and meadow. He is not thinking of climate as a purely external physical factor but as very much involved in and affected by human culture, so that it is climate subjectively conceived and culturally manipulated, not simply meteorology in which he is interested. He attributes various strengths and weaknesses to the different climates, holding that while the limitations can be overcome, one cannot, nonetheless, pretend that one can live in a different climate. With this theory Watsuji is seeking a rationale for handling problems of comparative culture and also for defending the necessarily Japanese nature of Japanese culture.

But the problem of space and climate is linked to other problems that get fuller treatment in *Ethics as the Science of Man* (1931) and *Ethics*, Volume 1 (1937). Besides being dissatisfied with Heidegger's exclusive attention to time at the expense of space, Watsuji is dissatisfied with his focus on the isolated individual at the expense of society. And further he sees these as related, holding that the temporal, historical aspect of existence is especially linked to individuals, and spatial, climatic existence to societies. Watsuji develops as the basis for his ethics a view of man that is fundamentally relational (*aidagara-teki*) and criticizes all Western ethics for starting with the isolated individual. Thus Watsuji makes two important contributions to his system, which is otherwise based heavily on Windelband, Heidegger, and Husserl—the notion of climate (*fūdo*) and of relation (*aidagara*). He even indulges in a little Heideggerian etymology by pointing out that the Japanese word for man (*ningen*) includes the notion of *between* men and the Japanese word for existence (*sonzai*) is composed of two characters, one emphasizing the aspect of time, the other of space.[49] Of course Watsuji wants to include the insights of Heidegger and others about individual existence, but in effect individual and group by negating each other give rise to the absolute whole that, when identified with the state, seems rather to tip the balance in the direction of society.

This brief glance at Watsuji's spiritual and intellectual development gives us some grounds for assessing his position as we found it in the wartime pamphlet of 1944. For one thing, it is evident that Watsuji is a long way from the fanatic traditionalists. He is completely in the group of Westernized intellectuals that Maruyama Masao indicates never gave themselves unreservedly to the fascist and militarist movement. (Indeed Watsuji was a very pillar of "Iwanami culture" having been closely associated with that publishing house from the beginning, an editor of the Iwanami periodical, *Shisō*, and an organizer of several Iwanami Kōza.[50]) He remained aloof from both Shinto and Confucian brands of nationalism and always explained the position of the emperor in very abstract philosophical language. Watsuji even claims that a right-wing Diet member demanded that he be dismissed by the Minister of Education in the late 1930s.

Like many in this group, he had a passing attraction to socialism in the 1920s and absorbed a certain amount of Marxism in his analysis of imperialism and capitalism. His support of the war was based on his definition of it as an anti-imperialist, antiracist war that would both defend Asia's millions against oppression and possibly lead to the establishment of a more equitable social system that would overcome the weaknesses of capitalism and socialism. In his enthusiasm for Japanese achievements he never lost sight of general cultural values and indeed always justified Japan in terms of its cultural role.

Yet Watsuji, as he himself was later fully aware, made no effective resistance to the tendencies leading Japan to disaster. Indeed, the position that he had worked out did not give any basis for individual or social resistance. Nowhere in my reading have I found Watsuji defending Japanese democracy in the 1920s and 1930s. Instead, by attacking the Enlightenment tradition of Fukuzawa Yukichi and the whole structure of *Gesellschaft* capitalist society in terms borrowed equally from socialist and conservative camps, he implicitly included the democratic structure, such as it was, in his attack. The new *Gemeinschaft* community that he held up as an ideal was no effective answer to any contemporary Japanese problem and in fact blended easily into the rightist rhetoric that was coming to dominate the country. Similarly, the absolute negativity Watsuji found at the basis of human existence gave no effective foundation for individual nonconformism. When, as in Watsuji's theory, the absolute is always actualized in groups, and most completely in the state, there is little basis for effective individual protest.

Even more fundamental, perhaps, is the lack in Watsuji's system of any universalistic or transcendental standard relative to which individual or social action can be judged. If the state is the most complete embodiment of human value, the state itself is expressed in the person of the Japanese emperor. In the wartime pamphlet, Watsuji exalted the emperor system above all the religions and philosophies of the world and found it the highest form of human cultural expression. The heart of his ethics, as he said himself many times, is the ethics of the emperor system. For all its sophistication Watsuji's theory is wholly committed to Japanese particularism.

In conclusion I would like to consider briefly Watsuji's postwar writings. Already in March 1945 when the bombings of Tokyo were becoming intense, Watsuji knew that the war was lost and decided to form a study group to "rethink the modern age [*kinsei*] from the beginning."[51] On March

7, after a bad night of bombing, the group met for the first time in a Shinjuku Restaurant. Meeting weekly when possible and moving from place to place as various members' homes were destroyed by fire, the group considered a wide variety of topics such as Machiavelli, Shakespeare, Prescott's *Conquest of Mexico*, Burckhardt's *Civilization of the Renaissance in Italy*, and the Christian culture of sixteenth-century Japan, continuing unperturbed by the surrender until February 1946. Out of this discussion group grew Watsuji's lectures that were eventually published as *The Closing of the Country*. The basic thesis developed there and elsewhere in Watsuji's postwar writings is that "Japan's Tragedy" was in large part the result of the closing of the country at the beginning of the seventeenth century, which had so many evil consequences for Japan's future. Perhaps the chief defect of the closed-country policy was that it greatly retarded the scientific spirit in Japan, says Watsuji, just at the time when it was making its greatest advances in Europe. The other side of the coin is that the closed-country policy allowed the vigorous development of an unusually narrow fanaticism, based on intuition rather than reason, which considered everything Japanese to be superior. It is evident that *Sakoku* marks a sharp break in some respects with "The Way of the Subject in Japan" and "America's National Character"; in the first of those essays the closed-country policy had been defended by Watsuji as justifiable in the face of imperialist aggression, and in the latter the spirit of modern science that he traced to Bacon was given a rather negative historical role.

What Watsuji now seemed to feel necessary was a new and vigorous dose of *kaikoku* (opening the country). He traced in the final section of his history of Japanese ethical thought the development of *jōi* ("expel the barbarians") and *kaikoku* strands of thought in the Bakumatsu period and strongly favored the *kaikoku* trend.[52] The treatment of Hirata Atsutane and his successors in the Meiji period is very violent, some of the harshest remarks going to Watsuji's old enemy Inoue Tetsujiro. But this change involves a whole series of reevaluations of earlier positions. In the postwar period it seemed to Watsuji a tragedy that the *bushi* managed to put down an incipient bourgeois bid for power in the sixteenth century. Thus the whole *chōnin* tradition and its European counterparts come in for rehabilitation. Watsuji even says that the shogunate would have collapsed except for the closed-country policy, because if the *chōnin* had been exposed to the ideas of the English and the French Revolutions they could not have been kept subdued. There is also a revision of his evaluation of the Enlightenment thinkers of the Meiji period, and Fukuzawa Yukichi is actually given half of the chapter on Meiji ethical thought where he is treated quite favorably. By contrast, the particularist tradition, which was defended in the prewar essay on "Japanese Spirit," now comes in for heavy castigation as the modern continuation of the closed-country policy.

This shift in thinking even affected the structure of Watsuji's magnum opus on ethics. He greatly revised the section on the nation that had been published in volume 2 in 1942, removing various statements about the absolute obligation of the individual to sacrifice himself for the state.[53] And in the final volume, which appeared in 1949, there is a long discussion of the ethical restrictions on the nation. No longer is the nation taken as an ethical absolute but rather is subjected to a general ethical norm deriving from mankind. And indeed Japan's errant behavior is seen to derive from its *sakoku* policy of isolation. A nation, like an individual, should be a good group member.

But as this last point makes evident, there is no basic change in the structure of Watsuji's thought. His central concerns continue and indeed get reexpressed in a series of essays on the emperor system. Watsuji wholeheartedly accepts the position of the emperor in the new constitution where he is held to be "a symbol of national unity." Indeed, this is what Watsuji claims he always meant when he said that the emperor was an "expression of the absolute whole." Watsuji argues for the essentially ethical and nonpolitical significance of the emperor all along and so denies that there is a change in the national structure (*kokutai*). However, he finds the word *kokutai* confusing and is happy to throw it out. In fact, in his postwar writings he refers to the *kokutai* theory as deriving from the Mito school of Confucianism in the Tokugawa period and as being essentially feudal and not applicable to a modern state.

But the fact remains that even in his postwar writings Watsuji never finds another standard of value that can transcend the emperor. The fusion of Japan, emperor, society, and individual, which he had held from the early 1920s as the highest good, remained at the core of his thought. In this, of course, he was merely giving theoretical expression to a way of thinking that is very old and goes very deep in Japan. But it is a way of thinking that has become profoundly and increasingly problematic in the course of Japan's modern history.

Whatever may be his final evaluation as a thinker, there is no doubt that Watsuji has made a permanent contribution to cultural history in Japan. As Shida Shōzō says, Watsuji's work is itself a many-sided cosmos.[54] A distinguished stylist, capable of bringing life and meaning out of the most diverse kinds of cultural material, often incisive in analysis, his work will instruct students of Japanese culture for years to come.

We may now turn to a consideration of what we can learn from Watsuji Tetsurō about our initial problem of national narcissism, or to use more neutral language, cultural particularism. Watsuji may be especially helpful in that he gives us not only an expression of cultural particularism but also a shrewd analysis of it.

For Watsuji there is no such thing as culture in the abstract. Culture always exists in a group. Thus there are no universal religions or philosophies but only group religions and philosophies. He attacks the so-called world religions for claiming a false universalism and praises the close union of culture and group in Japan as expressive of the true and proper relationship. Similarly, Watsuji attacks the notion of an abstract individual. All individuals are members of groups and take on real human meaning only when seen as such. The ideal situation is one in which culture, group, and individual are fused organically into a single body, a *Gemeinschaft* (*kyōdōtai*). The most adequate and comprehensive *kyōdōdtai* is the state, expressed most fully when embodied in the Japanese emperor who expresses in a mediate way, the only possible way, absolute value. This conception is, in Watsuji's view, neither doctrinaire nor narrow-minded. The Japanese emperor system can serve as a protective umbrella for all the world's culture, taking it up and utilizing it so long as it is willing to remain in its properly subordinate role.

Watsuji's negative image, a sort of negative cultural identity for Japan, is also instructive. It is summed up in Anglo-American culture that he sees as characterized by individualism, utilitarianism, legalism, science, and self-righteous intolerance. The essence of Watsuji's dislike is the *Gesellschaft* (*rieki shakai*) nature of Anglo-American society. It lacks organic unity. It exalts abstract mechanical ideals of which science is the type. It claims that the individual should be independent of social groups. It establishes society in terms of abstract legal rights rather than warm particularistic relationships. It relates to nature through mechanical manipulation rather than intuitive sympathy. In a word, it divides and separates where Japanese culture seeks to unite and fuse.

Without denying that Watsuji's characterization is overly schematic, it is nonetheless extremely suggestive and points to a crucial aspect of the problem of Japan's cultural identity. This is its profound resistance to the differentiation of the cultural and the social system and correlatively to the differentiation of social system and personality. Idea systems are seen as fused with, as ascribed attributes of social systems. Individuals are defined fundamentally as group members and have no identity independent of the group. It is then our hypothesis that it is this tendency for the individual to identify with his role, his group, and his culture in a relatively undifferentiated way that accounts for the cultural particularism described at the beginning of this chapter. This is not to say that such a situation is universal in Japan. But even when individual Japanese have renounced one or more aspects of this fusion in principle, it is often hard for them to avoid particularistic attitudes since they have been socialized in families and have lived in groups where the fusion was highly valued and indeed taken for granted. It is the experience of the Japanese collectivity structure, of the actually operative *kyōdōtai*, that lies at the root of these attitudes and makes them so persistent. The emperor system can be seen as a projection of the ideal pattern of collective life, the *kyōdōtai*, onto the nation as a whole. Though never able to overcome profound tensions and factional hostilities in fact, it was able to symbolize the deep unity of Japanese people, society, and culture. It thus provided a powerful symbolic reinforcement for the maintenance of cultural particularism.

This is not the place for an explanation of this Japanese pattern, but a few tentative suggestions about its historical background can be made. The type of fusion of culture, society, and personality that seems to be present in Japan is a normal feature of primitive and archaic cultures. It was found quite generally in the Bronze Age monarchies that existed throughout the civilized world until the first millennium B.C. At that time, however, a series of social and cultural revolutions broke up the archaic fusion and ushered in a new type of society that I have called elsewhere the "historic type."[55] One of the central features of this new type of society was the emergence of universal religions and philosophies that crosscut preexisting social groups and gave a new basis for the assertion of individual personality. It is fairly evident that Japan in the fifth century A.D. was a Bronze Age monarchy of classic type. However, in Japan both the monarchy and its associated ritual-religious system, which became known as Shinto, were able to survive and adapt to major institutional and cultural changes that took place under the stimulus of China, a society of historic type though with its own important legacy of archaism. Although taking on in many respects the features of a society of historic type, Japan did so gradually without major trauma. This is signaled by the persistence both of the organic type of collectivity structure with its very strong emphasis on kinship and pseudokinship and by the persistence of the ancient monarchy that continued to exist as it had "for ages eternal." The continuation of a near archaic type of fusion between culture, society, and personality was challenged by social disturbance and the importation of historic-type religion and philosophy. The Kamakura period, a time of great social instability, produced the great Buddhist thinkers Shinran and Dōgen, who did in principle break through the fusion. Japanese particularism, however, proved stronger than Buddhist universalism and gradually reabsorbed the Buddhist structure, as can be clearly seen in the subsequent history of the Shin and Zen sects. Confucianism through several vigorous thinkers of the Tokugawa period similarly challenged archaic structures of thought but was similarly unsuccessful.

The modern period brought much more serious challenges, some of which have been discussed above. Besides the cultural challenges stimulated by Western ideas, industrialization and bureaucratization created serious inroads in the traditional pattern of group life. But once again Japanese particularism proved remarkably resilient, as the work of Abegglan, Vogel, and others has shown.[56] Ideologically, however, Western universalism and individualism in several guises proved to be a powerful solvent. It won important converts who themselves have made major contributions to modern Japanese culture. It stimulated violent hostilities and movements to preserve the national essence. Where it roused neither enthusiasm nor hostility, it nonetheless unnerved and disturbed. In the case of Watsuji we have seen how an educated Japanese could be attracted by Western universalism and individualism, in his case through the work of Nietzsche and Kierkegaard, and yet find it finally unsatisfactory. Many other men—writers, scholars, social thinkers—went through a similar experience. In trying to find a solution for this situation Watsuji sought to reconcile Japanese particularism and world culture. Instead, we have argued that he succeeded merely in giving Japanese particularism a new Western-inspired philosophical rationale. The humane and gracious figure of a Watsuji Tetsurō would not be problematic for modern Japan were it not for the fact that partly behind the cloak of just such thinking as his, a profoundly pathological social movement brought Japan near to total disaster. The ideology of that movement, referred to by some Japanese scholars as emperor-system fascism, was the most explicit statement of Japanese particularism that had ever appeared.

This explicit version, inextricably bound up with Japanese defeat in the Second World War, was so deeply repudiated in the postwar period that it can probably never reappear. But it is of the essence of Japanese particularism that it exists as a tacit assumption far more than as an explicit ideology. And that tacit assumption remains embodied in Japanese collectivity structure, the myriad "small emperor systems." Whatever has happened in the realm of explicit ideology, it remains true that the "human nexus" continues to be more powerful and salient in Japan than either ideas or individuals. Neither the traditional *kyōdōtai* structure nor the monarchy has been radically disrupted, as might have happened if, for example, the Russians rather than the Americans had occupied Japan, but both have suffered serious attrition.

It is likely, given the continuation of present world conditions, that the attrition will continue and that antiparticularistic tendencies—universalism and individualism—will continue to grow. But it is far too soon for Japanese particularism, which has proven so viable over the centuries, to be counted out.

# 4  Notes on Maruyama Masao

## I. REVIEW OF 'STUDIES IN THE INTELLECTUAL HISTORY OF TOKUGAWA JAPAN'

Reading this book some fifteen years ago in Japanese I found it an extraordinarily powerful analysis of Tokugawa intellectual history, fully living up to its reputation as a landmark in its field. Reading it again in translation I now find it a profound work of political philosophy as well. It is difficult to think of another book one would welcome more in English translation, particularly, as in this case, in an excellent translation. Although more than thirty years old the book has not in the least lost its freshness. As intellectual history it naturally stands in need of some revision (some suggestions to that end are made in an author's introduction to the English translation) but as a work of political philosophy it will, I believe, occupy an enduring place in Japanese thought.

The book is a translation of *Nihon Seiji Shisōshi Kenkyū,* which first appeared in three parts in *Kokka Gakkai Zasshi* between 1940 and 1944. Professor Maruyama has added a new introduction that contains much valuable information about the context out of which the original work came. The three parts of the book consist of independent but parallel essays, each concerned with some aspect of the transition from traditional to modern forms of thought in the Tokugawa period. The first two essays concentrate on the conflict between the orthodoxy established by the Japanese followers of Chu Hsi and the critical perspective developed by Ogyū Sorai and his followers. Chu Hsi Confucianism tended to fuse the normative (ethical and legal) order with the natural (cosmological) order finding the same overriding Principle (*li*) at work in every sphere of life. Sorai attacked the metaphysics of Principle and dealt with each sphere of life—political, ethical, aesthetic, personal—on its own terms. By freeing the various spheres from the static dominance of Principle, Sorai contributed at least incipiently to the emergence of a dynamic, empirical, and critical consciousness that, like comparable tendencies in the West, was moving in the direction of modern culture. That is the theme of the first essay, "The Sorai School: Its Role in the Disintegration of Tokugawa Confucianism and Its Impact on National Learning."

The second essay, "Nature and Invention in Tokugawa Political Thought: Contrasting Institutional Views," specifies one of the mechanisms whereby the teachings of Sorai contributed to the disintegration of Chu Hsi Confucianism. Rather than deriving the normative order (*seido*) directly from the unchanging order of nature, Sorai saw it as an artificial human construct, an invention of men. Like Hobbes, Maruyama points out, Sorai does not give the inventive power to everyman, but only to the sovereign who creates a new political regime. The archetypal creators were the ancient sage kings of China toward whom Sorai expresses profound respect, but every founder of a regime must create new institutions in accord with prevailing conditions even though modeling himself after the ancient sage kings. Although developing his theory in order to shore up the old inherited order, precisely in the sense of a *Gemeinschaft*, that is, a natural community accepted without question, Sorai, according to Maruyama, developed the logic of *Gesellschaft*, social institutions created by the active intelligence and will of men, and therefore helped to undermine the old order. In his emphasis on active social creation in a concrete historical context Sorai without intending to was moving toward a modern rather than a traditional consciousness.

In both of the first two essays Maruyama points out that Sorai's criticism of Chu Hsi Confucianism opened up a space for other movements, notably National Learning (Kokugaku), which, in their empiricism, historicism, and naturalistic acceptance of human feeling, were also precursors of modernity.

The final essay, "The Premodern Formation of Nationalism," is a fragment that remained unfinished because the author was called to service in 1944 before it could be completed. It suggests that the emergence of an incipient national consciousness in late Tokugawa times is another sign of the emergence of modernity.

The virtues of the work as intellectual history are truly astonishing. I will mention only two: the extraordinarily subtle use of comparisons with Western thought, and the focus on general structures of thought rather than the biographies of individual thinkers. These two aspects are closely interrelated in that it is Maruyama's sense of the transformation of the structure of Western thought from late medieval to modern times that provides a constant backdrop of comparisons for the Japanese material. He is interested neither in linking particular ideas to particular "class forces" nor in discovering "progressive" intellectuals who were self-consciously urging a modern society. Rather, following suggestions from the work of Franz Borkenau, Maruyama is interested in the inner logic of systems of thought and their transformation over time, to some degree independently of the immediate pressure of productive forces and of the conscious intentions of the thinkers involved. In making his comparisons between Japan and the West Maruyama is reticent about claiming too much. He does not claim to have found Japanese equivalents to the revolutionary thought of the eighteenth- or nineteenth-century West. In the first essay he even hesitates to argue that there are Japanese equivalents to Renaissance thought but rather takes his analogy from late scholastic nominalism in its attack on Thomism, a Western analogue of Chu Hsi Confucianism. In the second essay he compares some of the consequences of Soraigaku to those of the teachings of Descartes or Hobbes. Everywhere he emphasizes the inhibitions characterizing the Japanese thought world, the difficulties in drawing radical conclusions, and the tendency to stagnation after significant critical achievements. But for all that by the end of the book we are convinced that Tokugawa thought provided valuable resources for the development of modern consciousness.

In the new introduction Maruyama qualifies the historical picture that he drew in the first two essays. Perhaps, he says, he was mistaken in seeing a well-established Chu Hsi orthodoxy in early Tokugawa times followed by its disintegration and annihilation in the middle and late Tokugawa period. Rather, it appears now, Chu Hsi thought, as a formal position, took shape only late in the seventeenth century at the same time as the emergence of Itō Jinsai and the school of Ancient Learning that was supposed to have been its critical negation. Chu Hsi thought only became an orthodoxy, to the degree it ever did, late in the eighteenth century after the first creative thrust of Sorai thought had spent itself, and Chu Hsi thought remained influential, along with other tendencies, right up to the end of the Tokugawa period. In saying, however, that "even if one discards the whole schema, several of the individual pieces of analysis ... still have a value " (p. xxxv), I think Maruyama's modesty gets the better of him. It does not seem to me that qualifications as to the temporal sequence of the emergence of modern tendencies alters the essential argument of the book ("the whole schema"). What Sorai and related schools called into question was not only the teachings of Chu Hsi, but more importantly that tendency of traditional Japanese thought that Maruyama has called "continuative consciousness."

Continuative consciousness makes little distinction between thought and the social context of thought, and the social context itself is taken as given, more a product of nature than of man. Even Chu Hsi thought, which was used in the Tokugawa period to provide a rational structure for traditional Japanese continuative consciousness, stands in tension with it to the degree that it is a conscious rational philosophical system. Of course the kind of rationality involved in Chu Hsi thought, the metaphysical monism of Principle, was, according to Maruyama, an effective mode of legitimation of the existing social order, whereas the irrational (empiricist and, paradoxically, supernatural) tendencies of Soraigaku and Kokugaku were potentially more critical. But in any case the incipient modernity that Maruyama is tracing is not dependent on the chronology of Chu Hsi thought in the Tokugawa period. It is the break with continuative consciousness that is decisive, not the break with Chu Hsi. In any case to remove the preoccupation with incipient modernity from the book would be to deprive it of its central thrust and would be faithful neither to the early nor to the late Maruyama.

The preoccupation with modernity raises the question of the philosophical stance of the book itself, its status as a work of political philosophy. In Japan Maruyama is widely known as a "modernist" or an advocate of "modernism," and certainly this book is deeply concerned with the modern, its emergence in Japan and its similarities and differences when compared to the West. But what is the nature of Maruyama's concern with the modern? Is it the same as the interest of American social scientists in the 1950s and 1960s in "modernization"? Does it involve the celebration of contemporary "modern" (industrial capitalist) society as the historical ideal?

I believe Maruyama's "modernism," if it can be called such, is profoundly different from that of "modernization theory." To suggest the difference I would like to turn to what at first glance might seem to be rather far afield: a passage from an earlier analyst of modernity, Alexis de Tocqueville, in *Democracy in America* (Volume II, Book III, chapter 21). In a traditional society, says Tocqueville, "generation follows generation without a change in man's position; while some have nothing more to desire, the rest have nothing better to hope. The imagination slumbers in the stillness of this universal silence, and the mere idea of movement does not come into men's minds." But in modern postrevolutionary commercial democracies, although men are in almost perpetual motion, dedicated to the search for an ever greater prosperity, "each individual is isolated, on his own, weak," and genuine intellectual vitality is almost as lacking as in the old traditional society. "But between these two extremes in a nation's history there is an intermediate stage, a glorious yet troubled time in which conditions are not sufficiently fixed for the mind to sleep. . . . That is the time when great reformers arise and new ideas change the face of the world." It is, then, the moment of transition from the traditional to the modern that is creative and liberating. Tocqueville was neither ecstatic about the "modern" society he was observing nor particularly hopeful about its future. If there was any historical moment with which he identified it would have to be called the "early modern," the heroic moment of the initial transition from bondage to freedom, before the new forms of unfreedom inherent in "modernity" had made themselves felt.

Another figure who takes essentially the same position and is even more appropriate because of his direct influence on Maruyama is Max Weber. Here we may cite Ōtsuka Hisao's interpretation of Weber, for Ōtsuka is a longtime friend and colleague of Maruyama and often associated with him as a "modernist." In *Max Weber on the Spirit of Capitalism* (Institute of Developing Economies, Tokyo, 1976) Ōtsuka stresses the heroic qualities of the early "spirit of capitalism" as a responsible and creative "productive ethic." But in contemporary capitalism, according to Ōtsuka, this spirit has almost completely disappeared and been replaced by the "mechanized petrification" of which Weber spoke. Maruyama, like Ōtsuka (and like Tocqueville and Weber, but unlike the "modernization" theorists), is deeply critical of modern society. He is, I believe, fascinated by that "glorious yet troubled time," the early modern, when new ideas changed the face of the world, not only out of historical curiosity but for insight and inspiration in dealing with the harsh problems of the present. In this respect he has always been deeply suspicious of "overcoming the modern" or "going beyond the modern" in either a fascist or a Marxist form. When the genuinely revolutionary insights of the early modern have not been understood or institutionalized, then moving into "postmodern" society promises only new forms of bondage.

It is this stance that gives Maruyama's position its peculiar pathos not only in the historical context of the early 1940s when the book was originally written, but even today. His analysis of Tokugawa thought is in a curious way tentative and ironic precisely with respect to the early modern. In important respects for Japan the "intermediate stage" of which Tocqueville spoke is not, as it is in the West, an "already" that stands in need of revivification, but a "not yet" that is still to come. The very subtlety of his analysis never allows us to forget that the modern tendencies in Tokugawa thought were never more than incipient and potential. But in the context of the early 1940s, as the new introduction makes abundantly clear, even the insistence on the incipiently modern was dangerous. At a time when the "modern" was being blamed for all of Japan's problems and many were raising the slogan of "overcoming the modern," in order to return to the traditional "Japanese spirit," Maruyama insisted on a positive evaluation of the modern and implied that Japan's problems arose not because it was too modern but because it had not become genuinely modern enough. Thus he wrote:

> As my final point, let me consider a very basic doubt that may be raised against this approach. That is to say, what is the value now of looking in this way for a modern consciousness in the internal disintegration of Confucian thought? Is it not this modern mode of thought that arouses the present cry of "crisis"? If we trace back the confusion and disorder that supposedly prevail in the modern spirit, shall we not find its origin here? To these doubts I can only reply as follows: What you say is true. But the question is, can the perplexities of modern thought be resolved by a return to premodern thought? Just as the citizen cannot revert to serfdom, the internally divided consciousness can no longer accept the innocent premodern continuative consciousness. Of course, each of these varied cultural values, although aware of its autonomy, cannot remain wholly unrelated to the others. For instance, it is undeniable that, deep down, art is linked with ethical values, but if these connections are held to be direct and immediate links, art ceases to be art. History, too, cannot be confined to a mere description of past events. But so long as history remains in any way the slave of moralistic standards, it cannot in any sense be called true history. (p. 184)

Here Maruyama does not glorify the modern or deny its profound problems and contradictions but insists that if these problems and contradictions are to be solved at all it will be in and through the modern, and not by some evasion of the actualities of modernity. In the "Author's Introduction" Maruyama describes the "almost physical revulsion" (p. xxvi) he felt as a young man toward the National Morality School (*Kokumin dōtokuron*) exemplified in the writings of Inoue Tetsujirō. It seems reasonably clear that that revulsion is rooted in the fact that Maruyama sees the National Morality school as the modern equivalent of Chu Hsi Confucianism (to whose heritage, in spite of his eclecticism, Inoue in part laid claim). The National Morality school is another form of rationalization for that continuative consciousness that prevents the emergence of early modern revolutionary consciousness. Of course the pervasiveness of continuative consciousness in modern Japan does not depend on the influence of intellectuals, but to the extent that intellectuals rationalize it (Inoue) or only ineffectually challenge it (Muraoka and Watsuji, but also Tsuda and Yanagita) they fail to contribute what they could to the desired transformation. There is little doubt that Maruyama sees his own work as a contribution to that transformation. The book we are reviewing is a delineation of that first faint movement toward a creative ethical individualism that Maruyama sees as the essence of the truly modern (to which industrial capitalism and bureaucratic socialism are just as much a threat as was feudal traditionalism).

As a compelling statement of a position that has permanent validity, this book will remain important for a very long time. It is itself not only a landmark in the study of Japanese thought; it is also a landmark in Japanese thought. Any easy criticism that would direct attention from the seriousness of the argument is to be avoided. But I would like to raise one point for consideration. Taking, as Maruyama does, the revolutionary early modern as his normative point of reference (and we have seen that in so doing he is in notably good company) seems to me deeply problematic. The very brevity and fragility of that moment, wherever it has occurred, the ease with which it disintegrates into its opposite, suggests the difficulty of building a political philosophy on it alone. Perhaps for contemporary man it is not viable to appropriate the early modern moment without a very deep appropriation of that against which the early modern was in revolt. To some extent Maruyama echoes Sorai's critique of Chu Hsi thought when he locates Chinese Confucianism in the context of Hegel's characterization of the static spatiality of nonhistorical oriental civilization (pp. 3–5). Can we accept that view today any more than we can accept Hobbes's caricature of Aristotle and scholastic philosophy? If, as Maruyama rightly says, we cannot in the face of the breakdown of modernity return uncritically to premodern thought, does that necessarily mean that the great philosophical and religious traditions that emerged in the first millennium B.C. have nothing further to teach us? It is my suspicion that the crisis of modernity is so profound that, without ignoring the moment of the heroic early modern transition, there is nothing in the human past that we will want to abandon a priori in the search for a rational alternative.

## II. MARUYAMA MASAO AS SCHOLAR AND FRIEND

I first came to know of Maruyama Masao when Tatsuo Arima, who had been a fellow graduate student at Harvard (and is now Japanese ambassador to Germany), made a translation of Maruyama's long review of *Tokugawa Religion* in *Kokka Gakkai Zasshi* (72, no.4, April 1958). That review already illustrated a tension with which I would become increasingly familiar as I got to know more and more of Maruyama's work: the tension between universalism and particularism. Maruyama's review was the most serious, searching, and passionate that I have ever received. *Tokugawa Religion*, Maruyama wrote, "aroused my appetite and my fighting spirit." What pleased him and what angered him were very much linked together: the fact that I had applied a universal theory to the understanding of Japan, but the fact that I had paid insufficient attention to Japanese particularity in so doing. What annoyed Maruyama most was my tendency to emphasize the contribution of Japanese tradition, as it was worked out in the Edo period, to modernization, without taking seriously enough its potentiality to oppose or distort a genuine modernization, that is, one that would embody universalistic principles. I had without knowing it, in my preoccupation with American modernization theory, touched on Maruyama's own deepest concern.[1]

The common designation of Maruyama in Japan as a representative of "modernism," although not altogether wrong, is unfortunate. The use of this term, by encapsulating him with a small number of like-minded thinkers who flourished at a definite time period, is a way of dismissing him. Such a polemical strategy is certainly not limited to Japan (I haven't enjoyed being classified and dismissed as a "Parsonian"), but it has been especially effective in Japan in circumscribing and blunting any critical challenge to the dominant consensus. It has often been pointed out that Maruyama's concern with modernism (*kindai-shugi*) is not to be equated with American modernization theory, and I would heartily agree. I would point out, however, that the version of modernization theory that I learned from my teacher, Talcott Parsons, was not the vulgar modernization theory common in American social science of the 1950s, in which economic growth was the almost exclusive concern. Rather, Parsons's modernization theory was more faithful to the thought of Max Weber and the neo-Kantianism that lay behind it. Thus, however much *Tokugawa Religion* was influenced and limited by its American environment, there was still something, for example, the concern with the universalistic aspect of religious belief, which struck a chord in Maruyama. Over the years I have only come closer to Maruyama in viewing the modern project in terms of ethical individualism and genuine democracy. Since neither of these dimensions of an ethically conceived modernity are securely institutionalized in the United States or in Japan, "modernism," so far as it has been applied to Maruyama, is not an outdated fad to be lightly dismissed, but rather an uncompleted project. Indeed, the prospects for the completion of that project are, if anything, cloudier today everywhere in the world than they were in 1950. Thus Maruyama's legacy is as vital and relevant as ever. In my meetings with

Maruyama in recent years I found that we continued to share the same fundamental commitments, even as we shared a pessimistic assessment of the potentiality of our societies to fulfill them.

Another trendy epithet has been used in both Japan and the United States to dismiss Maruyama in recent years: "Eurocentric." The ideological location of the term differs in the two societies: in Japan it is a negative term for the conservative upholders of *Nihonjin-ron;* in America for the radical defenders of "multiculturalism." Maruyama defiantly affirmed his Eurocentrism, arguing that European culture was a "universal legacy to humankind [*jinrui fuhen no isan*]." Perhaps his most consistent ethical insight, which came from Kant, was never to collapse too readily the distinction between the is (*Sein*) and the ought (*Sollen*). At moments Maruyama's love for things European (especially German) was almost comic. I remember once at Harvard in a small-group discussion Maruyama expressing disdain for Japanese poetry, which prompted one of the American professors to ask, "Don't you like Bashō?" Maruyama paused and then said, "I much prefer Goethe." Again once when he was spending some time in Berkeley he went to Seattle for a complete performance of the *Ring of the Niebelungen*. I teased him for keeping bad company because I had read in the newspaper that Henry Kissinger, not one of Maruyama's favorite statesmen, had also gone to Seattle for the same reason. Yet when Maruyama was in Berkeley in 1983 my wife and I easily persuaded him to go with us to see several Ozu movies being shown at the Pacific Film Archives. Maruyama admitted that he had enjoyed Ozu films all his life, not only the somewhat rebellious films of the thirties but also the rather sentimental family films of the fifties. Clearly Maruyama was more Japanese than he sometimes was willing to admit.

But what makes the charge of Eurocentrism finally trivial is the fact that Maruyama spent his life in the study of things Japanese. As far as I know almost everything he ever wrote was concerned with Japanese subject-matter. Of course, much that he wrote was critical, yet he was always concerned to discover the beginnings of modern consciousness among Japanese thinkers, whether in a Tokugawa figure like Ogyū Sorai or a Meiji figure like Fukuzawa Yukichi. While sometimes in near-despair over the perennial resurgence of the primordial "deep things" in Japanese culture (it is easy to imagine what he thought of *Nihonjin-ron*), he never ceased to nurture the seeds of ethical individualism and substantive democracy in Japan.

Much as I generally agreed with Maruyama, at the end of my review of the English translation of *Studies in the Intellectual History of Tokugawa Japan* (*Journal of Japanese Studies,* 1977) I raised one critical question for my old friend—one he never answered. I wondered if, by focusing so much of his work on the exciting moment of the early modern, the transition from primordial embeddedness to ethical freedom, whether in Europe or Japan, he had overlooked the resources of those premodern traditions, such as the great religions and philosophies of the first millennium B.C., that had broken with this-worldly affirmation in the direction of universalism and transcendence long before the modern era. Perhaps only the reappropriation of those resources in combination with the early modern initiatives can help us cope with the distorted modernity that has overtaken the developed world. I don't think Maruyama would mind if my last word to him is slightly contentious.

# 5 Intellectual and Society in Japan

At the beginning of the Chinese tradition as at the beginning of the European stands an intellectual who derived a conception of order in society from a conception of order in the Soul.[1] Both Confucius and Plato developed an idea of the Good (Chinese: *jen;* Greek: *agathon*) that provided a norm or measure for centuries of subsequent political thought. Although Confucian thought was long influential in Japan and much later Greek thought has not been without consequence, no such profound intellectual conception stands at the beginning of the Japanese tradition. Rather, the givenness of society, radically challenged in their very different ways by Confucius and Plato, has survived as the central focus of reflection in Japan.

I

Shōtoku Taishi (573–621), prince-regent under the Empress Suiko, is perhaps an archetype of the Japanese intellectual. A semilegendary figure associated with the beginning of the effort to establish a centralized imperial state on the Chinese model, he is credited with the first explicit statement of the normative order of Japanese society (the so-called Seventeen-Article Constitution) as well as with the first writings that give evidence of a profound grasp of Buddhism in Japan. For present purposes the authenticity of the documents is less important than their symbolic significance in subsequent Japanese thought. The Seventeen-Article Constitution ransacks the resources of Chinese culture to express the essential ideals of Japanese society.[2] Article One stresses harmony (*wa*), perhaps the quintessential Japanese social value, and subsequent articles extol in various ways the virtues of group solidarity, individual submission to group interests, and the self-sacrifice of high and low alike for group ends. Though almost all the language is in some sense Confucian, except for Article Two, which is explicitly Buddhist, the Confucian idea of the Good (*jen*) is mentioned only once, in Article Six, and that in passing.

Shōtoku Taishi has the peculiar distinction of being not only the first in a long line of intellectuals to express in foreign concepts the nearly inarticulate sociocentric emphasis of Japanese culture; he was also the first to use foreign ideas to cast doubt on the self-sufficiency of that emphasis. If he was the first "official intellectual" he was also the first "critical intellectual." The form of his criticism was his deep Buddhist piety expressed in his oft repeated phrase, "The world is empty and vain; only the Buddha is true."[3] Of course the dichotomy of "official" and "critical" is too simple. The proclamation that there is a transcendent reality that renders empty all earthly values had little sociological implication other than the establishment of a Buddhist monastic community (*sangha*) independent of political control. Yet the Seventeen-Article Constitution was obliquely critical in that it stated an ideal of general submission to the emperor when in fact Soga no Umako had dominant power at court and the Soga clan had for some decades effectively dominated the imperial family. Indeed the Constitution may have been written after 645 when the Soga were overthrown and attributed to Shōtoku Taishi in order to help legitimize the Taika reforms dating from that year. In any case Shōtoku's difficulties with the Soga seem to have been real enough, so that he found himself in the typical predicament of the Japanese intellectual: he would have to deal not only with the relation between foreign culture and the Japanese tradition, but also with the problem of arbitrary political forces that frustrate political idealism. His decision to withdraw more and more into Buddhist devotion in his later years was also prophetic.

There were clearly some remarkable minds at work in Japan during the seventh and eighth centuries when virtually the whole range of Chinese culture and social institutions were imported into Japan. Along with the rest came the Chinese (Confucian) idea of education and the competitive examination system for officials. But the educational and examination system was one of the earliest casualties of the process of erosion of Chinese institutions that set in almost at once. A secular intelligentsia oriented to bureaucratic office on the Chinese model did not develop, largely because the aristocratic clans managed to keep effective control of the land and to appropriate the newly established ranks and offices. The court aristocracy was literate as the rising local military families later would also be, but neither showed much interest in the theoretical aspects of the Chinese tradition, either metaphysical or political. Rather they inclined toward poetry and fiction if they became interested in literature at all. Their writings tended to be in Japanese rather than in Chinese and to be a vehicle more for emotion than thought. Theoretical culture was kept alive among the monks and was of course mostly Buddhist, though Confucian texts continued to be studied. The split between abstract foreign culture carried by relatively isolated intellectual coteries and emotional native culture more widely shared among the people has never been entirely overcome.

Until the seventeenth century intellectual life, with the partial exception of belles-lettres, was largely confined to the religious—Buddhist monks and later Shinto priests. Shinran (1173–1262) in the Pure Land tradition and Dōgen (1200–53) in the Zen tradition carried Japanese Buddhism to its highest peaks. Both broke through the givenness of Japanese society in their demand for absolutely transcendental loyalty, but it proved difficult sociologically to capitalize on these breakthroughs. Shinran's intense spirituality in the preaching of absolute "other power" had an electric influence during his lifetime but no very stable organization crystallized after his death. It was not until the time of Rennyo (1415–99), the so-called second founder of the True Pure Land sect, that a powerful organization was created and that was in part because Rennyo included a great deal of Confucian ethics in his teaching along with "other shore" piety. In the fifteenth and sixteenth centuries in some areas True Pure Land sect believers actually established independent political control, but not until they had come to mirror in large part the hereditary leader-follower social pattern of the environing feudal society. Loyalty and self-sacrifice were to be devoted to Amida and the sect leaders, not to the feudal lords, but the structure of relations was quite similar. Any chance that these religious structures might develop alternative patterns of social life was lost when the secular power of the religious sects was crushed by the great military dictators of the late sixteenth century, Oda Nobunaga and Toyotomi Hideyoshi.

The vigorous and independent life of the Zen monastery at the time of Dōgen later declined and the Zen monastery tended to become an educational center for the dissemination of Neo-Confucianism. Closely in touch with currents of thought in China, the Zen monks, particularly of the Rinzai school, were broadly educated and made excellent advisers for shogun and daimyo. In fact Zen became associated with the samurai class and made significant contributions to its gradually developing status ethic, later called *bushidō*.

To sum up the picture of Japanese intellectual life before the establishment of the Tokugawa shogunate in 1600 we may say that there were two periods of marked vitality and originality: poetry and fiction in the Heian period (794–1192) and religion in the Kamakura period (1192–1333). Some works of history were written from the early eighth century on, which contained some political and social reflection, but no major work of political or social philosophy was produced in the entire period. Confucian morality continued to percolate throughout the society, to rationalize leader-follower relations, and to alter some features of traditional Japanese society, such as lowering the status of women in the samurai class. But the givenness of society was largely its own justification. When in the course of the centralization of Japan leading up to the establishment of the Tokugawa shogunate the decision was made first to restrict and then to extirpate Christianity, the decision, paralleling as it did the decision to destroy the secular power of the Buddhist sects, arose partly because of the fear of the foreign powers behind the missionaries, but partly because Christianity was seen as a threat to the givenness of the social order. Fabian, Catholic apostate turned Buddhist, criticized the first of the Ten Commandments, "Thou shalt venerate *Deus* alone," as undermining the Japanese social order by advocating rebellion against lords and fathers. Rather, he said, "It is the way of man to live in accord with the rules of the Shogun who is the ruler of Japan, so long as one lives in Japan."[4]

II

Whatever the continuities, in its intellectual life, Japan at the beginning of the Tokugawa period was significantly different from the time of Shōtoku Taishi. Buddhism had stirred the hearts of the masses and had brought even the remotest villages into touch with universal ideas and national movements. In a somewhat inchoate way the needs of the peasants had begun to be articulated by the popular sects and resistance against samurai pressure had occurred, even though ending in defeat. Both Buddhism and particularly Confucianism had contributed to the development of a rigorous status ethic among the samurai and to the construction of a model of political relations that now had to be generalized to the whole country. Even if the emperor as descendant of the sun goddess still reigned and the round of village ritual with its Shinto observance only lightly colored by Buddhism continued as it had for centuries, the native tradition alone was far too inarticulate to provide a conscious conception of the new order that was to arise from the Tokugawa peace. One source from which ideas might have come was now excluded. The door had been firmly shut on a Europe, which was about to produce a Spinoza and a Descartes, a Hobbes and a Locke. The only available tradition that could provide a self-picture for the new society was

Confucianism, and it was to Confucianism that the early Tokugawa shogunate turned.

It should not be imagined, however, that the Tokugawa system was the
creation of intellectuals, Confucian or otherwise. As Ogyū Sorai later
pointed out, Tokugawa Ieyasu, the founder of the house, was a Sengoku
daimyo, a feudal lord of the warring states period, and the system he constructed was what you might expect from such a man.[5] Although it did not
meet the systematizing standards of Sorai, the system put together by
Ieyasu and his vassals and retainers, with only a modicum of advice from
intellectuals, was a powerful and effective one, as has so often been the case
in Japan. Warfare between feudal lords was eliminated and strong political
control, direct in the central domain of the shogunate itself, indirect elsewhere, extended throughout the entire country. The natural consequences
were a rapid advance in the agricultural and merchant spheres of the economy, rapid urbanization, and a general cultural efflorescence.

What the Confucian scholars were not asked to construct they were
asked to explain and defend. It is no accident that the school of Confucianism that Ieyasu chose to patronize and that later became the official
school of the shogunate was that of Fujiwara Seika (1561–1619) and his
pupil Hayashi Razan (1583–1657), followers of the Chu Hsi or Sung
Confucian school in China. Sung Confucianism had for some time been the
official orthodoxy in China largely because it gave nearly absolute endorse-
ment to established authority in family and state. The system developed by
Chu Hsi and his immediate followers was one of great complexity and profundity, but its use in later centuries, perhaps not unlike the use of Thomism
in the Catholic Church, was largely defensive. It tended to identify the existing social order with the order of nature itself and to preach an ethics of sub-
missiveness within the inherited status system. But as is usual in Japan no
single intellectual tradition provided the legitimation of authority. Ieyasu
made a great point, as Nobunaga and Hideyoshi had before him, of his reverence for the emperor. The Kyoto court, though deprived of any real power,
was lavishly subsidized and the emperor was recognized as the ultimate
source of legitimacy for the shogun. Seika and Razan duly included a
solemn exposition of Shinto myth (explicated in edifying Confucian concepts) as part of their teaching. In addition, Buddhism, though not contributing any appreciable element to the intellectual foundation of the
regime, was patronized organizationally. As part of the system of thought
control leading to the extirpation of Christianity all Japanese were required
to become members of a Buddhist parish. This "establishment" of Buddhism

among the masses was occurring just when Buddhism as a system of ideas was losing its hold among the elite.

Nonetheless it was only gradually that the intellectual role, almost identical with that of Buddhist monk in previous centuries, began to establish itself independently. Though sharply critical of Buddhism, Fujiwara Seika was himself a monk and it was not until 1691 that the head of the shogun's Confucian school was allowed to be a layman. The founder of the school of philological studies that resurrected the language and thought of ancient Japan, Keichū (1640–1701), was a monk and Matsuo Bashō (1644–94), the greatest of the haiku poets, lived a semimonastic existence. But by the end of the seventeenth century a number of independent secular bases for intellectual life had been established. The Tokugawa peace brought a new interest in education and literacy and the demand for teachers was high.[6] The samurai, no longer primarily warriors but civil administrators, were admonished to combine literary arts (*bun*) with the military ones (*bu*). Although the samurai class was largely a salaried bureaucracy, not, as in China, a landed gentry, it took on something of the character of a stratum of literati for the first time in Japanese history. Confucian scholars as teachers, advisers, and administrators became increasingly important throughout the period. Official schools of the shogunate or the fiefs provided employment to significant numbers of such scholars.

But in addition to the official intellectual world, urbanization and the growing cultural interests of wealthy townsmen and peasants provided the social basis for a "free intelligentsia," independent of either monastic or governmental structures, for the first time in Japanese history. Well-known scholars were able to establish their own schools in the cities and larger towns and to make a good living from their students and from lecture tours. Medicine was a high-status free profession that was followed by such diverse intellectuals as Andō Shōeki, Motoori Norinaga, and Yamagata Daini. Literacy, estimated to have reached approximately 40 percent by the end of the Tokugawa period, was sharply on the increase during the seventeenth century and provided a basis for the first time for a mass publishing industry that could support full-time writers.[7]

It would be surprising if in this welter of cultural activity we did not begin to see the emergence of "critical intellectuals." Political criticism and protest are evident during the Tokugawa period but they occur so spasmodically and in so devious and muted a form that their absence is a larger problem for explanation than their presence. Part of the answer, of course, is the oppressive hand of the shogunate. Its encouragement of the Chu Hsi school implied a criticism of other intellectual tendencies, though only when the shogunate perceived a direct political threat was there actual suppression of nonorthodox scholars and even then with nothing like the severity shown toward Christianity. Censorship of the theater and popular books was concerned as much with enforcing Confucian morality as with political orthodoxy. Perhaps as important in minimizing dissent as pressure from above was the view shared by all schools (in China as well) that political criticism was a form of faction, and faction a form of rebellion. Only with the greatest difficulty in the Tokugawa period would it have been possible to legitimize political dissent, criticism, and controversy. No conception of a free marketplace of ideas in this sphere existed.

One form of social criticism was allowed, however. Indeed it was almost required. This was the conservative form of criticism that denounced the present for not conforming to the purer customs of an earlier day. Both Chinese and Japanese governments welcomed such criticism, especially when it denounced sons for being insufficiently filial and retainers for being insufficiently loyal. Denunciation of the wealth and ostentation of prosperous townsmen and peasants was also highly approved. Only when such criticism became strident and led to insistent demands for government intervention, especially if the criticism and demands came from nonorthodox scholars, was the government inclined to crack down. Kumazawa Banzan (1619–91), a follower of the school of Wang Yang-ming, the Ming Dynasty rival of Chu Hsi, was placed under house arrest during the last years of his life; his protector, the daimyo of Okayama, was pressured into abandoning the teachings of his school after Banzan intemperately offered direct reform proposals to the shogunate.[8] Yamago Sokō (1622–85) opposed the teachings of Chu Hsi and argued for a return to the teachings of Confucius himself, unencumbered by later interpretations. He was thus one of the founders of what came to be called the Ancient Learning (*kogaku*) school. The vigor of his views earned him exile. Nonetheless neither the Wang Yang-ming nor the Ancient Learning school was suppressed and they continued to produce important (and occasionally critical) scholars in the eighteenth and nineteenth centuries.

Conservative criticism, unless it became too strident, was no threat to the status quo because it never questioned the givenness of the social order. It criticized latter-day fallings away from that order, not its fundamental principles. With Ogyū Sorai, however, criticism, though conservative on the surface, reached a profound level and the implications of his teachings changed the Tokugawa intellectual world in the eighteenth and nineteenth centuries.[9] Sorai was the son of a physician and was educated to follow his father's career. However, at a fairly young age he abandoned medicine for Confucian studies. Sorai was the greatest representative of the Ancient Learning school and like his predecessors he rejected the teachings of the commentators in favor of a return to the primary texts of Confucianism. His greatness, however, transcends membership in any school. Sorai was almost unique in the history of Japanese Confucianism in the extent to which he identified himself with the Chinese culture in which he was steeped. His Sinophilia was so great that he willingly called himself an "Eastern Barbarian" (a term used in China to refer to the Japanese) and upon moving his residence in Edo announced that he was pleased with his new residence in a more easterly quarter of the city "because it is closer to China."

Looking coldly at Tokugawa society and its problems from his Chinese perspective, Sorai was perhaps the first Japanese intellectual to subject the foundation of his own society to skeptical criticism. He developed his own conception of the Confucian Way. For Sorai the Way governing society was not derived from the natural order of the cosmos (as the followers of Chu Hsi taught) nor from the nature of the human heart (as the followers of Wang Yang-ming taught) but from the sage teachings of the ancient Chinese kings. The Way of society is a humanly constructed order and even though the ancient kings had the highest wisdom, every age must to some extent construct its own institutions. Sorai takes the Confucian notion of the Good, *jen*, as the most basic teaching, as a norm for social and personal order:

> In Confucian doctrine Jen occupies the most important place. Why is this so? It is because Jen is that which advances and embodies the Way of the Former Kings. The Way of the Former Kings is the Way of giving peace and security to the world.
>
> Jen is the term used to refer to those qualities in a man which promote the growth and development of mankind and give peace and security to the people. This is the great virtue which was possessed by the Sages. "The great virtue of the universe is life." The sage conforms to this.
>
> Jen is the Way of "nourishment." Hence in ruling the state one should "raise up the straight and set aside the crooked, and thereby make the crooked become straight." In personal conduct, too, the individual should nourish his good qualities, and thereby his evil qualities will disappear of themselves.[10]

While Sorai spent much of his life as an independent teacher with his own school, he served the daimyo of Dewa, a member of the shogunal government, for a period and late in life was a frequent adviser to the shogunate. Much of his thinking, therefore, was directed to problems of government and its reform. Perhaps the most profoundly shocking of Sorai's opinions was that the shogun was the legitimate ruler of Japan and the emperor was superfluous, an almost unheard of view before modern times. Sorai traced much of the troubles of the regime to its founder Tokugawa Ieyasu, also a rather shocking procedure in terms of the pieties of the period. Whereas Ieyasu should have founded a new regime on broad and systematic foundations, he was, said Sorai, after all just a Sengoku daimyo, and merely projected on a national scale the experience he had had in extending power from his own domain as a base. Sorai felt the time had probably passed when the regime could undergo a fundamental reform and went to his death full of gloomy forebodings about the future of the country under leadership he regarded as incompetent.

The particular measures that Sorai advocated were a mixture of radical and conservative elements. He advocated a strong central bureaucratic administration under the shogun with the feudal lords all but eliminated. Offices would be filled by merit rather than heredity, which meant primarily that lower ranking samurai would have a better chance, though Sorai had no objection in principle to townsmen or peasants holding office, providing they were men of talent. In these respects Sorai can be said to have anticipated the Meiji period. In other ways he was extremely old-fashioned. He was suspicious of the money economy and would have liked virtually to eliminate merchants and cities. The samurai would return to the land, and therefore no longer need money payments, and an idyllic rural existence would be enjoyed by a population of samurai and farmers. Such notions were reiterated by other thinkers of the period since they conformed to old Confucian ideals, but even many Confucian scholars recognized that they were utterly impractical. It was not, however, Sorai's particular proposals that were influential but rather his whole way of thinking that opened up for conscious reflection aspects of the cultural and social order previously closed to thought. The implications of Sorai's views had become sufficiently clear by 1790 to lead the shogunate to issue its famous ban on heterodoxy, aimed chiefly at the followers of Sorai, which led to the expulsion or conversion of scholars other than those of the Chu His school in the shogunal university and the fief schools. In various ways, however, the views of Sorai continued to influence thought in the nineteenth century, making a significant contribution to the open-minded reflection about institutional change that characterized the leaders of the Meiji Restoration.

The curious influence of Sorai's thought was paradoxically present in a man who was almost his opposite, Motoori Norinaga (1730–1801), the greatest figure in the National Learning school (Kokugaku), which was as radically committed to ancient Japanese culture as Sorai was to ancient Chinese.[11] The logic of Sorai's return to the ancient texts and the radical commitment to the Way he found in them was followed by Norinaga, even though the texts in question were different and commitment to them had different consequences. Norinaga was one of the best educated of Tokugawa intellectuals and was influenced by many traditions other than that of Sorai. Especially important to him was the philological tradition going back to Keichū, mentioned above, and the Confucian Shinto tradition of Yamazaki Ansai (1618–82). Whereas Sorai had been of samurai origin and became an adviser to the shogun, Norinaga was of merchant background and remained all his life a doctor and private teacher. Norinaga studied Confucianism in Kyoto with a teacher deeply influenced by Sorai. In the end, however, Norinaga concluded that the Confucian Way is the Way of governing the empire or a country and not the Way for an ordinary person or "small man" like himself.[12] Neither Norinaga nor later leaders of the school devoted themselves directly to political thought, partly because the leaders were all commoners and the movement appealed mainly to merchants and wealthy peasants, though it was not without influence among samurai especially late in the period.[13]

While remaining largely apolitical, the thought of Norinaga and his followers had at least latently radical consequences. The Way that Norinaga discovered in the ancient Japanese texts was not, like that of Sorai, a humanly constructed Way. On the contrary it was divinely instituted, indeed, a Way of the gods. Norinaga harshly rejected the notion that rulership should depend, as in Confucianism, on virtue. The Japanese emperor rules because of his descent from the sun goddess, regardless of virtue or the lack thereof. By implication the whole social order is validated by Norinaga's logic—not, as in Chu Hsi Confucianism, because it is alleged to conform to natural reason, but because it rests ultimately on arbitrary divine decree. Nonetheless Norinaga's critique of foreign, especially Chinese, culture had some subtle implications. For Norinaga, true Japanese culture is natural, emotional, and even "feminine," whereas Chinese culture (in Japan largely samurai culture) was artificial, calculating, and "masculine."[14] However much the latter might fit the Chinese it was, in Norinaga's opinion, pernicious in Japan. It was Norinaga's dissatisfaction with ruling-class culture that was for a long time the major subversive influence of the National Learning school. Norinaga's reverence for the emperor did not preclude profound loyalty to the Tokugawa regime, which after all also professed a high regard for him. Only at the very end of the Tokugawa period were National Learning school ideas used to undermine the Tokugawa regime, and then mainly by outsiders since most official teachers of the school remained steadfastly apolitical.[15]

Sorai's ideas had more explosive consequences in the hands of a man like Yamagata Daini (1725–67), who combined them curiously with the Shinto Confucian tradition of Yamazaki Ansai.[16] Daini agreed with Sorai that the samurai should be returned to the land, but as commoners. Daini argued that the whole period of military rule had been a mistake and that only an abolition of the samurai class and the combing of the country for talent under the restored rule of the emperor could solve the nation's problems. Daini, himself of samurai origin, had been an official of the shogunate as well as a private doctor and teacher. In 1766 he apparently planned an uprising against the shogunate involving samurai and armed peasants. He was arrested and executed. Daini had no immediate followers and the significance of his thought and action should not be exaggerated, but he was the first to move from critical thought to direct action and his example was not lost on the restorationist intellectuals at the end of the Tokugawa period.

The great fief of Mito, belonging to a collateral house of the Tokugawa family, had been the center of historical research even in the seventeenth century. The later Mito school under the leadership of Aizawa Seishisai (1782–1863) and Fujita Tōko (1806–55), and perhaps under the influence of an infusion of ideas from the school of Sorai, directed its attention to the Tokugawa institutional system and its need for reform. The Mito school, officially committed to Chu Hsi Confucianism and Shinto, worked out the theory of the National Polity (*kokutai*) and the duties and obligations of subjects (*taigi meibun*) that would become the major ingredients of the orthodox version of the Meiji emperor system after 1890. This did not mean that the Mito school was itself subversive. As in the case of the National Learning school, the ideas of the Mito school were not used against the regime until the shogunate began to prove unable to cope with the foreigners after 1853.

One significant late Tokugawa opposition intellectual did not apparently owe anything to Sorai. He is worth discussing as an example of the critical possibilities within the Wang Yang-ming school of thought, which would be influential at the end of the Tokugawa period and in early Meiji as well. His name is Oshio Heihachirō (1793–1837) and his influence is by no means dead even today.[17] Oshio was of samurai origin and a hereditary retainer of the shogunate. He served for some twenty years as a magistrate in Osaka, where he was noted for his zeal and honesty. After 1830 he passed on his post to his adopted son and occupied himself as a full-time teacher. His teaching took the form of a rather ardent monism in which the usual distinctions between inner and outer, self and nonself, active and passive are overcome. From this point of view self-cultivation is identical with public moral action and the evil actions of men in society is experienced as pain interior to the self. In the light of his radical monism he viewed evil in society as the result of mistaken distinctions and differences. The people and the emperor should be united in unbroken harmony but instead the shogunate and the samurai class stand between and oppress both emperor and people.

The intensity of Oshio's convictions finally led him to carry out an uprising that was perhaps the most significant in the Tokugawa period before the 1860s since, unlike numerous peasant rebellions, it had a conscious ideology. More religious than political, this ideology nonetheless broached themes that would have abiding significance. The rebellion itself was ill-planned. Although about one quarter of the city of Osaka was burned it took the troops of the shogunate only two days to restore order. Oshio and his son fled and about a month later committed suicide by sword and fire when capture was imminent. If Oshio expected success at all it was not through rational strategy but through the suasive effect of a pure moral act, striking enough to bring in a new dispensation at one blow. Conspiratorial planning would have been precisely the kind of "partial" and "separate" action that he was attempting to overcome. Similar problems, arising from the structure of Japanese values and, group life, affected many later activists, including Mishima Yukio, who took Oshio as his role model.

So far we have considered mainly elite thinkers and movements. There were also a number of movements in the Tokugawa period whose leaders were intellectuals of a sort even if they did not have a highly sophisticated education. Ishida Baigan (1685–1744) and Ninomiya Sontoku (1787–1856) who worked, respectively, among the townsmen and peasant classes are perhaps the best known.[18] Such movements, even though using mainly Confucian vocabulary, were concerned with inculcating self-discipline and self-respect among the common people and providing motivation for improving their material situation.[19] Similar in consequence though deriving more from Shinto and Buddhist concepts was the spate of popular religions that sprang up in late Tokugawa times: Tenrikyō, Konkokyō, Kurozumikyō, Maruyamakyō, and the like. None of these movements was explicitly concerned with political change and a number of them, for example, Shingaku in its later phases, were co-opted by the shogunate as part of its apparatus of ideological control. Most of them espoused an ideology of harmony and obedience that would have made rebellious actions almost unthinkable, but they did nonetheless give expression to the autonomous drive for self-improvement and dignity among the commoner classes and implicitly opposed the callous and utilitarian attitudes toward them of at least some samurai thinkers. These movements together with such mass phenomena as the periodic great pilgrimages to the Grand Shrine of Ise, sometimes involving several million people, also served to break down the narrow confines of village and fief and to develop the beginnings of a common consciousness among the Japanese people. In contributing to the development of an incipient national consciousness they did among the commoners what the major elite intellectual movements discussed above did for the upper classes.

A survey of Tokugawa intellectual life up to about 1850 would hardly make one believe that a regime was about to fall. On the contrary it would be more apt to convince one of the effectiveness and perhaps the oppressiveness of a regime, which was able to maintain the loyalty of the vast majority of its intellectuals and to blunt criticism so that it dealt more often with surface symptoms than with basic principles. Few of Sorai's successors had his critical perspicuity. From the vantage point of 1850 Yamagata Daini and Oshio Heihachiro could be viewed as isolated and insignificant figures. The main currents of intellectual life followed the channels that the regime had marked out for them. If leading thinkers did not loudly extol the shogunate, and most of them did, they at least proclaimed the virtues of harmony and obedience. In those few cases where opposition did break out it took the form of dramatic and, at least in the immediate outcome, futile expressive gestures—rebellion and/or suicide—rather than sustained organization of a political opposition, for which the society supplied few cultural or social supports.

It is no surprise then that there is little consensus on which Tokugawa intellectual movements provided the main impetus for the Meiji Restoration. None of them provided much impetus in that direction until the shogunate itself began to display flagrant incompetence in the 1850s and 1860s. Under pressure, most of the prominent traditions, including Chu Hsi Confucianism, could rationalize a change of regime. But what was presented as an alternative was neither very clear nor very radical. The idea of a restoration of the emperor was powerful emotionally (the Tokugawa shogunate had itself claimed to be an imperial restoration) but lacked content. The notion of a greater degree of centralization and greater utilization of talent from all classes had long been at hand in the well-understood system of Chinese centralized empire. Basic issues about Japanese society—the place of the emperor, the nature of authority, and obedience in family and state— were not raised.

It is difficult to state with precision what was the role of intellectuals in the process leading up to the Meiji Restoration. Certainly intellectuals, almost exclusively samurai intellectuals, first saw the need for a radical change of regimes and organized the first efforts to bring about such change. The initial attempts, however, were not much more effective than the earlier efforts of Yamagata and Oshio. Small groups of samurai or *rōnin* conspiring in the cities were unable to mobilize any effective support to sustain an opposition movement. Only when the great western fiefs turned against the regime was there a power base sufficiently strong to succeed. Of course the work of the intellectuals in creating a national climate of opinion favorable to restoration and a revival of national consciousness was essential. But the young administrators who moved into commanding positions in the new Meiji government were not among the most ideologically fervent. Behind the Meiji Restoration stood no Locke or Rousseau, no Marx or Lenin, no Gandhi or Mao Tse-tung, but only a group of open-minded young men, ready to learn, committed to Japan, but with no determinate vision of the future.

III

The curious thing about Japan compared to most non-Western nations is how well the young men succeeded. They and their successors have continued to rule Japan for more than one hundred years—through enormous successes and occasional severe setbacks. They have never been successfully challenged by a political opposition led by ideological intellectuals. They have never been overthrown. Unlike most major nations in the world the word "revolution" can be used in Japan with respect to the future or not at all.

It would not be correct to say that intellectuals had nothing to do with the formation of the Meiji state. Most of the Meiji leaders were themselves at least part-time intellectuals, but their ideas were put in the service of practical exigencies rather than vice versa. Their real creativity lay in organizational ingenuity rather than in the production of novel concepts. As was true in the Tokugawa period many of the autonomous intellectuals were co-opted by the government, especially in the early Meiji period, and served it well, including some who had begun as sharp critics of the regime such as Katō Hiroyuki and Mori Arinori. But the Meiji leadership was concerned with Japanese survival first of all and then with increasing wealth and power. It had no quarrel with the givenness of Japanese society except where it impeded these goals. It was not committed to a new conception of man or a new idea of society but rather to a defense of the old ones insofar as erosion of old conceptions and ideas threatened the more pragmatic goals.

Since the government was both effective and moderately repressive, intellectuals in the Meiji period and later have had some of the same problems as intellectuals in the Tokugawa period. The content of many of the modern ideologies has had a high degree of social relevance and has conceived of intellectuals as socially responsible, as did Tokugawa Confucianism. Since intellectuals have always been kept on the margins politically the tension has been severe. The traditional temptations of dramatically expressive but practically ineffective opposition or withdrawal into the private sphere of aesthetics or religion have remained strong throughout the modern period. The most powerful control on freewheeling intellectuals has been the strong sense of national identity, with its deep symbolic implication of life-giving maternal acceptance, that has been building up since the seventeenth century and has with almost mathematical regularity pulsated periodically ever since. Opposition that has not been justified in emotionally nationalist terms has been difficult to sustain, especially in periods, such as the present, when nationalistic sentiments are on the rise.

Even though there are important continuities in intellectual life between the Tokugawa and the modern periods there are of course very great differences. Above all, the range of cultural possibilities in Japan was enormously broadened by the reception of Western culture after 1868. The Japanese capacity to accept foreign culture without losing its own coherence and continuity, already severely tested by the reception of Chinese culture, was stretched to the breaking point. But in spite of enormous problems the flexibility of the Japanese pattern has once again been demonstrated.

Before discussing a few of the intellectual tendencies in modem Japan and the role they projected for intellectuals (even a sketch of Japan's convoluted modern intellectual history would be far too ambitious for this essay) we may consider briefly the occupational basis and career pattern of modern Japanese intellectuals.

Those few Japanese who could use a European language in 1868 were in an enormously advantageous position. Many were quickly taken into the government. Others established their own schools on the old Tokugawa private-school model, teaching English and European studies rather than Confucianism. Fukuzawa Yukichi (1835–1901) founded such a school in 1868 and it eventually became Keiō University, one of Japan's two greatest private universities. Other schools were much more transient. For awhile during the 1880s Christian schools and universities were predominant— they were the best financed and the best staffed schools in the country and ambitious young men flocked to them. But while private schools and universities continued to exist, the government system of higher education became preeminent after about 1890. Graduation from one of the great national universities was subsequently a necessary key for entry into the intellectual elite, and eventually for entry into any kind of elite, as is true in most modern societies.

While the universities had a certain degree of academic freedom and were not used, as were the lower schools, for nationalist indoctrination, there were still severe limits on intellectual life in the universities before 1945. In 1892 Professor Kume Kunitake of Tokyo University was dismissed for teaching that Shinto was a "survival of a primitive form of worship." In 1920 Professor Morito Tatsuo was dismissed from Tokyo University for publishing an article on the social thought of Kropotkin. During the 1920s further firings occurred, including the dismissal of most of the Department of Economics at Kyoto University. Many famous professors lost their jobs in the 1930s. In spite of these pressures the universities, especially after the growth of radical student movements beginning in 1918, were a major source of dissent until all opposition was silenced in the late 1930s. Even then students who could not read Karl Marx read Max Weber as the next best thing and continued to think radical thoughts. After 1945 the university has clearly been the main source of criticism and dissent with respect to Japanese society and politics.

Intellectuals have played an important role in the Japanese popular press, newspapers, and magazines, from the early Meiji period. Fukuzawa Yukichi was also one of the first to publish a newspaper and he wrote regularly for it during his lifetime. During the Meiji period many significant intellectuals lived mainly from their work on newspapers and magazines. Even as late as the 1920s and 1930s an outstanding intellectual such as Miki Kiyoshi (1897–1945) supported himself outside the university by journalism alone, and one could find a few examples in the postwar period as well. But after 1920 most influential intellectuals, however often they wrote for the popular press, tended to have a university appointment as their main occupation. Before 1945 government censorship was a constant problem. The press along with the universities was a major source of political and social criticism.

In the early Meiji period the intellectuals came mainly from the samurai class and there was much similarity of background between them and government officials. Even though the critical intellectuals tended to come from families who were formerly Tokugawa retainers or at least from fiefs other than Satsuma and Chōshū, which provided the main body of government leaders, there was some circulation between the two groups. The educational system had not yet crystallized and there was much movement between journalism, politics, and teaching. As late as 1917 Nagai Ryūtarō left Waseda University to go into politics, and in 1920 Nakano Seigo left a successful career in journalism to enter the Diet. But over time such transitions have become increasingly difficult. The vertical structures of Japanese society have become stronger and more differentiated and it has become more difficult to move between them.[20] This does not mean that intellectuals have become less influential. The vast expansion of higher education and of the mass media has tended to give intellectuals, professors and writers, larger audiences than ever. But such intellectuals are largely cut off from personal contacts with other elites. Even though in the late 1930s Prince Konoe, the last premier before Tōjō, collected a brain trust around him, the Shōwa Study Group, which supplied him with ideas and slogans, the wholesale movement of intellectuals into positions of administrative responsibility such as occurred in the American New Deal would have been impossible. Since the war the barriers have only increased. The government has its technical advisers, such as the "defense intellectuals," but significant use of intellectuals in executive and diplomatic posts in the manner of John F. Kennedy would be unthinkable in Japan. These developments represent general trends in modern Japanese society rather than any special encapsulation of the intellectuals.

These are, again, mainly elite intellectuals. Even when, as in recent times, elite intellectuals have been drawn from many class backgrounds, the samurai origin of the intelligentsia has continued to affect its attitudes. A certain aloofness and disdain toward the common people can be detected though the intellectuals are denouncing the government in the people's name. It has been possible for a Japanese Marxist to believe that he has a correct understanding of the role of the working class even if the workers themselves are too stupid to realize it. Compounding the aloofness of the intellectuals is the fact that they have been far more profoundly penetrated by Western culture than any group in Japan and suffer disequilibrium from this exposure. As before intellectuals were specialists in alien Chinese culture, now they are specialists in alien Western culture. Many have vacillated between extreme acceptance of some aspect of Western culture and wholesale rejection of it. The common man has largely escaped the inner agonies, the identity problems, and the (sometimes multiple) conversions from one to another intellectual position that have been the lot of the intellectuals. Alienation of intellectuals because of class differences and differences in degree of exposure to foreign culture are common in non-Western (and often Western) countries and not especially extreme in Japan. Since the war the gap has closed as ever larger percentages of the population attend college and as the media disseminate elite culture to the masses. Nonetheless many Japanese intellectuals have felt the obligation to "go to the people" as an uncompleted project.

There have also been, as in the Tokugawa period, secondary intellectuals, occasionally of great influence. These were secondary school teachers, village postmasters, and the like—men of some education but not graduates of the best national or private universities. Often they provided the local base for conservative or nationalist political or ideological movements. Suspicious of the city, foreign culture, and the modern sector of the economy, they sometimes contributed to the defeat of movements favored by the elite intellectuals. Occasionally such men have broken out of their anonymity to affect the national scene, as in the case of Makiguchi Tsunesaburo (1871–1944), founder, and Toda Josei (1900–58), postwar president and major organizer, of the phenomenally successful new religious and political movement, Sōka Gakkai. Makiguchi was the principal of an elementary school and Toda was one of his teachers.

The first major Western current of ideas to affect Japan in the early Meiji period was the democratic and liberal thought of France, England, and the United States. Perhaps the spirit of this new thought can be expressed in the famous opening words of Fukuzawa Yukichi's *An Encouragement of Learning* (*Gakumon no susume*), a book that sold more than 3,400,000 copies during Fukuzawa's lifetime and set the tone of an era: "It is said that heaven does not create one man above or below another man. This means that when men are born from heaven they are all equal. There is no innate distinction between high and low."[21]

According to Fukuzawa such distinctions as exist in the world are, or should be, now that the artificial status distinctions of the Tokugawa period have been swept away, based on real achievements, not on innate differences. And, since real achievements require knowledge, education—practical education, not merely the "study of obscure Chinese characters"—is the royal road to self-advancement and dignity in the world.[22] There are highly individualistic implications to Fukuzawa's teachings, but, as *Encouragement of Learning* quickly makes clear, there is a national context that, if anything, takes precedence over individual considerations. In a section entitled "National Independence Through Personal Independence" he writes, "As I have said above, all nations are equal. But when the people of a nation do not have the spirit of individual independence, the corresponding right of national independence cannot be realized."[23] Thus Fukuzawa's call for personal independence and achievement is as much or more for the sake of the nation as for the sake of the individual.

The political expression of such teaching as Fukuzawa's, and the many translations of Western liberal writings such as the Declaration of Independence and works of Rousseau and Mill, was the Popular Rights Movement (Jiyū Minken Undō) that demanded representative constitutional government in Japan. There is no question but that there was a genuine wide-spread enthusiasm for "freedom" in the early Meiji period, a natural response to the long period of narrowness and rigidity under the Tokugawas. What freedom actually meant of course varied from group to group. For some of the former samurai leaders of the movement it undoubtedly meant a new mode of access to political power from which they were excluded by the dominance of the Satsuma-Chōshū ruling clique. For many of the common people in the towns and villages it meant autonomous self-assertion of relatively oppressed groups in the face of arrogant and unresponsive bureaucratic control. Perhaps the major contribution of the movement was the way it swept ordinary Japanese all over the country into the arena of national politics and modern thought. Irokawa Daikichi has recently stressed the role of wealthy peasants (*gōnō*) as mediators of modern consciousness in the village context.[24] As he observed, involvement in the movement did not necessarily mean a break with traditional village collective consciousness but an intense autonomous concern to express that consciousness and defend that collectivity in the face of external powers and authorities. In a sense the Popular Rights Movement was the successor of late Tokugawa popular movements in breaking down village and local parochialism and bringing some kind of national consciousness to the common people. As such it contributed to what is currently called "political mobilization" more than any number of bureaucratic decrees from Tokyo could have done.

The widespread enthusiasm for the Popular Rights Movement in the late 1870s and early 1880s began to give not only the government, but even astute intellectuals like Fukuzawa, cause for alarm. Rules for political struggle did not exist and the dangers of "factionalism" in the Confucian sense were acutely felt. As early as 1875 Fukuzawa was pointing out that too great a concern for the part can lead to the destruction of the whole.[25] By 1881 he was turning his attention explicitly to the imperial house as the fulcrum of unity for the nation and people:

> At this moment we are most anxious about the imperial house. The groups called political parties each have different doctrines; some are termed liberal or progressive and some conservative. Although we say that these are struggling over issues, in truth they are struggling for power: each is trying to seize the handle of power for itself. . . . In Japan who can fully control the world of human feelings and preserve habits of virtue and righteousness? Only the imperial house.[26]

In that same year the government announced that a representative assembly would convene in 1890, thereby relieving much of the pressure for immediate constitutional government.

For our purposes the most important thing about the liberal movement of the first twenty years of Meiji is that it opened up, even if hesitantly and indecisively, some questions about the givenness of Japanese society that had not been asked before. Very few of the Popular Rights thinkers went so far as to advocate a republican system. Very few criticized the root values of loyalty and filial piety. But the whole idea that the political institutions of Japanese society might be radically restructured by a movement from below was dramatically novel. It gave a role to popular initiative and creativity that was certainly not present in the largely intraelite maneuverings that led to the Meiji Restoration itself. At the same time it led to serious questions about the viability of Japanese society, questions such as those raised by Fukuzawa. Much of the subsequent history of social thought and the involvement of intellectuals in politics in modern Japan has been organized around that point-counterpoint.

We cannot expect to trace in this essay all the subtlety of those developments. We are fortunate in having in Irwin Scheiner's *Christian Converts and Social Protest in Meiji Japan* an account of how Christian social thinkers deepened the conceptions of the Popular Rights Movement and gave them in the 1880s and 1890s a theoretical and religious basis alternative to the emperor system.[27] Kenneth B. Pyle has also made a significant contribution to our understanding of the rise in the period 1885–95 of a critical school of "Japanist" thought that was by no means a simple apologetics for the official governmental ideology.[28] But here we must confine our remarks to the so-called Meiji emperor system that was not fully worked out until the 1890s and that Maruyama Masao and others have argued remained a kind of orthodoxy from that time until 1945.

In the first place the simultaneous acceptance of the idea of a constitution and representative assembly and the construction of the mature emperor system is a kind of prototype of the way bureaucratic dominance has been maintained in modern Japanese society. It is echoed again in 1925 when the Diet voted for universal suffrage at almost the same time that it passed a greatly strengthened Peace Preservation Law, which severely hampered political dissent. Even in the postwar period the combination of democratic reforms (from on high) and continued bureaucratic dominance and unresponsiveness to popular needs shows much the same form. In each case the intellectuals have in a sense "lost while winning."

The Meiji government managed to make the constitution itself a keystone of the refurbished emperor system. Above all it made the constitution an expression of the givenness of Japanese society rather than a challenge to it. The preparation of the constitution was kept completely secret until it was unveiled on February 11, 1889. The day was significant for it was Kigensetsu, the national holiday celebrating the mythical founding of the nation in 660 B.C. The constitution was the gracious gift of the emperor and its preamble derived sovereignty exclusively from the "sacred and inviolable" imperial house. When Nakae Chōmin (1847–1901), leading Popular Rights thinker and translator of Rousseau, insisted in the first Diet session of 1890 that the constitution be submitted to the Diet and voted on article by article, he was ignored.[29] He later resigned in disgust. Even though it was obvious that the constitution was a carefully contrived document—and indeed Itō Hirobumi (1841–1909), its chief architect, had undertaken the most careful research, including trips to Europe to talk to constitutional experts—it was to be received almost as a natural object, protected from criticism by the charisma of the emperor. There was a tendency after 1890 to include under the term *kokutai* (national polity), defined as the unique Japanese relation between emperor and people, all those things which could not be touched, which university professors could lose their jobs for criticizing, which were to be forever removed from any popular tampering. Not only were the imperial house, Shinto religion, and the military establishment part of the *kokutai*, but later when socialist agitation became acute, private property also was declared to be one of its constituent elements.

It is important to disentangle to some extent the image of the emperor from the emperor system as such. The imperial institution is far older than the Meiji emperor system and has survived the collapse of the latter in 1945. It has indeed been argued by some that the emperor system was a perversion of the true imperial institution. At any rate it does seem possible to extricate two rather different symbolic pictures of the emperor which have had different consequences in modern Japanese social thought. What the Meiji government tried to create was what might be called a samurai image of the emperor. He was a man in a resplendent military uniform, riding on a white horse, remote and unapproachable. As such he stood for governmental authority and military duty. He was a heroic leader but a cold and demanding one. Credit for Japan's success in its first modern half-century was attributed to the genius and leadership of the Meiji emperor. This image might be called the image of the emperor as a father figure.

But even in the Meiji period, when the actual emperor came closer to this image than either of his two successors, this was not the whole story. Much in the emperor's role evoked an older and deeper image than the samurai or father-figure emperor. For one thing the commonest form of communication from emperor to people was the thousands of *waka* poems that he composed for many occasions. Unlike the stiff Chinese formality of imperial rescripts, the *waka* were written in poetic and emotional Japanese and spoke of cherry blossoms, autumn leaves, and other delicate things. Often they expressed deep concern for the welfare of the subjects and the future of the country. This was the emperor whom politicians were always wishing to "shield from anxiety" and nearness to whom, symbolically or actually, was the greatest reward in Japanese public life. Perhaps it is not going too far to see in all this an image of the emperor as a mother figure. Of course the Meiji leaders, probably without being consciously aware of the distinction I am drawing, also made use of this aspect of the emperor's image. But full control of this image evaded them, and repeatedly aspects of it were used by those in opposition.

Perhaps we can even argue that these two aspects of the emperor image represent two dimensions of Japanese social structure. The first image represents the external relations between groups of differing power in Japanese society. In particular it represents the samurai-bureaucratic-elitist notion that some groups should dominate other groups, that those below should submit with stoic obedience to those above no matter how heavy the demand. This was the military image of Japan that was very much part of the emperor system between 1890 and 1945. The second image, however, represents the internal nature of Japanese group life, its warm, accepting, *Gemeinschaft* (Japanese: *kyōdōtai*) nature. While the first image denotes separation, hierarchy, duty, the second denotes unity, fusion, fulfillment. The problem with the second image is that it is drawn from the structure of primary groups in Japan, or at most of particular institutional structures, such as a village or company or government ministry. The second model has never accurately described Japan as a national community, though, especially when conscious of the outside world, most Japanese do feel a strong emotional sense of Japanese identity overriding differences of status. The second model, then, even though it is thoroughly "traditional," operates in some degree of tension with the actuality of Japanese society with its strong elitist authoritarian tendencies. We have already seen that the *Gemeinschaft* model of Japanese society, the fusion of emperor and people, could lead to direct political action in the cases of Yamagata Daini and Ōshio Heihachiro. It has continued to do so in the modern period. Perhaps the 1877 rebellion of Kyushu samurai, led by Saigō Takamori, had something of this quality and was not simply a revolt of the disgruntled seeking to retain their ancient privileges.

Most modern Japanese intellectuals, with some notable exceptions, have been critical of the first, elitist and hierarchical, model of Japanese society. They have been much more ambivalent about the second, *Gemeinschaft*, model. Some contemporary Japanese intellectuals, called, with more than a little pejorative overtone by their critics, "modernists," have been as opposed to the structure of primary group relations in Japan as to the elitist authoritarian control structures.[30] Indeed they have argued that the two augment and complete each other. These modernists would stand outside both aspects of the traditional *kokutai* ideology and argue for the importance of universalism and individualism in a truly modern, democratic Japan. They draw mainly from Western sources, Christian, liberal, and radical, but they also refer to the more transcendent aspects of Buddhism and Confucianism for some support in the Japanese past. Whereas in the 1930s such modernists were being attacked for being too pro-Western and undermining traditional Japanese society ("overcoming the modern" was a major slogan among intellectuals during the Second World War), today they are attacked for being too pro-Western and undermining Third World values and solidarities.

But many Japanese intellectuals and intellectual movements have not been able to make up their minds on this issue. For populists, socialists, and even Communists the symbol of the "people" or the "working class" has been redolent of the warm, maternal fusion of Japanese *Gemeinschaft*. Through the mediation of this symbol, men who have been sharply rebellious and antiauthoritarian have been able to modulate themselves into a form of "restorationism" and start talking about the unity of emperor and people.[31] Highly sophisticated students of Japanese philosophy or art have been able to move from conceptions of the "unity of subject and object" in Japanese religious or aesthetic life to a social philosophy of harmonious union of government and people under the emperor.[32] Even a radical Christian like Uchimura Kanzō (1861–1930), whose followers were among the few Japanese consistently to oppose the militarist imperialist policies of the late 1930s and early 1940s, was in a state of tortured ambivalence whenever he experienced direct conflict with the national community.[33] Of the many leftists who underwent a "change of thought" (*tenkō*) in the 1930s under government pressure, most phrased their change as a return to the national community understood as *Gemeinschaft*.[34] The contemporary rise of what may be called a populist tendency in the Japanese intellectual world, though bitterly critical of the Meiji emperor system and bureaucratic arrogance, may also be a form of neo-*Gemeinschaft* thinking, a matter that becomes apparent from its attacks on "modernists" and dogmatic Marxists.

Perhaps the context of the two models of Japanese society, bureaucracy and *Gemeinschaft*, will help us understand the enormous popularity of Marxism among Japanese intellectuals since 1920. Many reasons have been adduced.[35] Marxism has been seen as a natural successor to Confucianism since both are collectivistic and concerned with social welfare. Marxism's claim to be "Progressive" made it popular in Japan where there has been a perennial desire to "keep up with the times." That Marxism would create a society *more* advanced than the West was an added inducement. Another feature of Marxism that made it attractive to politically marginal intellectuals was that it offered a powerful theory to oppose a powerful government. The breadth, abstractness, and coherence of Marxism as a system of total world explanation have worked in its favor. But one other feature of Marxism that has probably made it attractive in Japan (as elsewhere in the non-Western world) is its nostalgia for the lost world of *Gemeinschaft* and its promise of a new *Gemeinschaft* after the revolution. One thing that tends to reinforce this interpretation is that Marxism has been far more effective as a worldview or a theory than as a form of organization. In particular the Japanese Communist Party has always been small relative to the large number of Marxist intellectuals. The hierarchical, bureaucratic, disciplined nature of the party has been repellent to most of those for whom Marxism was an alternative to the bureaucratic authoritarian side of Japanese society.

The modernist critics of Japanese society hold that one of its greatest weaknesses, in either its bureaucratic or *Gemeinschaft* forms (the two are not mutually exclusive for Japanese bureaucracy is formed of a network of *Gemeinschaft* groups), is its lack of individualism. If by individualism one means, as they do, the kind of institutionalized individualism found in a civil society or voluntary organization, they are right. But Japanese society has developed its own forms of individualism not lacking a sense of autonomy (*shutaisei*). Japanese bureaucracy would not have been so effective if it could not stimulate and utilize a great deal of individual initiative, even though it maintains important constraints.

Even more striking is the kind of romantic individualism associated with "restorationism," the effort to make the whole society into a radical *Gemeinschaft*. Indeed some of the most remarkable individuals in modern Japanese history (as in Tokugawa history) fall into this category. Kita Ikki (1883–1937) wanted to "remove the barriers which have separated the emperor from the people."[36] After an adventurous life in the underworld of Meiji socialism, the Chinese revolution, and Taisho radical nationalism, he was almost against his will adopted as the intellectual mentor of the young officers who staged the attempted coup of February 26, 1936. Probably innocent of any knowledge of the coup he was executed with its leaders. Nakano Seigo (1886–1943) started out as an extreme liberal in the Taisho period.[37] During the 1930s he experimented with a variety of organizational forms designed to bring about the union of emperor and people and the overthrow of the oppressive bureaucrats and capitalists. For him the restoration of the emperor was a symbol of the release of autonomous individualism among the people. He was a devotee of Wang Yang-ming thought and Ōshio Heihachiro was one of his heroes. He was one of the few Japanese openly to criticize the Tōjō government during the early years of the war and committed suicide under police pressure in 1943. The latest example of this Japanese form of romantic individualism is, of course, Mishima Yukio, who was influenced by both Ōshio, and Nakano. He preached a "positive nihilism" that would sweep away all the corruptions and distortions of postwar Japanese life and return the Japanese people to a pure unity with the emperor.[38] Organizational ineffectiveness and the dramatic expressive gesture (standing alone against the entire nation even if it means death) are the hallmarks of this tradition.

Much more could be said about forms of intellectual protest and opposition in modern Japan. But it is the bureaucracy that has continued to rule. It has shared its power with some other groups. First it created the great corporations, known before the war as the *zaibatsu,* and allowed them to have a continuous influence on subsequent policy. Then it created a parliamentary system and eventually political parties to go with it. Not without strain it accommodated itself to sharing political power with the established parties. In the postwar period the alliance of bureaucracy, corporations, and the Liberal Democratic Party has been singularly successful. The 1946 Constitution was almost as much a meteorite from the sky as the Meiji Constitution had been. It, together with other reforms of the Occupation period, made important gains in the fields of civil liberties and popular rights. The arbitrariness of the bureaucracy has been seriously hampered by these gains, but the givenness of Japanese society has not been broken through. Postwar democracy was not the popular enactment of the democratic visions of the Japanese intellectuals. It came from the Occupation through the hands of the bureaucrats. Although enjoying an unprecedented degree of freedom, the Japanese intellectuals have most of the same problems they have always had. They have yet to find the organizational forms through which they can have a decisive impact on their own society.

IV

If there is one among the many omissions in this essay that is more serious than the rest it is the degree to which I have ignored the apolitical tradition among Japanese intellectuals. That tradition is in many respects more important than the political traditions and more revealing as to the interior structure of Japanese life. Perhaps I can make up in small measure for this defect by quoting the poem by Dōgen with which Kawabata Yasunari began his Nobel Prize acceptance speech in 1968:

In the spring, cherry blossoms,
In the summer, the cuckoo,
In autumn, the moon.

And in winter,
Cold, clean snow.[39]

# 6  The Japanese Emperor as a Mother Figure

*Some Preliminary Notes*

The following "preliminary notes" approach the status of free associations on an idea that occurred to me when reflecting on the "family-state ideology" of the Meiji and subsequent periods. One can, of course, dismiss the entire "official" ideology of the pre-1945 period, an ideology in which the family-state idea was central, as sheer window dressing for the really important economic and political forces that have shaped modern Japanese history. Or one can accept this ideology in its own terms as an important key to understanding. In these remarks I would like neither to dismiss nor to accept but to take the family-state ideology seriously as a guide to important cultural and motivational problems but also as partially obscuring and distorting the real dynamic factors in the situation.

It is not necessary here to give more than brief reminders as to the historical development of the official ideology. There were of course strong ideological factors at work in the overthrow of the Tokugawa Bakufu and the Meiji era began on a markedly ideological note. This emphasis was soon scrapped, however, for more pragmatic preoccupations until the 1880s. In the face of rapid social change and the influx of Western ideologies many Japanese, influential government leaders among them, began to worry about the ethical foundations of Japanese society. The Meiji Constitution of 1889 and the Imperial Rescript on Education of 1890 were important landmarks in the reemergence of an ideological emphasis on the part of the Meiji government. During the debate on the new civil code, which occurred in the 1890s, the concern for strengthening traditional ethics and the peculiar stress on family-state ideology became increasingly evident. Professor Kawashima in his book on the family system as ideology has given numerous examples from these debates. One conservative speaker said, "If we speak of family the nation too is a family; the nation is a sort of family and the family is the nation. Our nation has a familistic national structure [*kazoku-shugi no kokutai*]." Indeed the family and the nation were seen as literally identical: all Japanese families are branch families from the imperial family as the main family. Thus the nation is a hierarchically organized kinship group with the emperor at its head. The civil code that emerged from these debates reflected a hierarchical authoritarian conception of family structure and gave great authority to the household head, though somewhat inconsistently allowing a rather individualistic conception of property rights. The family-state ideology got incorporated in the ethics textbooks used in all public schools, especially after the Russo-Japanese War. It was also propagated by many private groups and applied to a variety of situations including the relation of landlord and tenant as well as capitalist and worker. In fact the industrial version spoke of "one enterprise, one family."

In all of this official and semiofficial ideological material the tone is authoritarian, patriarchal, and moralistic in the Confucian sense. The prime virtues are loyalty and filial piety, involving selfless devotion and unquestioning obedience from those below to those above. Examples of rigorous self-discipline and self-sacrifice are lauded. The atmosphere generally is very *bushi-teki*, very samurai, insofar as it has roots in pre-Meiji Japan. Occasionally this samurai model became very explicit as in Hozumi Yatsuka's maxim for drawing up the civil code: "The customs of farmers are not to be made general customs—instead we must go by the practice of samurai and noblemen." He went on to argue that the customs of ordinary people are not really customs at all. The cultural source of most of this rhetoric was a rigoristic Confucianism with perhaps a touch of Zen Buddhism (long a component of establishment ideology in Japan).

From the ideological material we get, at first glance, a picture of a strongly patriarchal, hierarchical, and authoritarian social structure in both family and state. In it we recognize the so-called feudal social organization, the *dōzoku* family system, and the *bushi* social ethos. What seems to be happening is that the traditional family structure is being used as a model for building a strong state ideology.

Yet we know that Japanese social organization, including the family, even the samurai family, was not adequately described in this ideology. While there are parts of Japan, especially the Northeast, where strong patrilineal *dōzoku* structures survive even today, bilateral kindreds have long been important even in those areas. And in other parts of Japan, especially in the Southwest, a small family system with a great emphasis on age grading and lateral cooperation in age groups goes back for many centuries. This is not just a case of earlier and later stages in the process of modernization, as some observers have perhaps too hastily assumed. Vertical ties have long been strong in Japan, but so have lateral ties and associations. Even in that early charter of Japanese values, the Seventeen-Article "Constitution" of Shōtoku Taishi, Article III, which says, "when the superior acts, the inferior yields compliance," is balanced by Article X, which advises us to "follow the multitude and act like them."

But if the official ideology distorts social reality in Japan by emphasizing too exclusively the vertical over the lateral aspects of Japanese society, then it errs perhaps even more seriously in its emphasis on the patriarchal and masculine at the expense of the maternal and feminine aspects of Japanese culture. Again this masculine bias derives from samurai and Confucian sources. Yet women were not nearly so marginal in the family, even the samurai family, as the *bushi* family ideology implied. Indeed there is reason to suspect that the mother may have been a central or even the central figure in the Japanese family even in the Edo period. Our best evidence is much more recent, being based on projective tests and depth interviews that cannot be administered to Japanese of the Tokugawa period. George DeVos has shown on the basis of projective tests the motivational centrality of the mother. Ezra Vogel has confirmed that the father is often emotionally marginal, even though he makes the decisions, at least overtly, and there is an implicit coalition of mother and children against him. Since the child-rearing practices and socialization experiences that underlie this in some ways mother-centered family are not recent there is considerable reason to believe that what contemporary social scientists have discovered is an old pattern in Japan.

But of course the emphasis on the feminine side is not something recently discovered by social scientists. Who is the most important figure in Japanese mythology? Of course the sun goddess, Amaterasu o mikami. Not only is she female but, unlike some more Amazonian types in other mythologies, her influence is exercised in a very feminine way. She is no patriarchal despot like Jehovah. She is often portrayed as confused; she relies on the advice of her counselors; she asks the will of higher gods through divination. She is often shown as relatively weak and defenseless, for example, compared to the willful Susa no o no mikoto. She is a peacemaker, conciliator, mediator, not a despot.

It is my contention that through Amaterasu we can understand the emperor in Japanese ideology, the very emperor who is the focus of the whole austere Confucian family-state cult. Even in the Kojiki, which recounts the semilegendary history of the early emperors, the emperor is not portrayed as a heroic warrior. Often he is saved in the nick of time by others who are more powerful militarily. He is often portrayed as weak, confused, and submissive to the will of the *kami*. Now all through history this picture of the emperor has remained relatively constant. It would seem then that the Japanese emperor, based on the model of the divine ancestress Amaterasu, has been more of a mother figure than a father figure. Like the mother in the Japanese family, he has been emotionally central even when actually powerless, exercising a powerful motivational attraction even when giving no effective command.

The actual rulers, the aggressive strong men, soldiers or politicians, are the father figures or older brother figures. From the Soga to the Fujiwara, Taira, Minamoto, Hōjō, Ashikaga, Nobunaga and Hidesyoshi, Ieyasu and his Tokugawa successors, on to Ito Hirobumi and Yamagata Aritomo and up to Tōjō Hideki and who knows next, the actual leaders have been admired, envied, hated, but seldom loved. They have not attracted the deep affection that on the whole has gone to the imperial house. Motoori Norinaga was one of the profoundest students of the specifically Japanese component of Japanese culture and few have stressed more strongly the feminine side. For him the relation to the emperor is based on kinship and emotion, not on politics and ethics. A Confucian scholar once criticized Norinaga, saying that "to revere and serve the ruler without questioning his good and evil is merely the way of women." Norinaga replied that even if it was the way of women it was the Japanese way.

We cannot of course deny that there is some truth in the picture of a hierarchical, authoritarian, patriarchal social organization that seems to be implied by much of the official ideology. But it is also true that many dynamic features of Japanese social action are hard to derive from the purely patriarchal model but become easier to understand if we develop a more complex picture of Japanese intrafamilial relations and their political reflection.

It is true, for example, that the authority of the father was underlined legally and stressed in the moral teachings of the ethics textbooks. But even in those textbooks, if we look at the illustrative stories and not just at the injunctions, we see a somewhat different picture. Many stories in the Shūshin textbooks tell of cases where the father is dead and the son cares for the mother and younger siblings, or the father is sick and the son cares for the family. The focus is not on a powerful authoritarian father but on an able vigorous son. The relation between parents and children is portrayed as warm and emotional rather than as highly authoritarian. Further the maxims of pure self-sacrifice for the glory of superiors do not come through undiluted in the stories. The filial son is in the end highly rewarded. He gains general recognition and becomes himself a significant ancestor.

The structure of the traditional Japanese lineage partially helps us to understand why the conservative and traditionalist implications of the explicit values were not always determinative. After all, only the eldest son would inherit the ancestral occupation and status. The younger sons, even in premodern times, often had to enter new fields and unconventional activities. Bright younger sons were traditionally admonished in some parts of Japan to "become an ancestor," that is, to establish their own family lines in some new occupation. In the Meiji period, when opportunity was so much greater, the number of sons, even eldest sons, striking out on their own in new undertakings was greatly increased. But if the stereotyped picture of the overwhelming authoritarian father and the submissive, obedient son was accurate one must ask why the sons were so often innovative, iconoclastic, and competitive, able not only to compete with their fathers but easily abandoning them as role models. I would suggest that one factor that helps to make this situation intelligible is that even when the father was formal, forbidding, and authoritarian, he was to some extent balanced by a warm, supportive mother who provided the basis of emotional security from which the son could go forth into a competitive world and whose generalized expectations of high achievement were not tied to the specific details of the father's actual occupation and status.

But not only was there a base in the family (the mother) that provided emotional security for breaking with all traditional identifications of status and occupation, there was also an external base, namely, the emperor. All kinds of aggressive and innovative behavior could be legitimated if it were for the sake of the emperor. Thus naive statements by Meiji industrialists that everything they produced and everything they sold was really for the sake of the emperor should not be entirely dismissed. The emphasis on the emperor not only legitimated innovation but it also provided a framework of national morality, which partly checked the tendencies toward familistic aggrandizement deriving from the intrafamilial motivational structure.

The commitments to both family and nation had religious dimensions that require brief consideration. We have already alluded to the dynamic aspect of family religion when we mentioned the injunction to "become an ancestor." Kamishima Jirō in his very stimulating book on the spiritual structure of modern Japan (*Kindai Nihon no Seishin Kōzō*) cites an essay of Lafcadio Hearn written in 1895 as an indication of the spiritual atmosphere of that period. In it Hearn quotes a young Japanese soldier about to depart for the Sino-Japanese War as saying, "We think that after death we shall still be with our families. We shall see our parents, our friends. We shall remain in this world—viewing the light as now. . . . One who has a son can die with a cheerful mind. . . . Every man needs someone to love him after he is dead." Success in the world, when it leads to the establishment of a family line, thus ensures a happy immortality. This is the "payoff" side of the enormous stress on filial piety that is a self-aggrandizing as well as a self-abnegating notion depending on one's structural position in the life cycle. This powerful familial motivation for achievement is of course not unique to Japan but exists wherever Confucianism has been influential, certainly in China.

In Japan, however, the dynamics of the family cult are carried over into the emperor cult in ways that are probably unique in East Asia. As in the case of the family cult the austere self-abnegating aspect of emperor worship only thinly disguised more self-centered orientations. In this regard we may follow Kamishima in a further reference to the 1895 essay of Hearn. The young man in Hearn's story had expressed as a schoolboy his desire to die for the emperor and Hearn is seeing him the night before his departure. The boy says,

> Those of us who fall in battle against China will also be honored. They will be revered as Kami. Even our emperor will honor them.
> There will be monuments set up to honor our dead in their own native villages and towns and the bodies of our soldiers will be burned, and the ashes sent home to Japan.
> We shall be loved and worshipped by all the people.

Quite similar sentiments were expressed as late as the Second World War. The point is that dying for the emperor involves not just an abstract moral duty but a warm personal relation. Not only will I die for the emperor but the emperor will worship *me*. Yasukuni Jinja, so closely associated with the emperor, was the center of the cult of the war dead, but there were also memorials in villages and towns. Even in the family the war dead were singled out as individuals for worship. In this way, while calling on parallel motivational patterns, the national cult competed with and in some ways surpassed in intensity the familial cult. Entering the Yasukuni Jinja was a kind of "success" greater than simply "becoming an ancestor." (Indeed there was a board game in the Meiji period in which the goal was to ascend gradually through the ranks until reaching the Yasukuni Jinja. If one landed on certain designated spots indicating death in battle, even though at a relatively low rank, one then jumped immediately to the goal [Yasukuni Jinja] and "won" the game.) The war dead became especially associated with the emperor; and if I am right that the emperor is more a mother figure than a father figure, then entering Yasukuni Jinja meant nearness to mother's love. It also meant becoming the continuing focus of national concern. Maruyama reports Tōjō as saying, "If we compromise with the Anglo-Americans how would we be able to face the myriad spirits of the war dead?" or how could we "sleep facing the Yasukuni Jinja?"

Quite aside from the context of the war dead, nearness to the emperor was a powerful motive, as Maruyama pointed out. Some of the Meiji oligarchs, quite unsentimental men, were overcome with emotion in personal encounter with the emperor. Tōjō's reply to a Diet member's question as to whether he was becoming a dictator early in the war years is instructive:

> It is only when I am exposed to the light of His Majesty that I shine. Were it not for this light I should be no better than a pebble by the roadside. It is because I enjoy the confidence of His Majesty and occupy my present position that I shine. This puts me in a completely different category from those European rulers who are known as dictators.

The entire vocabulary of political reference to the emperor in the prewar period is indicative of the emotional constellation with which I am concerned. Politicians accused each other of making the emperor anxious or causing him concern. They claimed themselves to wish to protect him, put his mind at ease, and so forth. There were few references to the emperor's will or anger or the possibility of punishment coming from him.

The emperor, then, both in recent times and in the far distant past, has been primarily an emotional point of reference. He stands for no policy, no rules, no institution, and no constitution. The men who rule and who build institutions may come and go. The imperial house is unaffected. This pattern has had the function of providing what Maruyama has called an empty envelope or empty bag. Anything can go in—there is almost infinite receptiveness and flexibility—yet also a stable point of reference unrelated to the particular cultural content of the moment. The difficulty is that this pattern makes it extremely difficult to establish higher-order universalistic cultural controls and reinforces the prevailing particularism of Japanese culture.

I am suggesting, then, that the family-state ideology be taken even more seriously, if anything, than it has been previously. The fusion of familial, political, and religious motivation, which we have been discussing, provided enormous energy for development and a uniquely Japanese way of fostering flexibility, innovation, and aggressive activism without breaking the mold of traditional values. This fusion has also created very serious problems of social and cultural control, which are by no means entirely solved.

In conclusion I night mention two major reservations about the idea of the emperor as a mother figure. One is that the emperor was partly also a figure of austere masculine authoritarianism. The ideological fiction fostered especially during the war that the emperor was indeed the ruler had some success. The apparently very considerable feeling at the end of the war that the emperor should take responsibility for the defeat and abdicate is an indication of this side of his symbolic valence. Yet that feeling did not prevail and most Japanese accepted the long-standing theory of wicked advisors who misled the innocent emperor. And the postwar "humanization" of the emperor has led to a marked decline in his significance as a symbol of masculine authority. The widely used diminutive appellation "Ten-chan" is perhaps only the most striking indication of this recent trend. The emperor's symbolic significance is obviously some balance between the masculine-authoritarian and the feminine-emotional. A total shift to the latter meaning could undercut the entire traditional significance of the emperor, which is perhaps what is going on now.

This last point leads to our final consideration. We have spoken a great deal about paternal and maternal but we have not mentioned the key Japanese concept of *oya*, that is, "parent" with sex not specified. (Motoori Norinaga gave philological reasons for believing that the original significance of *oya* was maternal rather than paternal, but if that is true, the point has long been forgotten in actual usage.) All Japanese authority figures have a maternal succoring aspect to a greater extent than would be the case in many other cultures. We must thus talk in terms of relative emphases rather than of an either/or. But with all these qualifications it nonetheless seems to be true that the Japanese emperor has been much more a focus of emotional attachment than an effective wielder of power. From this point of view there is warrant for a particular stress on the maternal aspects of his role.

# 7    Continuity and Change in Japanese Society

How does it happen that the nation with the highest average economic growth rate for the last hundred years is also the only complex society with a Bronze Age monarchy, where the emperor until recently was believed to be the lineal descendant of the sun goddess and, in some sense, himself divine?[1] How does it happen that in the nation with the third highest gross national product, the most important modern novel, Tanizaki Junichiro's *The Maki-oka Sisters*, resembles the great eleventh-century novel of Murasaki Shikibu, *The Tale of Genji*, not only in its sensitivity to nature and human feeling, but also in the structure of personal relations and the anxiety about gossip and criticism?[2] How does it happen that in spite of the Industrial Revolution, life in the agricultural villages is so much like that of the late prehistoric period some fifteen centuries ago?[3] These questions are meant to suggest only a few dimensions along which the great continuities of Japanese life can be measured, even when one must also note the drastic series of structural changes that characterize Japanese history. The paradox of continuity and change in Japan stretches to the limits any functional theory of society and any theory of change in terms of structural differentiation. If societies are functioning systems, then how can the same structural features accommodate such major organizational and cultural changes? If structural differentiation accounts for the changes, then what explains the immunity of so many important features of Japanese society from this process?

Talcott Parsons has developed with considerable subtlety a conception of Western social development that involves long-term continuity at the level of value orientations combined with great structural change.[4] This example may not be entirely relevant because the element of universalism, so important in allowing this process to occur in the West, is singularly weak in Japan, and besides the continuities are by no means limited to the highest

184

level of value orientations. Nevertheless it may be useful to try to unravel this apparent enigma by considering the Japanese value system where indeed continuity has been most impressive.

## THE JAPANESE VALUE SYSTEM

In *Tokugawa Religion* I characterized the values of the Tokugawa period in terms of the pattern-variables of particularism and performance, a combination that according to action theory can be seen as "political."[5] Although at that time I believed this pattern was considerably older than the Tokugawa period (1600–1868), more recently Randall Huntsberry has shown convincingly that at least from the formation of the Japanese state in the seventh century "political" values of particularism and performance were central, though he points out certain variants and alternatives that were also influential.[6] Ezra Vogel has found the same pattern virtually unchanged in the postwar new middle class.[7] Thus, this pattern seems to be almost continuously dominant from the beginning of historic times to the present. Rather than repeat the technicalities of the description of Japanese values in *Tokugawa Religion* I would like to cite a later somewhat more discursive statement:

1. Value is realized in groups that are thought of as natural entities. The community (*Gemeinschaft, kyōdōtai*) is the locus of value.

2. These groups are thought to be integrated with the structure of reality and thus are endowed with a sacred quality.

3. There is a divine-human continuity in which the symbolic beads of groups have an especially important place, being especially endowed with a sacred quality. One of their functions is to relate the group to the divine ancestors and protective deities. This pattern applies at many levels: for example family (and its ancestor worship), village (and the local deity, *ujigami*), and ultimately the whole country at whose head is the emperor (and above him the imperial ancestors).

4. Individuals exist because of a continuous flow of blessings from spirits and ancestors through the symbolic heads of groups. The individual is obligated to work in order to repay in small measure the blessings he has received and to sacrifice himself for the group if necessary.

5. Science, ethics, philosophy, and virtually all aspects of culture are valuable only insofar as they contribute to the realization of value in the group, not as ends in themselves. Ethics consist mainly in acting as one should in one's group—there is no universal ethic.

6. In spite of how completely the individual is merged in group life there

is one place where he can be relatively independent: the realm of personal expressiveness including art, mysticism, recreation, and skill. But this sphere does not legitimize failure to fulfill group expectations. It actually helps reconcile the individual to group demands.[8]

Despite the importance of this pattern certain elements within the Japanese tradition do not entirely fit. Especially significant are the universalistic and individualistic components of what I have called the "tradition of submerged transcendence." [9]

## JAPANESE GROUPS AND NATIONAL INTEGRATION

The earliest Japanese groups of which we have knowledge, the warrior bands who carried out the conquests establishing the primacy of the Yamato court in central Japan, illustrate the value pattern described previously. Society was divided into tightly knit local groups known as *uji* and *be*, whose members were united by strongly particularistic ties. There was a kinship group at the core but nonkinsmen were included as well.[10] Heroic action was defined by selfless devotion to the defense or aggrandizement of one's group. The Japanese state as we see it crystallizing in the early historical records, the *Kojiki* and the *Nihon Shoki*, capitalized on these values by concentrating loyalty on the Yamato ruling family and regulating the status of other groups by the service they rendered to the Yamato court.[11] Part of the formative structure of the new Japanese state was partly provided by a system of court ranks and bureaucratic offices of Chinese inspiration. This was superimposed on the *uji* system, which continued to provide the real vitality in Japanese social organization. Even though the behavior of particular groups toward the imperial family did not always meet the ideal standards of the mythographers, the inner coherence of groups and the integration of the national polity tended to be mutually reinforcing. As John Hall has written, "In its most generalized form, perhaps, the sense of group served to heighten the Japanese consciousness of the political community as a whole, reinforcing that particular pattern of unity around the imperial family which the Japanese have labeled 'the polity' (*kokutai*)."[12] By contrast, with the continuity of the imperial family it has been possible to form and reform other groups beneath it. The later rise of the feudal lords and their groups of warriors (*bushi*) completely destroyed the old *uji-be* system. But the feudal groups had the same basic value pattern as the earlier groups, namely, one that stressed particularism and performance—group loyalty and selfless service to its ends. Hall explains how the circulation of elite groups could combine with strong national continuity:

Historically the imperial family was once a party to the violent struggle for power in Japan. But once the initial hegemony was established, and although the imperial family gradually lost real military and political power, its symbolic position as mediator between the members of the oligarchy and as the prime source of legitimacy remained of such importance that the emperor could never be assailed. . . . Five times powerful military families arose to political hegemony in Japan. . . . Yet in each instance these families achieved their victory as the result of a military conquest which carried through from within the oligarchic structure rather than attacking it from without. . . . Even during the age of great feudal wars no group was able to obtain a base of power outside the polity from which it might have attacked and destroyed the system of legitimacy over which the emperor presided. In the fifteenth and sixteenth centuries the emperor was reduced to a condition of near oblivion and outright economic distress, yet the idea of the national hierarchy remained. As new military leaders fought to the top they looked to the emperor for tokens of legitimacy and to the system of court ranks over which he presided for a means of ritualizing the pyramid of power. It is no accident that Japan entered the modern era following a political coup d'etat carried out in the name of the emperor.[13]

One important difference between the *bushi* groups and the earlier *uji* and *be* is that the element of kinship was of less importance in their organization. The family line of the feudal lord was focal, but the followers were united to the lord through loyalty rather than kinship. It was possible to organize new feudal alliances and extend their power rather more easily than in the earlier system. From about the tenth century on, the feudal organization penetrated even the remotest parts of Japan and provided the basic social organization for many centuries.

In the Tokugawa period the group structure characteristic of the *bushi* permeated wider sections of the population and notably influenced both the townsmen and the peasants. The same type of tie that linked feudal lord and samurai also came to characterize the relation of merchant and clerk. In many parts of Japan the village consisted of one or more *dōzoku*, a hierarchically organized group of families not necessarily linked by kinship. Thus the pervasive influence of tightly organized hierarchical groups extended throughout the population.

The Meiji Restoration of 1868 completely abandoned the feudal system and introduced modern economic and political organization. But within the pores, so to speak, of government ministries and industrial firms Japanese group life continued to thrive. Tightly organized all-embracing groups demanded the complete loyalty and devoted service of their members. As in the past such groups formed and reformed, justifying their existence by the larger polity. The power struggles between elite groups went on largely within the framework of the imperial system, though in recent decades, especially with the American occupation, political elements entirely outside the traditional *kokutai* finally began to enter the scene. But even such groups as the Zengakuren factions who are currently battling for control of the university campuses exhibit much the same group structure that has been so typical in Japan, though their ideology questions every accepted tenet of Japanese society. Tightly cohesive and all consuming in their demands, they receive intense loyalty and devoted service from their members.

We now can summarize some implications of the Japanese group life pattern for the problem of continuity and change. The basic loyalty in Japan is to the group rather than to a status or an abstract ideal or a notion of self-fulfillment. This means that many particular status systems such as the *uji-be* system of ancient Japan or the feudal class system of Tokugawa times could be abandoned without changing the basic value pattern. Indeed particular groups themselves were not considered eternal. As total as any group's demands might be, the group itself was justified by its performance and might be displaced by other groups if it did not succeed. Further, groups were not closed or isolated. They were linked in vertical chains of loyalty that ultimately brought them all within the structure of the national polity. This meant that when there was strong direction from the top, Japanese groups could be mobilized for vigorous new lines of action. Nonetheless it is hard to see in this structure, either in its value or its organizational components, any powerful internal drive toward innovation and differentiation. Indeed the universalism and individualism that are usually associated with strong rationalizing tendencies were severely limited by this pattern. If we look at the periods of most rapid and radical change in Japan, the seventh and eighth centuries and the nineteenth and twentieth, we see that they are associated with the wholesale importation of a more rationalized foreign culture. This phenomenon requires further inquiry.

## JAPANESE CULTURE AND FOREIGN CULTURE

No complex society has maintained a stronger sense of what is native and what is foreign than Japanese society. This consciousness did not begin in modern times but goes back to the centuries immediately after the large-scale importation of Chinese culture. It seems likely that if a statistical comparison were made Japan would be found to have "borrowed" no more than other countries have, and possibly Japan would be well below the average on a "borrowing index." The concern with this issue is in the meaning of native and foreign culture, not in the amount of borrowing. The heart of specifically Japanese culture is the value system and group structure described previously. The native religion, Shinto, can be seen as the religious dimension of every Japanese group, but especially of the nation itself with its divinely descended emperor. Part of the problem in defining Shinto, or indeed of defining purely Japanese culture, is that it seems to be contentless. This "contentlessness" led Nishida Kitarō to define Japanese culture as a "formless form" (*katachi ga nai katachi*) and Maruyama Masao to call Japanese tradition an "empty bag," or an "unstructured tradition."[14] Japanese culture as the "container" is less easy to define than the heterogeneous "contents" of largely foreign origin, but it is the container that tenaciously persists while ever-new contents are received and often later abandoned. This pattern has led Maruyama to say that there is no history of Japanese thought as such but only a history of the reception of various foreign systems.[15] These systems have existed for a while, usually in isolation from each other, and then have either died out or continued as the property of small and specialized groups. The same arguments can to some extent be extended to institutions as well.

The first great period of receiving foreign culture was in the seventh and subsequent centuries, when Chinese thought and institutions were consciously and deliberately imported on a massive scale. It was perhaps the most systematic effort in world history before modern times of a less developed society to learn from a more developed one. A written language, a classic literature, a complex religion, a political theory, a legal system, an elaborate bureaucracy, a system of coinage, forms of land tenure, and much else were imported wholesale. Some of these cultural importations became so indigenized that they merely gave conscious expression to the native tradition. This is obviously the case where abbreviated forms of certain Chinese characters were used to write the Japanese syllabary (*kana*), but it was also true in the realm of thought where Confucianism supplied the rationale for the close personal bonds of kinship and loyalty that were already central in Japanese social organization. Other elements borrowed from China added a new dimension to the generalization of social communication and social control, as in the bureaucracy and the legal system. Even where the Chinese patterns were eroded by Japanese particularism a residue remained that left Japan permanently different from and more differentiated than Japanese society in late prehistoric times.

Much the same argument can be made for the massive reception of Western culture in the last hundred years. Political, legal, economic, and educational systems have been imported, largely replacing previous institutions in these areas. New philosophical, religious, and artistic movements have entered the country and have competed with earlier systems of thought. All these new importations have been indigenized to some extent but all bear the clear marks of their foreign origin. As a result of conscious systematic importation and adaptation Japan has been transformed from a poor agricultural society to a powerful industrial one. Once again importing foreign culture has gone hand in hand with a rapid advance in structural differentiation. It should be noted that this second transformation, like the first, was carried through under the aegis of the emperor system by groups organized in typically Japanese ways.

The lack of individualism and universalism in the Japanese pattern and the subsequent weakness of the drive toward rationalization would seem to be made up for by the ease with which it has been possible to import and adapt more rationalized forms from other cultures. Because the indigenous pattern, being relatively "formless," is not committed to any dogmatic set of beliefs or institutions but only to a pattern of group life, it does not place any barriers to importing foreign culture, as Islamic or Confucian orthodoxies did. The native Japanese pattern was simple and flexible, sufficiently generalized to sustain new and complex features and not so specialized as to limit new developments.

Of course, Japan's geographical position helped to make this mode of adjustment possible. Japan was just far enough from the continental mainland to make conquest extremely difficult, as the Mongols learned to their own cost. But, Japan was close enough so that she was within easy reach of the latest cultural advances in China and, indirectly, India as well. This continuous borrowing (the seventh and nineteenth centuries are only the most dramatic instances) kept Japan from ever getting too far behind the more "advanced" societies so that she was not in great danger of being overwhelmed by sheer technological superiority.

Japan's pattern of particularistic groupism not only allowed the relatively smooth acceptance of more rationalized thought and institutions, but also it provided the motivation for it. The constant effort to improve the position of one's own group relative to others within the society was generalized to a competitiveness between Japan and other societies. The necessity for Japan's equality with or superiority to other nations is not a product of modern nationalism. Concerns of this sort lie deep in Japanese history. They are related to the national integration under the emperor mentioned previously and helped provide in Japan an apparently easy fit with the model of the Western nation-state, though in fact the basic structure was quite different. In particular it should be noted that rationalization and rational forms are in the traditional Japanese view merely means to nonrational ends given by the immutable structure of Japanese group life.

Another dimension in understanding the paradox of continuity and change in Japan should now be evident. The continuity is mainly in the realm of values and the structure of group life. The change is mainly in cultural content and large-scale institutional and organizational forms. The relatively isolated, insular Japanese position accounts for some continuities, particularly in material culture, but the nature of Japanese society accounts for many more. Yet the rapid change and increase in structural differentiation result from importing and adapting more complex patterns developed abroad.

## FUNCTIONS AND DYSFUNCTIONS
## IN THE JAPANESE PATTERN

Many positively functional features of the Japanese pattern have already been mentioned—its flexibility, openness to adaptive improvements, and at least incipient national integration. The tight discipline of the groups over the individual allowed a ready mobilization of effort when required, though it caused strains for personality that require a later section for their consideration. Two features that have had severe dysfunctional consequences and that seem to be inherent in the Japanese pattern are *factionalism* and *xenophobia*.

The essence of the tightly organized Japanese groups is that they are linked primarily through vertical loyalty ties.[16] Between groups of the same order that are not linked together by a relatively close superordinate power there is apt to be competition verging on open conflict. This feature of Japanese society has its positive side because the competition and conflict of various groups have contributed to the dynamism of Japanese society and the circulation of Japanese elites. But, especially when the higher levels of integration are weak, the resulting factionalism can have severe consequences. Civil disturbances caused by the rivalry of the most prominent *uji* and *be* were common in the ancient period. Conflict between feudal lords kept the whole country in endemic warfare from about the tenth to the sixteenth centuries. Even when such group conflicts did not result in actual violence, as they tended not to do in the Tokugawa period and in modern times, they have produced many situations of insubordination and lack of responsible control. The great feudal domains of Satsuma and Chōshu actually endangered the national safety by attacking foreign warships against the orders of the Tokugawa regime toward the end of its rule. In the period from the 1931 Manchurian incident through World War Two numerous examples of factional strife and insubordination could be cited, actions that rendered leadership ineffective so that the nation first drifted into a war that nobody planned and then fought it less effectively than was possible.

Xenophobia too seems to be an inherent feature of the Japanese group. Students of Japanese village life have noted that even neighboring villages may view each other with grave suspicion. The tight group structure makes a sharp distinction between "us" (*uchi no mono*, literally "inside persons") and "them" (*yosomono*, outsiders).[17] The feeling is so strong that the outsider is sometimes considered less than human. When generalized to the national level this tendency can result in extreme xenophobia. Two periods of xenophobia had severely pathological consequences for Japanese society: the closing of the country (*sakoku*) near the beginning of the Tokugawa period and the period of ultranationalism in the 1930s and early 1940s. We have noted the usual openness of Japanese society to foreign culture and have linked this to the strong competitiveness associated with the performance values in the Japanese pattern. Foreign culture is endlessly assimilable as long as it does not affect the Japanese pattern itself—as long as it is only "contents" and not disruptive to the container. But when the foreign threat seems to endanger the fundamental pattern itself the reaction can be extreme—in early Tokugawa times almost total withdrawal after a period of vigorous intercourse with and borrowing from the West, and in the 1930s and early 1940s external aggression, again after a period, the so-called Taisho Democracy, of exceptional openness. These extreme reactions were not mainly triggered by foreign aggression, though both periods were dangerous for Japan. Other periods of foreign danger have had the opposite effect. Rather what seems decisive is the fear that significant groups within the country have been converted to ways of thinking incompatible with the traditional structure of Japanese society. Thus both periods of xenophobia were marked by vigorous persecutions. The persecution—including the large-scale execution—of Christians in early Tokugawa Japan was among the greatest religious persecutions in world history. The ban on Christians continued throughout the Tokugawa period and even the first Christian converts at the end of the Tokugawa period still had to face the irrational hostility that Christianity aroused. In the later period, severe persecution of liberals and Marxists followed. In both cases a renunciation of the alien commitment and a return to purely Japanese group life were primarily demanded. Only if the victim refused to recant was he executed or imprisoned. In both cases the persecuted groups were felt to have had loyalties that transcended and were incompatible with the Japanese *kokutai*.

These xenophobic periods were dysfunctional or pathological not merely because of persecution, unpleasant though that is. In both cases communication with the outside world broke down, leading to serious miscalculations that endangered the whole society. At the beginning of the Tokugawa period, Japan was a military match for any European power and the strongest nation in East Asia, having overwhelmed Korea and undermined the Ming regime in China. At the end of it Japan was so weak, comparatively speaking, that she could have been successfully invaded by any determined second-rate power in Europe. The complete isolation from the development of Western scientific and democratic thought from the beginning of the seventeenth to the middle of the nineteenth centuries probably had even more severe consequences. The disastrous consequences of Japan's military adventures in the 1930s and 1940s hardly need mention.

In less powerful doses Japan's xenophobia has undoubtedly been functional in promoting national pride and a vigorous effort to maintain national independence and autonomy. But Japan has also suffered from an opposite malady—extreme xenophilia. On occasion at least some Japanese, overwhelmed by a sense of Japan's backwardness, have seemed willing to jettison the entire national heritage. There were those, for example, in the early Meiji period who wanted the nation to abandon the Japanese language and learn English instead or to abandon Buddhism in favor of Christianity. More common has been a gnawing doubt and self-derogation about Japanese culture. On the whole a moderate amount of self-doubt and a willingness to learn from others have been greatly beneficial to Japan's cultural advancement.

To point out certain dysfunctions in the Japanese pattern is certainly not to derogate it. Every society has severely dysfunctional elements as Americans at the present moment know very well. Over the long haul the Japanese pattern has produced a dynamic, flexible, and effective society. This does not mean that it has not, as have all such patterns, exacted its price.

## PERSONALITY IN PREMODERN JAPAN

Japanese groups place great demands on the personality of the individual. They also provide great rewards. Considering the infrastructure of Japanese groups is necessary to obtain further insights about stability and change in Japanese society.

We have spoken of the hierarchical nature of Japanese groups. Concretely this means that a primary group is composed of a leader and his followers, often conceptualized as a pseudokinship relation as when the leader is referred to as a parent-person (*oyakata*) and the followers as children-persons (*kokata*). It is worth pointing out that the leader in this terminology is called "parent" rather than "father" (in ancient Japanese "*oya*" probably meant "mother" first and "parent" only as a derived meaning, but this is forgotten today) and his functions are diffuse, having to do with the general welfare of his followers. A high degree of dependency on the mother is generated by Japanese socialization patterns and this dependency is later partially transferred to the leader who must "care for" his followers and not merely direct them in specific tasks. Secondary groups in Japan are composed by linking together vertical chains of loyalty. A national political leader today, or a feudal lord of old, has his direct followers who in turn have their followers down to the lowest level primary groups. Although great initiative and dynamic activity of a very "masculine" sort are necessary to put together large groups organized in this way, and such a leader may develop a great following because of his ability to come through for his followers or to coerce them into obedience, such masculine dynamic leaders are not greatly loved. The leadership that excites the strongest emotion and the greatest devotion is more passive and even feminine. Symbolically this more emotionally positive leadership focuses on the mother at the family level and the emperor at the national level. Both stand for nurturance and benevolence rather than domination and control. Those who dominate and direct gain their legitimacy as defenders or protectors of the more feminine leader type. Even when the hierarchical dimension is not strong, as in some traditional groups and perhaps increasingly today, the group itself is felt as nurturant, accepting, and in a sense feminine.[18]

All this means for individual personality that high levels of performance are demanded by and supported by nurturant, accepting groups and leaders. Instead of being crushed by despotic patriarchal authority the individual is encouraged to work hard to gain maternal favor. He is manipulated more by rewards than by threats and punishments. Although completely dependent on the group and its leader he is nonetheless not crushed by external authority but may exhibit remarkable initiative and creativity. This pattern helps to explain how the strong Japanese emphasis on the group nonetheless goes along with rapid adaptiveness and flexibility.[19]

Despite the great rewards, the rigors of group life are considerable. Social obligations may directly contravene personal feelings and needs, and there was no justification in premodern times for any outcome but personal submission to the group. The conflict between love based on personal feeling and marriage based on the convenience of the family line epitomized this kind of conflict and the only possible outcome other than submission to the social demands was love suicide. But the group could be frustrating not only because it frustrated personal feelings, but also because it aroused but did not fulfill the need for perfect fusion, loss of personal identity in the group. When human relations prove frustrating, Japanese for many centuries have thought of merging with nature as a solution to personal problems.[20] The benevolent all-encompassing beauty of nature in which one can completely submerge one's own identity has been a symbol of personal fulfillment. Much in the Japanese aesthetic tradition has concentrated on this kind of expression. But even the aesthetic appreciation of nature has not always been satisfactory and the Japanese have many times been led to a religious quest for enlightenment to overcome the last remnants of the troublesome individual self.

In our discussion of Japanese values we have already seen that aesthetic and religious pursuits did not undermine the commitment to the group but actually reinforced it by providing a means for handling unbearable tensions that the group itself could not absorb. But this is not quite the whole story; the social structure of aesthetic and religious life in Japan should be further considered.

It would certainly be a mistake to give the impression that the aesthetic sphere was one of purely personal expression divorced from a social context. Poetry, the most ubiquitous Japanese literary expression, was a form of social communication. This is clearly true in the Heian period when love affairs were carried on through indispensable poetic exchanges, but even in modern times when, as Tanizaki shows in the relation between Sachiko and her husband in *The Makioka Sisters*, poetry continues to play a role. Indeed the brevity and allusiveness of Japanese art forms are in part explained by the fact that they are not meant to be taken as isolated objects set apart for solitary contemplation but are part of an ongoing stream of interaction and take their meaning only from that context. A simple ink painting hung in the appropriate spot in a Japanese room says something about the season, the character of its owner, and the nature of the occasion. It will frequently be replaced by other pictures for other contexts, unlike a Western painting that exists as an independent element in a room. Thus, no "frame" separates the Japanese work of art from its surroundings. In poetic diaries, a peculiarly Japanese art form, prose and poetry are intricately related and flow out of each other.[21] In a Japanese room the painting is complemented by the flower arrangement, the bamboo and wood of the interior architecture, and the view of the garden. The boundary between art and life is blurred and ideally life itself is turned into art so that everything, from the clothes one wears to the way one enters a room, has a kind of formal perfection and expressive subtlety. Then group life and artistic expression have no break and each intimately reflects the other.

Yet perfection of artistic form always carries a certain autonomy. The more completely the individual was committed to artistic expression the more he or she tended to withdraw from the normal group obligations of Japanese life. In the Heian period the greatest writers tended to be widowed or semiretired gentlewomen of the lower nobility. In the Middle Ages the greatest painters and poets were Buddhist monks. The great seventeenth-century haiku poet Bashō ran away from his feudal post and spent much of his life in wandering and semiseclusion. Even in the modern period one can think of Tanizaki Junichirō writing *The Makioka Sisters* during World War Two, utterly unaffected by the current nationalist propaganda, or Nagai Kafū writing his petulant and utterly apolitical diary entries in the same years.[22] The pervasive Japanese groupism is the organizing principle of the artistic world as well—schools of painting, flower arranging, tea ceremony, as well as such professions as acting, dancing, and music tend to be organized along kinship or pseudokinship lines. Even in the modern period the Japanese art world has divided into the usual collection of warring cliques. Yet the greatest artists and the most innovative ones have seldom been produced by the conventional schools. They have usually been those who, like Bashō, broke loose from some earlier life course to devote themselves to a new and autonomous expression.

Although artistic expression was integrated with the ongoing pattern of everyday life perhaps more completely than in any other advanced society, it often took the form of a covert protest against that life. The poetic tradition is full of disillusionment with human society and often reflects the turn to nature or religion as a consolation. Both the drama and the novel have frequently focused on the conflict between social obligation and human feeling. This is not to say that social protest or social analysis has an artistic tradition. The social problem drama or novel has received only uncertain experimentation in the modern period and did not exist at all traditionally. Japanese art forms generally concentrate on feelings more than ideas, but feelings may rebel against a social order even when no set of ideas supports them. This is exactly what happens in the longer literary forms where such situations become most explicit. The unhappy protagonists have no hope of openly challenging their sad fate and go to their death amid the tears of the audience. But even a seventeen-syllable poem or a flower arrangement may be an expression of and an emotional protest against personal unhappiness.

No culture has more richly cultivated the life of feeling and its aesthetic expression, and only here Japanese culture transcends its particularism and speaks to the universal human spirit. In poetry and painting, novels and plays, as well as in house architecture, garden design, and flower arrangement, Japanese culture breaks through the limitations of its social organization and has exercised far-reaching influences on other cultures.

Religion is the one other sphere where Japan has been able to transcend its cultural particularism and for much the same reason. For many centuries the religious life was a refuge, often the only refuge, from the unbearable pressures of group life. It was always possible for even the most distinguished person to shave his head and enter a monastery when faced with an irresolvable dilemma or when overcome with unbearable remorse. The upper classes were more apt to follow the meditation practices of Zen Buddhism, perhaps in some exquisite mountain temple where each change of season brought new beauties of nature. The masses were more apt to cast themselves on the mercy of Amida, the Boddhisattva who vowed never to enter nirvana until all sentient beings are saved. Japanese religion like Japanese art is aesthetic and emotional rather than intellectual, but it too provides an oasis of personal autonomy and of access to universal values in a desert of particularism.

I have called that aspect of the Japanese artistic and religious tradition that stands in tension with the existing social reality the "tradition of submerged transcendence." It is transcendent because it breaks through the strictures of the given social order but submerged because it lacks the ability to call forth any alternative. It is expressive of dissatisfaction without providing the basis for constructing anything new. The continuity of this tradition from Murasaki Shikibu to Tanizaki Junichirō or from Shōtoku Taishi to Suzuki Daisetsu itself indicates the basic continuity of the Japanese group structure to which it is so closely and so ambiguously related.

## THE RELATION BETWEEN TRADITION
## AND MODERNIZATION IN JAPAN

The relation between tradition and modernization in Japan is peculiarly complex. I would argue, though this is not the place to marshal the evidence, that no inherent trend toward modernization existed in any of the current usages of that term in Tokugawa Japan. Social change in the Tokugawa period can best be understood as the working out of the pattern possibilities of the Japanese culture of approximately 1600 through two hundred and fifty subsequent years of peaceful isolation. I see no fundamental challenge to the basic pattern of Japanese culture nor any inherent drive toward a radically different society. Nevertheless, much dynamism of Japan's modernization can be attributed to the traditional culture and society *once it had sustained the material and psychological shock of the Western impact.* This means that potentialities that did not in the Tokugawa period drive toward modernization could be mobilized in its support once new necessities and new models entered the picture. This limits the usefulness of Japan as an "example" for other modernizing nations with quite different traditional cultures.

Let us review quickly the elements that made the transition from feudalism to nation-state (the chief unit and vehicle of modernization in the West), an at least superficially easy one for Japan.[23] Japan already had a semicentralized government in the Tokugawa shogunate. It also had an ancient tradition of national political unity as well as a tradition of reshuffling actual power under the unchanging legitimacy of the emperor. A political elite had a strong Confucian ethic of governmental responsibility and considerable experience of government at the local and provincial level. This elite (the *bushi* class) had already become a salaried bureaucracy and thus was disembedded from the involvements in local landholding that limited the effectiveness of its Chinese counterpart. No significant regional, linguistic, religious, or cultural divisions stood in the way of national integration and national geographical boundaries were of the most unambiguous sort. The general populace was schooled in the discipline of tightly organized groups, competitive but open to direction, and quickly responsive to strong leadership. There was no significant tradition of organized opposition to political authority. Except for an occasional peasant revolt, usually brought on by extreme famine conditions and utterly lacking in political program or organization, there was no form of alienation from authority other than purely private withdrawal and escape.

By and large the early Meiji state was built on these elements. It can be said to resemble the Western European nation-state only superficially for these reasons: there was no way of changing the top effective leadership (under the emperor) except through the open violent clash of political power groups. The choice of national goals depended entirely on the intelligence of the top leadership—there were few regular channels of representation, interest aggregation, or even consultation. Only the *bushi* class was conscious and responsible at the national political level, and members of that class could enter the government only with personal connections, often involving coming from the same feudal domain, with the top leadership. Communication flowed easily from the top down but with difficulty the other way. There was no ideal of the political participation of a nation of citizens, but rather the political role of the general population was limited to that of self-sacrificing subject. The whole modern Japanese political history is the history of attempts to open up this structure (which as described would apply only to early Meiji Japan) to new groups and new modes of political communication and participation and of opposition to such attempts. The major problem in any substantial alteration of this structure was that this structure itself was the very basis of Japan's rapidly growing national strength. Thus measures to strengthen the traditional pattern often went hand in hand with efforts to increase participation and develop the mechanisms of democratic government. Both these tendencies were seen as aiding modernization at least insofar as that is measured in wealth and power. Thus strengthening tradition in Japan was a component of modernization rather than necessarily in opposition to it.

Strengthening the traditional components of Japanese society took place at two primary points—the *kokutai* or national polity, and the primary group, whether in family, village, or factory. Through the mass media and compulsory education the *kokutai* ideology of the family-state was widely inculcated.[24] It stressed the obedient subject and very secondarily the participant citizen. Through the civil code and governmental sponsorship of various associations, such as youth groups and veterans groups, the state attempted to reinforce the tight hierarchical nature of Japanese primary group relations. Also from the second decade of Meiji the government attempted to repress strictly any ideology or group that seemed to challenge openly the *kokutai*. But at the very same time important steps were made in the direction of representative government. A constitution was granted to the people by the emperor in 1890 that opened the way to legislative participation in government and eventually (1919) to a party cabinet. Although effective participation was only opened to a relatively small group, the trend was for gradually increasing inclusion. But at virtually every step strengthening the traditional structure went hand in hand with growing participation, as when in 1925 universal suffrage was passed at the same time as a Peace Preservation Law that outdid all previous Japanese legislation in limiting free speech and repressing allegedly subversive groups.

During the 1930s and early 1940s the balance was tipped toward the "traditional," though it should be remembered that this was a period of continued economic development and growing egalitarianization of Japanese life. Since 1945 the balance has shifted toward representative government and popular participation, though the cohesive primary group is far from dead and even a shadowy form of *kokutai* lingers on. The most interesting questions about Japan's modern century are: How far has the traditional *kokutai* and primary group really been undermined? How far have genuinely alternative modes of organization been established? And how have the traditional forms survived in modern guise? If we could answer these questions we would begin to know whether the centuries-old Japanese pattern with its balanced stability and change is still viable or whether it may be shifting in a radically different direction. The evidence is certainly insufficient but some speculations may perhaps be allowed.

## CULTURAL RESOURCES FOR VARIANT PATTERNS

We have already commented at length on one aspect of Japanese tradition, the "tradition of submerged transcendence," which is deeply ingrained at the very heart of Japanese culture and personality, especially in the aesthetic and religious spheres, but which has only an ambiguous relation to the central value system focusing on the predominance of the group. On one hand, these aesthetic and religious activities have provided a safety valve for the dominant system, in that alienative motivation has been drained off without threat to the social order. On the other hand, the deep-going universalism and individualism of the tradition of submerged transcendence cannot help but implicitly call into question the dominant pattern. There has been, however, no political means whereby this subversive potentiality could be realized. The religious-aesthetic tradition has been not only apolitical but almost amoral. This does not mean that resources from this tradition cannot be utilized to construct an alternative system of social values, but it does mean that most work in such an enterprise is still to be done.

Another element in Japanese tradition, however, was strongly political and ethical in orientation but was not entirely at peace with the dominant pattern. Confucianism also contains an element of "submerged transcendence," even though it existed in some tension with the religio-aesthetic components of the tradition for which earlier in this chapter I have reserved that term. Much in the Confucian tradition does reinforce and rationalize the dominant pattern. Confucian ethics stresses particularistic obligations to parents, teachers, and rulers. It has been used to justify existing social orders in all East Asian societies. But at the same time in its notion of Heaven (*Ten*) and of the Way (*Dō*), Confucianism contains universalistic overtones that have clear political and moral implications. Moreover in the Confucian tradition, the conception is that the man of moral virtue, whatever his worldly position, may act to embody the transcendent moral order no matter what existing authorities may say. This freedom of moral action was very closely hedged and denied altogether by the most establishment-oriented Confucians, but it was not entirely lacking in China or Japan. It combined with a Confucian pragmatism enjoining retainers to act in the "best interest of" their superiors even when the superiors didn't know it, to provide an intellectual and moral justification for many great innovators at the end of the Tokugawa period who had to engage in dangerous missions often expressly forbidden by parents and feudal lords.

Confucianism provided much of the scaffolding for the modern ideology of the *kokutai,* or emperor system. It is also true that explicit reference to Confucianism in modern Japan has been almost exclusively the property of the right-wing. Confucianism almost nowhere in East Asia has been able to disentangle itself from its involvement with the old regime. But we must also point out the many ways in which Confucianism supplied a bridge to Western universalistic ideologies like Christianity, liberalism, and even socialism. It is well known that the Puritanical Yankee missionaries made such an impression on many young samurai in the late nineteenth century because they seemed the very embodiment of Confucian self-mastery and ethical idealism. Most early liberal and socialist thinkers had started as rather idealistic Confucians. Even as late as World War One, Yoshino Sakuzō's term *minpon-shūgi* (literally "People-as-the-basis-ism;" but more loosely "democracy"), has a distinctly Confucian ring.

Nor, indeed, was Confucian universalism entirely confined to ideology. It was to some degree embodied in institutions, particularly in the educational and bureaucratic institutions of Tokugawa Japan. And of course the universalism embodied in those and other institutions of modern Japan has to some extent this same Confucian lineage. Both here and in the ethical idealism that has such a long history in Japan our figure, "container and contents," cannot be taken too literally. The particularistic "container" has been permanently bent by the centuries-old "content" of Confucian universalism. Nevertheless, for reasons already stated, Confucianism lacked either the dynamism or a sufficiently clear alternative model to challenge fundamentally the basic pattern of Japanese values. Those fundamental challenges that have arisen in modern times may draw from Confucian universalism or from the religio-aesthetic tradition of submerged transcendence, but they have always also involved some significant influence from the newly available Western culture.

Maruyama has made the case for the largely instrumental use to which borrowings from Western culture have been put—means at the service of group goals but without value in themselves—but he is quite aware that that is not the whole story.[25] At least some components of Western culture standing in tension with Japanese group values have evoked profound commitment, including Christianity, liberalism, German Idealism, and Marxism. To give a complete account of these four tendencies would be to write much of the intellectual history of modern Japan. Here we can consider only a few ways that they combined with or challenged the Japanese tradition.

German Idealism more closely resembles the Japanese tradition of submerged transcendence than any other of these four tendencies. It is no accident, therefore, that Nishida Kitarō, Japan's most influential modern philosopher, combined an attachment to Zen Buddhism and the "Oriental" philosophy of absolute negativity with an interest in German Idealism. The particular synthesis that Nishida developed has been called the "orthodoxy of emperor-system thought," but this seems gratuitous. It is true that Nishida never developed a social or political ethic and never openly criticized the status quo. In this apolitical stance he resembled much of the German philosophy that had influenced him. Yet his espousal of a Kantian personalism clearly extended the implications of the Japanese religio-aesthetic tradition in an ethical direction and was an important first step toward an altered conception of society even if it never went any further. These implications remained implicit and some of Nishida's disciples wrote the most intellectually respectable apologetics for the Japanese war policy. But it would be as absurd to blame Hitler on Kant as to blame Tōjō on Nishida. Nishida Kitarō and other ethical personalists who flourished in the 1920s remain an important resource for building an ethic both genuinely Japanese and genuinely universalistic.

Christianity has had a perennial appeal in modern Japan. Christianity made more explicit the transcendental implications of Confucianism and demanded an ultimate loyalty to Christ rather than the emperor or the state.[26] Christianity also contained certain resemblances to the Pure Land tradition of Buddhism, as Uchimura Kanzō recognized when he said that he worshipped Christ not as Wesley and Moody did but as Hōnen and Shinran worshipped Amida. Christianity, at least in the American Protestant strand that had the most influence, carried a much more explicit social ethical concern than did German Idealism. Japanese Christians have been involved in every reform movement for the last century and were especially in the vanguard in the Meiji period. Modern Japan has produced at least one authentically new Christian movement—the so-called Nonchurch Christianity of Uchimura Kanzō. Especially interesting about this movement is that although starting as a protest against the dominance of the missionary church even as a model for Japanese Christianity, it has developed a deep-going criticism of Japanese group structures as well.[27] Paradoxically, organized on a teacher-disciple basis, it yet demands of its followers that they worship Christ directly without mediation through the teacher. One leading Nonchurch teacher, a former president of Tokyo University, dissolves his Bible class every year so that the students will not form too strong and permanent a relation to him. Although small, the Nonchurch movement has had influence out of all proportion to its numbers, like the Quakers in America.

Liberalism, a somewhat vaguer tendency than the other three, has been of pervasive influence in modern Japan. It has produced such important government leaders as Shidehara Kijūrō and such influential social thinkers as Kawai Eijirō. Although the Marxist critics accuse the liberals of not being "thorough" in their criticism of the emperor system, undeniably most liberals were committed to universal ethical values that transcended the Japanese nation. They tried to interpret the Meiji Constitution in a liberal direction and to reduce the emperor's role to that of a conventional constitutional monarch. They contributed much to the genuine successes of prewar Japanese democracy. They were unable to halt the drift to fascism, a tendency that many courageously fought, less because of defects in their ideology than because of the structural weakness of their political position and their lack of allies in defending parliamentary democracy.

Marxism has been a powerful movement in modern Japan. Since World War One, it has been the largest movement whose value position stands outside the traditional *kokutai*. Marxism is based on a theoretical understanding of reality in general and history in particular that grants no special position to the Japanese people and its emperor. It has also represented to many Japanese a struggle for social justice often at great personal sacrifice to those involved, which has deep ethical meaning. Marxism is explicitly anti-individualistic, but at least in prewar times considerable individualism was necessary to persevere in the Marxist movement. The Japanese have not been entirely satisfied with the objectivist and cognitive stance of orthodox Marxism, and the somewhat heterodox Marxist Miki Kiyoshi even before the war discussed *shutaisei*, or "subjectivity" in social life and political action.[28] Since the war this element has come to be more and more emphasized so that Marxism too has contributed to a kind of ethical personalism.[29] Present-day student groups are very much concerned with this issue. Just as Christianity has been far more influential than the Christian church so the Marxist influence in Japan has been far wider than the Communist or Socialist Parties.

All these tendencies were well established in prewar Japan and all helped to give some grounding to "Democracy," the officially proclaimed new value system after the war. The minor success in institutionalizing liberal demo-

204 / Continuity and Change in Japanese Society

cratic values that had been made by the 1920s was partial and almost completely swept away during the period of ultranationalism. Nonetheless, the new institutional order, which was derived largely from American liberalism and established by command of the occupation authorities, had some real grounding in previous Japanese experience. No direct challenge to the traditional *kokutai* from within has ever succeeded. The postwar institutional system did not result from the maturation of an alternative value pattern that finally gained the social support to institutionalize itself, but was imposed from without—and that imposition by no means destroyed the *kokutai* or the traditional Japanese group structure. Both were too amorphous and too pervasive to be annihilated by a mere change in official ideology or even by changes in the legal order. The confession documents written by Japanese Marxists and liberals in the 1930s when they renounced their former errors show that they do not by and large expand on the superiority of a native Japanese ideology. They tend to renounce ideology altogether and signal their intent to return to the primordial loyalties of family and nation.[30] They ceased being Marxists not to become some other kind of "-ist," but to be once again simply Japanese. Because the traditional Japanese pattern has never rested primarily on explicit verbal formulation (has never had, for example, a formal creed), it cannot be considered abandoned when new verbal formulations are adopted. Only changes in ways of thinking and feeling and in patterning interpersonal relations can tell us that the traditional pattern is changing. Here the evidence remains ambiguous.

VALUE CHANGE IN POSTWAR JAPAN

So far we have been discussing cultural resources for constructing a new value system. Now we must consider how structural changes and historical experiences affected value change in postwar Japan.

Defeat in the Pacific war and foreign occupation were unprecedented experiences for the Japanese people. Not in historic times had the Japanese islands been successfully invaded. Never before had Japanese society been at the mercy of a foreign power. The entire modern fabric of ideology known as emperor-system thought collapsed before these eventualities, and the personal charisma of the emperor was dealt a severe blow. The explicit ideology of the pre–1945 period is most unlikely ever to be successfully revived again, though nostalgic echoes of it have been heard increasingly in recent years. But the basic value system in Japan, including the *kokutai* broadly understood, has never depended primarily on explicit formulation and, as we have seen, is able to survive ideological collapse.

Perhaps the profoundest change in postwar Japan has been the shifting balance between public and private values, which has had wide repercussions. When the terrible sacrifices that the state had exacted from the people, especially in the closing phases of the war, proved to be utterly without meaning or effect a terrible revulsion set in.[31] Whereas before the war any pursuit of purely private happiness was considered almost criminal, postwar society has been heavily oriented to a family-centered consumer hedonism. A good job, a pleasant home (with television, refrigerator, automobile, and so forth), and a happy marriage have become the great desiderata. This exaltation of private ends has been criticized as selfish and materialistic not only by the old right but by the new left. Yet unlike private values in earlier times the new emphasis on the private sphere is not apologetic, does not defend itself as a mere complement to public values, and is much more closely integrated into the main centers of social life. Even the sense of Japan as a nation, which continues very strong, has been affected by the new values, Japan's economic productivity is proudly compared to other nations, not its military might or its imperial rule. The events that concentrate and symbolize national identity are things like the 1966 Olympics or 1970 Expo. The competitive element is strong in these occasions but they symbolize consummatory gratification more than political domination. This shift from sacrifice for public ends to private gratification has been clearest in the relation between state and people, but it has influenced group life at every level. One way to say this is that the vertical dimension of Japanese and group life has been weakening. The ubiquitous "boss" in Japanese society has not disappeared, but it has become necessary for him to moderate the nature and extent of his demands.

To some extent this tendency has gone hand in hand with the institutionalization of a democratic political order and an egalitarian legal system. In recent years attempts to strengthen the arbitrary powers of the state have been consistently resisted as possible infringements on the growing sphere of private interest. But the shift toward the importance of the private sphere is not to be interpreted as identical with an institutionalized individualism. Consciousness of individual rights remains relatively low. In many ways the individual is as dependent on the group as ever but group power is exerted through conformist pressure from peers more than through hierarchical authority.[32] In many spheres vertical controls remain strong but are exerted in a more subtle and roundabout way than would formerly have been the case. In other words, the typical structure of Japanese life is by no means broken. Nor is it quite right to say that the national collectivity has been smashed and Japanese society has been split into its constituent groups, for national consciousness remains strong and a powerful bureaucracy continues to provide direction over a surprisingly wide range of activities.

Many aspects of structural change in modern Japan seem to favor individualism and universalism, the perennial solvents of Japanese group particularism. Universalistic criteria have long been fundamental in the vast educational system as well as in much of the legal and governmental system. Though pockets of particularism held out in the economy even there universalistic criteria are becoming ever more decisive. All these changes are bound to have a long-run influence on values. And yet exposure to urban life, modern industry, and advanced education does not in itself create universalistic and individualistic values. "Mass society" theorists have shown how these advanced conditions can lead to the creation of pseudo-*Gemeinschaft* and "other-direction." In Japan where *Gemeinschaft*, pseudo-*Gemeinschaft*, and other-direction have always been strong, much in modern society strengthens rather than undermines them. Thus, structural conditions alone do not seem to be determinative. They reinforce traditional patterns as well as providing some support for alternatives. The future of the Japanese value system will be determined by the creative action of the Japanese people and will not simply be dictated by existing economic and social structures, important though they may be.

As part of the shift from public to private dominance has come the increasing unwillingness to put up with the traditional split in consciousness between personal desire and social duty. The issue of subjectivity (*shutaisei*) referred to here has been raised by those who insist on integrating personal impulse and public action. Many educated Japanese have come to rebel against living in a society where social obligations act like steel cables pulling and controlling one's acts regardless of what one's own feelings are. One element in the student revolts is an almost apocalyptic desire to determine the social conditions under which one will live, rather than docilely accept a fixed and preexisting network. The most constructive expression of this new impulse is the growth of genuine voluntary associations in postwar Japan. Much so-called voluntary association has been in fact government-inspired and government-dominated. Long before the war various government ministries cultivated special interest groups that they then patronized and subsidized. This pattern is still very much alive. Veterans groups, farmers groups, and even religious groups tend to gravitate to the appropriate ministry and obediently accept direction. Yet more and more in recent years genuinely autonomous groups have emerged to give a social expression to the private sphere and to nurture a genuine individualism.[33] But for many who have little hope of reconciling personal desire and group obligation Japanese society continues to provide a range of the most exquisite aesthetic and sensual diversions, sufficient perhaps in themselves to explain why Japan has never had a social revolution.

Some Japanese intellectuals have recently realized that abstract ideologies, particularly of Western origin, can have little hope of transforming Japanese life unless they are deeply indigenized so that they affect the feelings and unconscious thoughts of the masses.[34] However true this may be, indigenization has almost always meant in Japanese history the loss of universalism and the submergence of transcendence. From Buddhism to Christianity, from Confucianism to Marxism, the more the foreign ideology has penetrated Japanese group structure the more it has come to serve the interests of Japanese particularism. This situation has made the "synthesis of East and West" illusory in modern Japan, for the synthesis has almost always involved the loss of vitality of the more universalistic partner. And this situation has tended to divide Japanese intellectuals between Japanese purists and thorough Westernizers. Although some at least partially successful syntheses have been achieved—for example, in the work of such philosophers as Nishida Kitarō and Miki Kiyoshi, of such novelists as Soseki, Akutagawa, and Tanizaki, of such religious leaders as Uchimura— the very limitations in these syntheses as well as their rarity leads one to be cautious about the future. Japan continues to be Asian but not Asian, Western but not Western, and in the very paradoxicality of its situation, acutely self-conscious.

At the moment what must be said about Japanese values is that there is a variety of competing possibilities. Socially effective particularistic values continue to contradict proclaimed universalistic ones. A society that talks a great deal about individualism continues to be dominated by groupism. The present ambiguities can continue partly because of delicate balances in political forces both within and outside the country. But history is unlikely to allow such tightrope-walking forever. Political or economic crises could force decisions that would propel the society in a more decisive direction. Several possibilities suggest themselves.

One possibility that seems partially to be realizing itself is the classic Japanese response to periods of weakening central control, namely, the emergence of several strong competing power centers. This situation in the past has led to open power struggles in the country. At the moment only the radical student groups seem bent on an all-out challenge to governmental authority. It does not seem likely that this tendency will spread to broader segments of the population, but the possibility exists. A tightly structured and totalistic group like Sōka Gakkai, for example, is a potential base for an independent power play. Another possibility is that the conservative government party, which is far from weak, may exert a more overt effect on ideology by resurrecting some old slogans and jettisoning some of the democratic rhetoric, which could be done without resorting to the extremism of the ultranationalist period. Still another possibility is that a coalition of reformist forces spearheaded by the newer voluntary associations and the more democratic elements in the Diet might succeed in seriously weakening the hold of particularistic and especially hierarchical groupism through both formal political changes and informal behavioral changes.

It is possible, then, that certain deep patterns of Japanese social life, which have existed since the formation of the Japanese state, may be breaking up and quite different patterns may be emerging. But the enormous tenacity and adaptability of the Japanese pattern indicate that any such conclusion is quite premature. In any case the conflict is not between "tradition" and "modernity," for the traditional pattern has been highly favorable for many kinds of modernization. Rather the question is: What kind of modernity? Only the Japanese people themselves can answer that question.

# Notes

## INTRODUCTION: THE JAPANESE DIFFERENCE

1. In spite of the similarity in title, this book has a quite different intention from Ronald B. Inden's book *Imagining India*. Inden mounts a full-scale critique of "Orientalism" in the study of India, including an analysis of received ideas and influential scholars in the field of Indology. My focus is much more selective and concentrates on a few Japanese intellectuals. The closest parallel to Inden that I have found in the Japanese field is Harry Harootunian's *History's Disquiet: Modernity, Cultural Practice, and the Question of Everyday Life*, though Harootunian shares Inden's intent only in part.

2. Bellah, "Civil Religion in America"; reprinted as chapter 9 of Bellah, *Beyond Belief*. Here I might note that the many invitations to speak and write on related subjects that the *Daedalus* article stimulated, and my feeling that turning them down in a period of national crisis (the Vietnam War) would not be responsible, led me to an intensive period of self-education in American studies, because I had no serious scholarly preparation for what was to come. Unfortunately for my work on Japan, the momentum of my involvement in American studies has scarcely ceased until today.

3. Bellah, *Tokugawa Religion*.

4. Ibid., p. 57. In *Tokugawa Religion* I spoke not only of particularism but of a kind of "generalized particularism" that could substitute in some ways for universalism. S. N. Eisenstadt has developed this idea somewhat further in an article, "Trust and Institutional Dynamics in Japan: The Construction of Generalized Particularistic Trust."

5. I make no claim to originality in seeing Japan as similar to and not merely different from other countries. Indeed it would seem that the near exclusive preoccupation with the theme of uniqueness, at least in the popular literature in both Japan and the West, is rather recent. Johann Arnason has indicated how long-standing has been the interpretation of Japan as similar to as well as different from the West, the case of "feudalism" being an obvious example. Arnason considers most of these earlier interpretations to be "pretheoretical"

and attempts to raise the theoretical level of the discussion, a project to which I hope to contribute in this introduction. See Arnason, "Comparing Japan: The Return to Asia," pp. 33–54.

6. Bellah, "Values and Social Change in Modern Japan," pp. 13–56. The second and third lectures were published under the same title as chapter 7 in Bellah, *Beyond Belief.*

7. Eisenstadt, *Japanese Civilization.*

8. Most of the essays in this book were published in the 1960s and 1970s and represent a series of efforts to explore further the meaning of Japanese identity as it was perceived primarily by major Japanese intellectuals of the mid-twentieth century. The essays on Ienaga, Watsuji, and Maruyama (Chapters 2, 3, and 4) stand on their own—there is little I would revise in them today. Nor would I change Chapter 1 on an earlier group of Japanese intellectuals, the great figures of Kamakura Buddhism, although, as I will point out below, the scholarly understanding of Buddhism in Japanese history generally and the Kamakura period in particular has changed dramatically since that essay was written. The essays on intellectuals and society and on continuity and change (Chapters 5 and 7) are the ones most limited by the time of their first appearance. I am keeping them in their original form (although I will be suggesting in this introduction some ways in which they might be reconsidered) because they do provide a helpful context for the treatments of individual intellectuals, and also because they represent an important phase of the American social scientific study of Japan, namely that of functionalist modernization theory, so much derided today. This tradition is clearest in the essay on continuity and change (Chapter 7), which was, after all, a contribution to a *Festschrift* for my teacher, Talcott Parsons, but it is also implicit in the essay on intellectuals and society (Chapter 5). What I think these essays suggest is that at least some of the criticism of this phase of American social science is misplaced. My treatment of Japanese society is neither ahistorical, that is, concerned with the timeless equilibrium that functionalist theory is supposed to posit, nor without an interest in the coercive use of power. Particularly the essay on intellectuals and society is constantly aware of the atmosphere of coercion within which Japanese intellectuals worked.

9. Bellah, "Religious Evolution"; reprinted as chapter 2 of Bellah, *Beyond Belief.*

10. Randall Collins develops his own version of social evolution by speaking of three kinds of market dynamics: kinship markets, agrarian-coercive exchange, and capitalism. See, in particular, his "Market Dynamics as the Engine of Historical Change," in his *Macrohistory,* pp. 177–208.

11. Jaspers, *Origin and Goal of History.*

12. Among many relevant works one might mention especially Eisenstadt, *Origins and Diversity of Axial Age Civilizations.*

13. Weber, *Protestant Ethic and the Spirit of Capitalism,* p. 181.

14. Arnason, *Social Theory and Japanese Experience.*

15. For a careful analysis of the evidence concerning the rather gradual process of development of the Japanese early state, perhaps beginning in the

third century A.D. in Kyushu and moving to the Yamato region somewhat later, see Wheatley and See, *From Court to Capital*.

16. Tambiah, *World Conqueror and World Renouncer*, pp. 102–31; and Tambiah, *Culture, Thought, and Social Action*, pp. 252–86. Tambiah describes the galactic polity as follows:

> The concentric-circle system, representing the center-periphery relations, was ordered thus: In the center was the king's capital and the region of its direct control, which was surrounded by a circle of provinces ruled by princes or governors appointed by the king, and these again were surrounded by more or less independent "tributary" polities. . . . If we keep in mind the expanding and shrinking character of the political constellations under scrutiny, a central, perhaps the central, feature to be grasped is that although the constituent political units differ in size, nevertheless each lesser unit is a reproduction and imitation of the larger. . . . Thus we have before us a galactic picture of a central planet surrounded by differentiated satellites, which are more or less "autonomous" entities held in orbit and within the sphere of influence of the center. (*World Conquerer*, pp. 112–13.)

It should be borne in mind that Tambiah contrasts the galactic polity with a centralized polity like that of dynastic China. Thus my use of the term is only analogous to his. But even though the Chinese polity was much more centralized than the Southeast Asian polities Tambiah describes, on its outer peripheries it shows many of the same features. Geoffrey Samuel applies Tambiah's model to Tibet in his *Civilized Shamans: Buddhism in Tibetan Societies*, pp. 62–63, but he also speaks of the eastern part of Tibet as belonging to the galactic polity of China.

17. On the T'ang version of the galactic polity in the early eighth century:

> T'ang power extended over a vast area from southern Siberia to Southeast Asia and westward through Tibet and Central Asia to the Caspian Sea. Around the borders of China proper clustered vassal states, controlled by six protectorates. Four of these were named for the cardinal points, as in An-hsi ("the pacified west") in the Tarim Basin, An-tung ("the pacified east") in the Korean area, and An-nan ("the pacified south"), from which Annam, the usual Chinese name for Vietnam, was derived. Beyond these vassal states were others, such as Japan and various kingdoms in Southeast, South, and West Asia, which recognized a vague Chinese suzerainty by occasionally presenting tribute. T'ang rule thus, from the Chinese point of view, was virtually worldwide. (Fairbank, Reischauer, and Craig, *East Asia*, p. 98.)

18. This is a point rightly emphasized by Arnason. See his *Social Theory*, pp. 145–49. For more detail, see Grapard, *Protocol of the Gods*.

19. For a suggestive discussion of these issues, see Abé, *Weaving of the Mantra*, pp. 315–22.

212 / Notes to Pages 12–18

20. Abé, *Weaving of the Mantra*. See also Hakeda, *Kūkai: Major Works Translated*.

21. See Groner, *Saichō*.

22. Kasulis, "Kūkai," pp. 131–50.

23. Ibid., p. 140.

24. For an excellent recent treatment of *hongaku* thought, particularly in the Tendai tradition, see Stone, *Original Enlightenment*.

25. Arnason speaks of "pseudo-archaism" in this connection, meaning that the archaic was consciously constructed, not simply an unconscious heritage, though he also stresses that the archaic aspect is still genuinely so. See Arnason, *Social Theory*, pp. 130–32.

26. Maruyama, "Structure of Matsurigoto," pp. 27–43.

27. Arnason quotes Sir George Sansom as referring to Kamakura Japan as "the astonishing spectacle of a state, at the head of which stands a titular emperor, whose vestigial functions are usurped by an abdicated emperor, and whose real power is nominally delegated to an hereditary military dictator, but actually wielded by an hereditary advisor to the dictator" (*Social Theory*, p. 208).

28. Arnason, *Social Theory*, ch. 3.

29. The term *kenmon* derives from the work of Kuroda Toshio and was introduced in English as "influential parties" by Neil McMullin in his *Buddhism and the State*, p. 8.

30. Grapard, *Protocol of the Gods*. Besides this major work on the Kasuga complex Grapard surveys the major Heian institutions in his article, "Institution, Ritual, and Ideology," pp. 246–69.

31. The development of monastic complexes that were virtual states in themselves in Tibet is described by Geoffrey Samuel in *Civilized Shamans*. Here too an amalgamation of Mahayana and native beliefs and practices under the organizing influence of Tantric (Esoteric) Buddhism is to be found, with chief officials of the complexes often coming from aristocratic lineages. A careful analysis of the similarities and differences in the two cases would be of great interest. Samuel's title, *Civilized Shamans*, suggests the extent to which the pattern in Tibet (and probably Japan as well) represents a compromise formation between archaic and axial materials.

32. Grapard, *Protocol of the Gods*, p. 186.

33. Abé, *Weaving of the Mantra*, pp. 417–22. Here Abé is summarizing the ideas of Kuroda Toshio on the "*kenmitsu* system." Shugendō, a movement that fused esoteric Buddhism with Japanese folk religion, originating in the eighth century but spreading widely until modern times, is an example of the degree of penetration of the Esoteric tradition. It is discussed in a book I received too late to take fully into account here: Miyake, *Shugendō*. See especially chapter 7, "Cosmology of Shugendō: Shamanism and Shugendō Thought," pp. 131–42.

34. These new movements are described in more detail below in Chapter 1.

35. The element of world denial in each of the new Kamakura sects is emphasized below in Chapter 1. But each of them contained the potentiality of compromise, most obviously the Zen sect whose spiritual discipline could be

used in the context of samurai culture as a kind of psychological technology for the more efficient acting out of the samurai role. Similar uses of Zen have even been noted among company employees in contemporary Japan. Within the Pure Land sect, not only did a hierarchy based on lineage develop, but reliance on Amida alone could become a kind of apolitical quietism. Nichiren sects were always in danger, when they identified Japan as uniquely the land of the Buddha, of fusing religion and state. In these ways powerful moments of world denial could become forms of world affirmation. On the significance of world denial in Weber's thought, and religious evolution more generally, see Bellah, "Max Weber and World-Denying Love," pp. 277–304.

36. On this point, see Foard, "What One Kamakura Story Does," pp. 101–15.

37. See, in particular, Payne, *Re-Visioning "Kamakura" Buddhism.*

38. McMullin, *Buddhism and the State*, p. 71. For further discussion of Nobunaga's idea of *tenka*, see Katsumata , "Development of Sengoku Law," pp. 119–24.

39. McMullin's excellent book, *Buddhism and the State*, describes in detail this great transformation.

40. McMullin, *Buddhism and the State*, p. 257.

41. Ooms, *Tokugawa Ideology.*

42. Ibid., pp. 170–71.

43. Ooms gives a good summary of the Pure Land and Buddhist cases in *Tokugawa Ideology*, pp. 30–38. Stone gives a helpful discussion of the extent to which the radical trends in the "new" Kamakura Buddhism, deriving from the "single condition" necessary for salvation, undercut all existing forms of political legitimation. She notes (in *Original Enlightenment*, pp. 250–51) Nichiren's willingness to condemn even an emperor for failing to protect the true Dharma (that is, the Lotus Sutra) and his belief that all earthly authorities owe their power ultimately to Sakyamuni (an idea that would get Nichiren followers in trouble as late as World War II). She quotes Taira Masayuki as arguing that the new Buddhism "relativized the social hierarchy and established religious equality," but notes that Nichiren did not envision "an egalitarian restructuring of society—a modern idea" but rather a reversal of the outsider status of himself and his community (*Original Enlightenment*, p. 262).

44. The best treatment of the persecution of the Christians is Elison, *Deus Destroyed.*

45. Wakabayashi, *Anti-Foreignism*, pp. 64–68.

46. Frank, *ReOrient*, pp. 145–46. Frank shows that silver exports were particularly large in the early seventeenth century but continued well into the eighteenth century, while copper exports continued high after silver exports declined. He shows that these exports contributed to world economic liquidity alongside the metal exports from the New World. See also Collins, "An Asian Route to Capitalism," in his *Macrohistory*, pp. 209–37, for an argument that Japan had an advanced capitalist economy in the Tokugawa period. Collins also argues that Buddhist monastic institutions in the Kamakura and Muromachi

periods provided a chrysalis for the development of capitalist forms of economic life, analogous to the role of Christian monasteries in the European Middle Ages, that was the precondition for the generalized capitalist economy of the Tokugawa period.

47. On the nature of indirect rule in the Tokugawa period, see Ikegami, *The Taming of the Samurai*.

48. Ooms, *Tokugawa Ideology*, pp. 5, 80. Matsudaira's "ban" was really a directive intended to enforce Chu Hsi orthodox Neo-Confucianism only in the shogunate's own official Confucian school, though it was later extended to include the official schools of the feudal domains, but it was never enforced against private schools devoted to other kinds of Confucian teaching. See Ooms, *Charismatic Bureaucrat*.

49. Ooms, *Tokugawa Ideology*, pp. 182–86.

50. Ibid., ch. 6. Maruyama Masao in the 1980s wrote the introduction to a volume on the Ansai school in a series on Japanese intellectual history published by Iwanami. He found that working on this project gave him "unbearably painful headaches," headaches that ceased when he had completed the work. His reason for spending time on this school was that it was one of the sources of "ultra-nationalism and cultural essentialism" to quote from Tetsuo Najita's description in his "On History and Politics," p. 15.

51. Ooms, *Tokugawa Ideology*, p. 247.

52. Najita, *Tokugawa Political Writings*, pp. xiii–liv.

53. Najita, "On History and Politics," p. 11.

54. Najita, *Visions of Virtue*.

55. Najita, "Ambiguous Encounters."

56. Najita, "Some Comments on the Theme of Translation," pp. 7–8.

57. Moore, "Japanese Peasant Protests," p. 325.

58. Hardacre, *Shinto and the State*, p. 12.

59. Davis, "Pilgrimage and World Renewal," Part I, pp. 97–116; Part II, pp. 197–221.

60. Ooms, *Tokugawa Ideology*, p. 192.

61. Arnason, *Social Theory*, ch. 7.

62. Dore, *Education in Tokugawa Japan*.

63. Keene, *Japanese Discovery of Europe*.

64. Arnason, *Social Theory*, ch. 9.

65. The best fine-grained analysis of this process remains Craig's *Chōshū in the Meiji Restoration*.

66. Arnason, *Social Theory*, ch. 9.

67. Collins, *Macrohistory*, p. 47.

68. Ibid.

69. See the charts on pp. 419 and 503 of Jansen, *Making of Modern Japan*. Jansen indicates the dominance of Chōshū in the army and Satsuma in the navy as follows: "The list of seventy-two full generals down to 1926 shows 30 percent from Chōshū; while of the forty full admirals 44 percent were from Satsuma. In

the central bureaucratic and command structure that preponderance was stronger still. No navy builder, however, dominated the scene to the degree that Yamagata did the army during his lifetime" (Jansen, *Making,* p. 397).

70. As we will consider later, even the cut-off date of 1945 will have to be seriously reconsidered. Wasn't General MacArthur a kind of "shogun" and wasn't there a continuation of a kind of "military rule" even after the Occupation ended under the aegis of the Japan-United States Security Treaty?

71. Tsunoda, de Bary, and Keene, *Sources of the Japanese Tradition,* pp. 643–44.

72. Tsunoda, *Sources,* pp. 705–6.

73. Ibid., 646–47.

74. Bellah, *Tokugawa Religion,* p. 158.

75. The book edited by Stephen Vlastos, *Mirror of Modernity,* is a useful application to Japan of the idea of the invention of tradition most influentially set forth in Hobsbawm and Ranger, *Invention of Tradition.* The Vlastos book, like all such efforts, in attempting to correct the "uncritical use of tradition" (p. I), runs the risk of misunderstanding tradition altogether and the extent to which any living tradition is always being invented.

76. Jansen, *Making,* p. 393.

77. Ibid., p. 394.

78. Gluck, *Japan's Modern Myths,* pp. 58–69.

79. For a description of these tours, see Fujitani, *Splendid Monarchy,* ch. 2.

80. Fujitani, *Splendid Monarchy,* ch. 3.

81. Garon, *Molding Japanese Minds,* p. 64.

82. The best treatment of Shinto since the Meiji Restoration is Hardacre, *Shinto and the State.*

83. Fujitani, *Splendid Monarchy,* ch. 4.

84. Gluck in *Japan's Modern Myths,* ch. 8, gives a good description of how diversity and conformity could both be found in the language of Meiji ideology.

85. Barshay, *State and Intellectual in Imperial Japan,* p. 40.

86. Ibid., pp. 35–122.

87. Garon, *Molding Japanese Minds,* p. 19.

88. Rubin, "Soseki on Individualism," p. 24.

89. Natsume, "My Individualism," pp. 41, 40.

90. Ibid., p. 44.

91. See "German-Bashing and the Theory of Democratic Modernization," in Collins, *Macrohistory,* pp. 152–76.

92. Harootunian, *Overcome by Modernity,* p. xxviii.

93. Germaine A. Hoston discusses Sano Manabu and several of the other Communist Party leaders who underwent *tenkō* in her *State, Identity, and the National Question,* pp. 327–60. Sano, who had been a long-standing defender of the Commintern line before his *tenkō,* went on to develop a "national socialist" position combining a call for popular (nonviolent) revolution with nationalism and emperor-system particularism.

94. Hoston, *State, Identity, and the National Question,* pp. 356–57.

95. On these issues see, in particular, Hoston, *Marxism and the Crisis of Development in Prewar Japan.*

96. Barshay, *Social Sciences in Japan,* forthcoming, ch. 4.

97. Barshay, *State and Intellectual,* p. 202.

98. Harootunian, *Overcome by Modernity,* p. 38.

99. Barshay, *State and Intellectual,* pp. 114–20.

100. Ibid., pp. 95–96.

101. Dower, *Embracing Defeat,* p. 531. Maruyama Masao has the following to say about responsibility for starting the war:

> Whatever may have been the causes for the outbreak of war in 1939, the leaders of Nazi Germany were certainly conscious of a *decision* to embark on hostilities. In Japan, however, the situation was quite different: though it was our country that plunged the world in to the terrible conflagration in the Pacific, it has been impossible to find any individuals or groups that are conscious of having started the war. What is the meaning of the remarkable state of affairs in which a country slithered into war, pushed into the vortex by men who were themselves driven by some force that they did not really understand? (*Thought and Behavior,* p. 16.)

102. Maruyama points out that the emperor entirely lacked the freedom of the absolutist monarchs in early modern Europe because he too was "saddled with a burden—in his case a tradition that derived from an infinitely remote past" (*Thought and Behavior,* p. 20).

103. Dower's splendid book, *Embracing Defeat,* is the main source for my treatment of the Occupation period.

104. Dower points out the Occupation's serious tampering with the procedure of the war crimes trial in Tokyo from 1946 to 1949 in order to avoid any testimony that might incriminate the emperor. See *Embracing Defeat,* pp. 443–84 and elsewhere.

105. Dower, *Embracing Defeat,* p. 389.

106. If we take seriously Collins's definition of revolution by its results, "wholesale transformation of the ruling elite accompanied by political and economic restructuring" (see Collins, *Macrohistory,* p. 47), we will have to say that it was a less radical revolution because, although it did indeed involve political and economic restructuring, it did not involve a wholesale transformation of the ruling elite. Except for a small number of people purged as war criminals and a much smaller number executed, the ruling elite continued largely unbroken. Most of those purged were quickly rehabilitated after the Occupation ended and some of them reached high office, as for example Kishi Nobusuke who became prime minister.

107. Maruyama, *Thought and Behavior,* chs. 1 and 2.

108. Koschmann, *Revolution and Subjectivity.*

109. On the establishment of MITI, see Dower, *Embracing Defeat,* pp. 541–

60, but more generally on all three dimensions described here. The classic treatment of MITI is Johnson, *MITI and the Japanese Miracle*.

110. John Dower emphasizes the institutional continuity between the prewar and postwar periods in many fields: bureaucracy, especially economic bureaucracy, business organization, labor organization, even farm tenancy where wartime regulations already greatly reduced the control of landlords over their land and its produce, making the postwar land reform relatively easy. See Dower, "Useful War," pp. 49–70.

111. Dower, *Embracing Defeat*, p. 559.

112. Barshay, *Social Sciences*, ch. 5.

113. Dale, *Myth of Japanese Uniqueness*; see also his *Myth of Japanese Uniqueness Revisited*.

114. Yoshino, *Cultural Nationalism in Contemporary Japan*.

115. Ibid., p. 141.

116. Ibid., p. 142.

117. Ibid.

118. This account is based on Field, *In the Realm of the Dying Emperor*.

119. Sakamoto, *Emperor System as a Japan Problem*, p. 23.

120. Ishida, "Emperor Problem," p. 47.

121. Ibid., pp. 54–56.

122. Andrew Barshay raises the interesting possibility that "*Tennosei* may not require a *Tenno*" in an unpublished paper, "The Problem of the Emperor System in Japanese Social Science," p. 19.

123. Broadbent, *Environmental Politics in Japan*.

124. The remaining paragraphs of this Introduction draw in part on my epilogue to Madsen, Sullivan, Swidler, and Tipton, *Meaning and Modernity*.

125. See Eisenstadt, "Mirror-Image Modernities." For survey data that show the United States and Japan as polar cases on many dimensions, with other industrial nations in between, see Lipset, "Pacific Divide," pp. 121–66.

## CHAPTER 1: THE CONTEMPORARY MEANING OF KAMAKURA BUDDHISM

This paper was read originally at a symposium in Honolulu sponsored by the Department of Religion at the University of Hawaii and the Hawaii Buddhist Council. The symposium, extending from January 21, 1973, to April 15, 1973, was entitled "Kamakura Buddhism: The Buddhist Reformation, Retrospect and Prospect." During this period the symposium hosted a series of lectures and discussions exploring the meaning of the variety of Buddhist movements initiated in the Kamakura period of Japanese history (1185–1332). The effort was undertaken to celebrate several anniversaries: the 800th anniversary of the founding of the Jōdo school by Hōnen, the 800th anniversary of the birth of Shinran, and the 750th anniversary of the birth of Nichiren. The symposium was under the leadership of Professor Alfred Bloom, then of the University of Hawaii. It was published in the *Journal of the American Academy of Religion*, 42, no. 1 (1974): 3–17.

1. *Rekishi Tetsugaku* in *Miki Kiyoshi Zenshū*. See also his essay "Nin-gengaku no Marukusu-teki Keitei" (The Marxist form of anthropology) in vol. 3. My discussion follows the spirit of Miki's analysis but does not attempt to reproduce his much more complex terminology.

2. See Futaba, *Shinran no Kenkyū* (Shinran studies).

3. On the three marks, see Conze, *Buddhist Thought in India*, ch.3, passim, but especially p. 34.

4. Ibid., p. 37.

5. Ibid., p. 60.

6. Ibid., pp. 75–76.

7. Bielefeldt, "Shōbōgenzō-sansuikyō."

8. Nakamura, *History of the Development of Japanese Thought*, 1:90. The passage is from Dōgen's *Bendowa*, which is translated in its entirety by Waddell and Abe in *Eastern Buddhist*. For their translation of the passage quoted, see p. 144 of that issue.

9. Bielefeldt, "Shōbōgenzō-sansuikyō," p. 74.

10. Futaba, *Shinran no Kenkyū*, the chapter entitled "Shinran no shin to jiritsu-teki jissen no kankei" (The relation between Shinran's faith and autonomous practice), pp. 279–310.

11. Bloom, *Life of Shinran Shōnin*, p.18.

12. Bloom, *Shinran's Gospel of Pure Grace*, pp. 43-44. (Japanese characters contained in the original manuscript have been omitted from this text.) D. T. Suzuki gives a somewhat looser translation of this difficult passage on pp. 171–72 of his *Mysticism, Christian and Buddhist* :

> Ji means "of itself," or "by itself." As it is not due to the designing
> of man but to Nyorai's vow [that man is born in the Pure Land], it
> is said that man is naturally or spontaneously (*nen*), led to the Pure
> Land. The devotee does not make any conscious self-designing efforts,
> for they are altogether ineffective to achieve the end. *Jinen* thus means
> that as one's rebirth into the Pure Land is wholly due to the working of
> Nyorai's vow-power, it is for the devotee just to believe in Nyorai and
> let his vow work itself out.
>
> *Hōni* means "it is so because it is so"; and in the present case it means
> that it is in the nature of Amida's vow-power that we are born in the
> Pure Land. Therefore, the way in which the other-power works may be
> defined as "meaning of no-meaning," that is to say, it works in such a
> way as if not working [so natural, so spontaneous, so effortless, so
> absolutely free are its workings].
>
> Amida's vow accomplishes everything and nothing is left for the
> devotee to design or plan for himself. Amida makes the devotee simply
> say "Namu-amida-butsu" in order to be saved by Amida, and the latter
> welcomes him to the Pure Land. As far as the devotee is concerned, he
> does not know what is good or bad for him, all is left to Amida. That is
> what I—Shinran—have learned.

13. Blyth, *Haiku*, 1:195. I have altered the translation of the last two lines.
14. Ibid., 1:332. Blyth translates *asagao* in the plural.
15. Ibid., 1:179
16. Ibid., 1:333.
17. Ibid., 1:349.
18. Ibid., 1:345.
19. MacKenzie, *Autumn Wind*, p. 71. I have altered the translation.
20. Kobayashi, *Oraga Haru* (The year of my life), pp. 139–40. The prose text is unchanged but I have altered the text of the haiku after consultation with the Japanese text in MacKenzie, *Autumn Wind*, p. 104.
21. Nishida, *Intelligibility and the Philosophy of Nothingness*, p. 130.
22. Ibid., p. 133.
23. Ibid., p. 137.
24. Summarized in Chapter 2, below.

CHAPTER 2: IENAGA SABURŌ AND THE SEARCH
FOR MEANING IN MODERN JAPAN

This chapter was first published in Marius E. Jansen, ed., *Changing Japanese Attitudes Toward Modernization* (Princeton, N.J.: Princeton University Press, 1965), pp. 369–423. It was first presented at a conference in Bermuda in January 1962, at which Maruyama Masao and other Japanese and American scholars were present.

1. Ienaga, "Watakushi no dokusho henreki," in *Rekishi no kiki ni menshite*, p. 241
2. He would later write an important essay on Sōseki.
3. This was, of course, before the attack on Minobe's theories, which developed in the 1930s.
4. Ienaga, "Watakushi no dokusho henreki," in *Rekishi no kiki ni menshite*, pp. 240–41.
5. Ienaga, "Waga chojutsu to shisaku o kataru," in *Rekishi no kiki ni menshite*, pp. 231–32.
6. Ibid., p. 241. The book was first published by Iwanami in 1918.
7. Private communication, July 9, 1961. The date was 1932 or 1933.
8. Private conversation, 1961.
9. According to an article by Ienaga in *Shūkan dokusho*, May 5, 1961. In the preface, dated November 1941, of his *Jōdai Bukkyō shisōshi* (1942), later reissued more correctly as *Jodai Bukkyō shisōshi kenkyū*, he said he read the *Tannishō* "about ten years ago."
10. Ienaga, *Rekishi no kiki ni menshite*, p. 232.
11. Maruyama has said that Japan never had an "orthodoxy." This is true in the sense that what was ultimately sacred was always a system of social relations rather than a system of ideas. But the word "orthorelational" is too barbarous to use. See his *Nihon no shisō*.

12. Ienaga himself has pointed out (private conversation) that what most of the followers of Neo-Kantianism in Japan picked up was its cultural historical emphasis, not the theory of value, which interested him. Nevertheless one should perhaps be cautious in assigning German Idealism or the Kyoto school to the category of "establishment" philosophy. Actually one might make out a case for inner breakdown of "orthodox" philosophy in modern Japan from Inoue Tetsujirō to Nishida Kitarō to Tanabe Hajime along lines quite analogous to that described by Maruyama for Tokugawa orthodox thought (see his *Nihon no shisō*). The process involves the differentiation of previously undifferentiated elements in which the distinction between social order and moral order is central in both cases, though of course in quite different ways.

13. Minobe's theories clearly had no revolutionary meaning for Ienaga when he first read them. They were attacked as being out of keeping with the *kokutai* in 1935 approximately twenty-five years after they had originally been enunciated. Part of the reason for this is that the *kokutai* notion itself was changing. The ultranationalism of the 1930s may in a sense have been "implied" in the Meiji family-state notion but it was not there in all its virulence. On the special characteristics of this ultranationalism, see Maruyama, "Chōkokkashugi no ronri to shinri," pp. 7–24. This essay has been translated by Morris as "Theory and Psychology of Ultra-Nationalism."

14. Ienaga, "Watakushi no shojo shuppan," in *Rekishi no kiki ni menshite*, p. 235. The incident occurred in the summer of 1937.

15. This paragraph is based on Ienaga's article in *Shūkan dokushojin*, July 15, 1961.

16. On the basis of the preface to *Jōdai Bukkyō shisōshi kenkyū* mentioned above, it is probable that the thought of Shinran also became central at this time. He says that it was the reading of the *Tannishō* (which undoubtedly first occurred in higher school) that drew his interest to the practice and thought of Buddhism and determined his scholarly interest in this field.

17. Although I believe there were Christian elements directly or indirectly in the background, for reasons that will become clear later.

18. A number of elements in Ienaga's early experience are not unrelated to some of those described for postwar Japanese youth by Robert Jay Lifton in his article "Youth and History," pp. 172–97.

19. The major books are *Nihon shisōshi ni okeru hitei no ronri no hattatsu* (The development of the logic of negation in the history of Japanese thought) (1940) ; *Jōdai Bukkyō shisōshi kenkyū* (Studies in ancient Buddhist thought) (1942) ; *Nihon shisōshi ni okeru shūkyōteki shizenkan no tenkai* (The development of the religious view of nature in the history of Japanese thought) (1944) ; and *Chūsei Bukkyō shisōshi kenkyū* (Studies in medieval Buddhist thought) (1947, enlarged edition 1955). In the same period he published several works on ancient Japanese painting (of which the most important was *Yamatoe zenshi*, published in 1946) but these fall outside the central concern of this chapter.

20. The last quote in the book (p. 116) is from Nishida Kitarō's *Tetsugaku no kompon mondai*, p. 90, where he is cited as saying that for a new philosophy of

negation "there must be a basic change in logic." See also Tanabe, *Tetsugaku tsūron* (1933), ch. 2, sec. 8, pp. 170–236, for a discussion of dialectical method in which many of the terms in Ienaga's book appear.

21. Here Ienaga attributes to Shōtoku Taishi the same series of differentiations—of morality from social system and religion from morality—that we posited he experienced in his own development.

22. Elsewhere Ienaga asserts the essential similarity of the views of Paul and Shinran, See "Nihon Bukkyō no kongo no seimei," in *Chūsei Bukkyō shisōshi kenkyū,* p. 229. Other aspects of Ienaga's evaluation of Christianity will appear below.

23. Ienaga, *Nihon shisōshi ni okeru hitei no ronri no hattatsu,* p. 108.

24. In the above, highly condensed summary I have tried to maintain as much of the flavor of the original as possible and many phrases are direct translations.

25. I shall discuss below other elements in the Japanese tradition that receive positive evaluation from Ienaga in his work after the war, but these do not include Shinto, Confucianism, the *kokutai,* or even any of the schools of Buddhism except those in the Pure Land tradition.

26. If there is a third hero for Ienaga, taking the whole of his work and not just this one book, it would probably be Uchimura Kanzō.

27. Arima, *Failure of Freedom,* p. 16.

28. The former book deals with aspects of the thought of Shōtoku Taishi (including his Pure Land thought) and of Nara and Heian Buddhism. The latter book is especially interesting in that it presents a new way of thinking about Kamakura Buddhism. Ienaga vigorously opposes the tendency to view Hōnen, Shinran, Nichiren, and Dōgen as simply parallel "great religious leaders" without carefully analyzing the relations between them and their different positions relative to earlier Japanese Buddhism. Ienaga reserves the notion of Kamakura Buddhism as a "new" Buddhism exclusively to the Pure Land tradition. For him Hōnen represents a drastic break with previous tradition—a rejection of the earlier eclecticism and the formulation of a powerful and radical religious insight. This is carried to thorough completion in Shinran with his "absolute faith alone" position. But the various "old" Buddhist sects did not simply remain passive or merely react with a negative persecution of the "new" Buddhism, though they attempted the latter. They instituted a series of reforms and doctrinal innovations in every case, Ienaga argues, *derived from the influence of the "new" Buddhism* but with the aim of combating it. There were such movements not only within Tendai and Shingon but also in the Nara sects, which were more vigorous by far in the Kamakura period than they had been since ancient times or ever were again. This even included a revival in the Ritsu (Precepts) sect and an outburst of enthusiasm for adhering to the Hinayana rules for monks. Nichiren is treated as the most powerful of these "counter-reformation" leaders, but one so deeply influenced by the new Buddhism that he actually breaks out of the forms of the old, even of the Tendai, which he so dearly loved. But, while attaining many of the insights of the "new" Buddhism (even though derivatively, Ienaga feels) Nichiren was not "thorough." Many magical elements that

were purged by Shinran remain in his system, such as the magical use of prayer. Further, he continues the old *honjisuijaku* theory of the relation of the Buddhas and the Shinto deities, rather than radically eliminating any syncretism with Shinto as the Pure Land thinkers did. Ienaga traces the nationalistic and contentious spirit of Nichiren to this lack of thoroughness even though he does not deny to Nichiren a real participation in the universalism of the "new" Buddhism.

Ienaga treats Kamakura Zen Buddhism and its greatest exponent Dōgen in somewhat different terms. However radical the new Kamakura Buddhism of Hōnen and Shinran was, it grew entirely out of the inner dialectic of *Japanese* Buddhism, as did of course the "counter-reformation" movements that defined themselves relative to it. Zen, by contrast, in Kamakura times was something absolutely out of the blue. It was the latest import from China without roots or historical relevance to the Japanese situation. Nonetheless, once entering the Japanese scene, it could not but be influenced by it. Ienaga contrasts the eclecticism of Eisai for whom Zen was perhaps merely one more embellishment in his stock of Esoteric practices to the single-mindedness of Dōgen for whom *zazen* (Zen meditation) became the only way. In this latter point Ienaga sees the influence of the new Buddhism on Dōgen (and cites texts to prove it). But for Ienaga Zen lacks thoroughness since *zazen* must after all be practiced in the meditation hall and not in the midst of the actualities of life. While highly appreciating Dōgen (whom he likes much more than Nichiren, I feel) he must conclude that there remains about him a monkish smell when compared with Shinran.

It remains to be seen to what extent future research will validate this scheme, but it illustrates the suggestive power of Ienaga's scholarship in bringing a new level of order to a great deal of complex material and thus suggesting the directions that future research can most fruitfully take.

29. Published together with three other essays in the book that bears the same title in 1944.

30. See Arima, *Failure of Freedom*, passim.

31. Ienaga, *Shūtkyōteki shizenkan no tenkai*, pp. 4–6.

32. Unlike the logic of negation, the religious view of nature is treated as being unique in its Japanese form. In the last analysis, however, this for Ienaga is perhaps more of a liability than an asset.

33. Ienaga, *Shūtkyōteki shizenkan no tenkai*, pp. 20ff.

34. Ibid., pp. 48ff.

35. Ibid., pp. 60–61.

36. Ibid., pp. 43–47, 74–78. The complexities of Ienaga's argument are only suggested here.

37. Ibid., p. 80.

38. Ibid., p. 85.

39. Ibid., p. 84.

40. Ibid.

41. Ibid., pp. 87–88.

42. Ibid., p. 88.

43. Ibid., pp. 89–90.

44. Ienaga, "Shisōka to shite no Natsume Sōseki, narabi ni sono shiteki ichi," in *Nihon shisōshi ni okeru shūkyōteki shizenkan no tenkai*, pp. 149–221.

45. Ibid., p. 158.

46. Ibid., n. 3, pp. 198–99, 220.

47. Ibid., p. 162.

48. Ibid., p. 197. It will be remembered that in *The Logic of Negation* Ienaga had said that the suffering that can be solved by sudden enlightenment is not real suffering.

49. Ibid., pp. 175–83. Once again the subtleties of Ienaga's argument suffer from the extreme compression of the summary.

50. Ibid., p. 186.

51. For this translation I am indebted to Valdo Viglielmo's *The Later Natsume Sōseki*, p. 12; also in that work, see p. 212.

52. Ibid., p. 220.

53. In "The Future of Japanese Buddhism" (in *Chūsei Bukkyō shisōshi kenkyū*, expanded edition, 1955) Ienaga makes his criticism of Christianity only after the most extensive demolition job of religious self-criticism the writer has seen outside of the Christian West. Not only does almost every aspect of traditional Buddhism go down the drain, but Amida and the Pure Land itself are found to be meaningless in the present age (p. 230). Only the recognition of human sinfulness and the understanding that salvation can come in no other way than through that recognition remain. It is at this point that Ienaga turns to Christianity to note that its apprehension of the same truth is blurred by its own mythical forms and its theism. Actually Ienaga is only pointing to something of which a number of contemporary Christian theologians are aware, Rudolph Bultmann and Paul Tillich being examples. In conversation with Ienaga I questioned him about his use of Christian references to explain the thought of Shinran. He said that he had been criticized for this but that he felt this was perfectly defensible and that in fact in the modern period Shinran had become understood only after the impact of Christian theology—in Tokugawa times Nembutsu thought had been understood only magically. Ienaga's criticism of Christian theism in this conversation (1961) was, as I understand it, as follows: Theism makes an illegitimate initial affirmation that does not arise out of the experience of absolute negation and may actually prevent the attainment of that experience. Ienaga also discusses Christianity in a long essay on Buddhist-Christian controversy in Japan ("Waga kuni ni okeru Bukki ryōkyō ronsō no tetsugakushiteki kōsatsu," in *Chūsei Bukkyō shisōshi kenkyū*, pp. 111–80) in the last section of which he discusses views of Tanabe Hajime, which are probably not far from his own.

54. From the preface to *Nihon kindai shisōshi kenkyū* (1953) dated September 30, 1953. The article referred to in the first paragraph above, "Kinsei ni okeru hanfukkoshugi shichō," was reprinted in *Nihon shisōshi ni okeru shūkyōteki shizenkan no tenkai*, pp. 122–47. One result of his wartime labors was his *Essay on the History of the Reception of Foreign Culture* (*Gairai bunka*

*sesshushi ron*) subtitled, "An Intellectual Historical Investigation into the Reception of Modern Western Culture." In the preface to this book he says that he began the research for it around the beginning of 1942 and completed the manuscript in March 1945. Due to difficulties in obtaining materials at that time, illness, and the external pressures of the atmosphere, Ienaga states that he is not entirely satisfied with this work (preface, pp. 3–4). It consists largely of copious quotations illustrating various reactions of Tokugawa and early Meiji figures to foreign culture. There is also a section devoted to the earlier reception of Buddhism and Chinese culture.

55. Personal communication, July 9, 1961.

56. Ienaga, *Rekishi no kiki ni menshite*, pp. 233–34.

57. In his most recent, as yet unpublished, work he is turning to a consideration of the thought of "Taishō Democracy." He has published a few brief studies on Tokugawa thinkers (most of which appear in *Nihon kindai shisōshi kenkyū*) and a number of brief complete histories of Japan, but his monographic publications since the war are exclusively on Meiji figures.

58. Ienaga, *Rekishi no kiki ni menshite*, p. 234. Also personal communication of July 9, 1961. In this respect Ienaga probably stood close to the position of Tsuda Sōkichi, whom he quotes as saying not long after the war that the absolute uniformity of all that he reads and hears reminds him of the absolute uniformity of what he read and heard during the war and makes him think that the situation in Japan has not changed. ("Tsuda shigaku no shisōshiteki kōsatsu," in *Nihon no kindai shigaku*, p. 154. This article was first published in June 1953.) At the time he published this article, however, Ienaga was already critical of this attitude in Tsuda and presumably in his own past.

59. Ibid., and personal communication of July 9, 1961.

60. Ienaga, "Atarashii shisōshi no kōsō," in *Kokumin no rekishi*, 2:14–18.

61. Ienaga, "Nihon shisōshigaku no kako to shōrai," in *Nihon shisōshi no shomondai*, pp. 149–239.

62. Ienaga, "Shisōshigaku no tachiba," in *Nihon no kindai shigaku*, pp. 24–44.

63. Ibid., p. 29.

64. Ibid., pp. 32–33.

65. Ibid., p. 40.

66. Ibid., pp. 41–44.

67. "Bunkashi to bunka isan no mondai," in ibid., p. 15.

68. Personal communication, July 9, 1961.

69. Ienaga, *Kindai seishin to sono genkai*, p. 9.

70. Ibid., pp. 173–74.

71. Ibid., pp. 202–3.

72. Ibid., pp. 204–5.

73. Ibid., pp. 60–84.

74. Ibid., pp. 60–64.

75. Ibid., pp. 65–67. Maruyama Masao has argued what seems to be the opposite position, namely that there was no sphere of *private* morality in tradi-

tional Japanese thinking (*Gendai seiji no shisō to kōdō,* 1:11–12). This, however, does not seem to be a real contradiction for what both Uchimura and Maruyama are pointing to is the *undifferentiated* nature of the traditional point of view. This becomes clear when we take the concrete example of the "family-state concept" described by Ishida Takeshi (*Meiji Political Thought*). From Uchimura's point of view this is a pervasively private concept that leaves no room for a universalistic public ethic. From Maruyama's point of view it is a pervasively public morality that allows no moral legitimacy to the private sphere. These are two sides of the same coin.

76. Ibid., pp. 69–73.

77. Ibid., pp. 73–79.

78. Ibid., pp. 79–86.

79. Ibid., pp. 86–117.

80. Ibid., p. 103.

81. Ibid., p. 112.

82. Ibid., p. 114.

83. Ibid., p. 130.

84. Ibid., p. 136. Ienaga highly appreciates Uchimura's views on religion, starting from the point that this world is not its own end but exists for the sake of eternity. But also he notes the fact that Uchimura was as critical of the church as anything else. He quotes Uchimura as saying, "Heresy, heresy, they say. But truly there is nothing as honorable in the world as heresy. just because there is heresy in the world there is progress. The prophets were heretics. Jesus was a heretic. Paul was a heretic. Luther was a heretic" (p. 110). Similarly Uchimura was no biblical fundamentalist. He wrote, "I do not say this is the truth because it is in the Bible. I say it is the truth because it is the truth. I study the Bible. I don't blindly follow the Bible" (p. 123). Ienaga also emphasizes the positive side of Uchimura's doctrine of "no church," namely, that all mankind is the church. He notes Uchimura's openness to other religions, and cites these interesting words of Uchimura: "My friends are Hōnen rather than Wesley, Shinran rather than Moody. Those of the same religion do not necessarily have the same direction of faith. The heart with which I turn to Jesus is like the heart with which Hōnen and Shinran relied on Amida. It is not like the heart with which English and Americans believe in Christ" (p. 123).

85. Ibid., pp. 137–66. Ienaga returns to this theme in the essay "Historical Reflections on Anti-Modernism," in *Nihon kindai shisōshi kenkyū,* where Uchimura is one of the prime examples, but this does not represent a revision of his earlier analysis.

86. Ibid., p. 166.

87. Ibid., p. 167.

88. The essay on Taguchi is an appreciation of his early contribution to an economic and social interpretation of history such as had already been hinted at in Fukuzawa. Kitamura Tōkoku, by contrast, occupies a position similar to that of Uchimura in Ienaga's view. He shared many of the antifeudal and liberal values of Fukuzawa (pp. 13–23), but like Uchimura he went beyond that to criti-

cize the utilitarian and nontranscendent side of the modern spirit itself (though Ienaga sees the self-criticism of the modern spirit as itself in a sense truly modern), also on the basis of a Christian position. One of his contributions somewhat different from Uchimura was his "romantic" spirit that stressed the emotional and expressive side of human life and opposed an exclusively intellectualist or scientific preoccupation (pp. 24–44). Ienaga's final estimate is as follows: "Even though he cannot escape the criticism that he was weak in the power of judging social reality and, fleeing to the world of art, lost a broad social view, nevertheless not only did he fulfill a historical mission in giving an important spiritual backing to one side of the development of modern society, but he left behind an eternally imperishable heritage in grasping the essence of the human condition" (p. 45). Kitamura came to his understanding of life through his own suffering and discovered its essence to be suffering. Since he thought that the true meaning of human life was in suffering itself, he rejected "enlightenment" (*gedatsu, satori*) as an escape from the truth (pp. 46–48). Here we see a close approximation to "the logic of negation," though Ienaga does not use the term. Through Kitamura Ienaga even seems to be repeating his old antipathy to a Zen-type mysticism.

89. Ienaga, *Ueki Emori kenkyū*, pp. 401–3.

90. Ienaga, *Shin Nihonshi*, pp. 306–7.

91. Ienaga, *Rekishi no kiki ni menshite*, p. 234.

92. Reprinted in Ienaga, *Rekishi no kiki ni menshite*, p. 115.

93. Besides these he published a high school textbook, *Shin Nihonshi* (I have the fourth printing of 1961 and have not been able to ascertain the date of the first edition. From the following book, which is a supplement to the *Shin Nihonshi* for more advanced students, I surmise the date to be 1949 or 1950), *Shinkokushi gaisetsu* (1950), *History of Japan* (in English, Tourist Library Series, 1953, but too condensed to be very revealing about Ienaga), and *Kokumin no Nihonshi* (1959, a revised edition of *Shin Nihonshi* not for textbook use).

94. In this respect the *Nihon dōtoku shisōshi* is reminiscent of the great work of Tsuda Sōkichi, to whom Ienaga acknowledges a significant debt (p. 276).

95. First in the article on Ueki's thought in *Nihon kindai shisōshi kenkyū* (1953), then in the small Iwanami Shinsho volume on him called *A Pioneer of Revolutionary Thought* (Kakumei shisō no senkusha, 1955) and finally in the compendious *Ueki Emori kenkyū* (1960), 792 pp.

96. This was my initial impression.

97. Ienaga, *Sūki naru shisōka no shōgai*.

98. Ibid., p. 192.

99. Ienaga, *Ueki Emori kenkyū*, pp. 396–403. In a note (p. 406) he points out the parallel lack of self-criticism in the Japanese communist militants up to 1955. It is clear that Ienaga would see in the recognition of Stalin's evil the beginning of wisdom.

100. Ibid., p. 403.

101. Arima, *Failure of Freedom*.

CHAPTER 3: JAPAN'S CULTURAL IDENTITY

This essay was first published in the *Journal of Asian Studies* 24, no. 4 (1965): 573–94.

1. DeVos, "Role Narcissism."
2. See Keene, "Hirata Atsutane and Western Learning," 353–80.
3. Tsunoda, de Bary, and Keene , *Sources of the Japanese Tradition*, p. 596.
4. Nakamura, *Ways of Thinking of Eastern Peoples*, ch. 35.
5. This is a point that has been stressed by Maruyama Masao. See his *Nihon no Shisō* (Japanese thought).
6. The interpretation of Fukuzawa and Uchimura owes much to conversations with Maruyama Masao and Ishida Takeshi, as well as to Ienaga Saburō's *Kindai Seishin to Sono Genkai* (The modern spirit and its limitations).
7. See Ishida, *Meiji Seiji Shisōshi Kenkyū* (Studies in the history of Meiji political thought).
8. For a stimulating treatment of several aspects of Japanese fascism, see Maruyama, *Thought and Behavior in Modern Japanese Politics*.
9. Blacker, *Japanese Enlightenment*, ch. 7.
10. Inoue, *Chokugo Engi* (Commentary on the rescript). His *Waga Kokutai to Kokumin Dōtoku* (Our *kokutai* and national morality) was prescribed for use in the public schools by the Ministry of Education in the prewar period.
11. These works on the Yōmei, Shushi, and Kogaku schools of Confucianism were published in 1897, 1915, and 1918, respectively, by Fuzambō. Armstrong, *Light from the East*, is based largely on Inoue.
12. *Nishida Kitarō Zenshū*, 12:271, as cited in Arima, *Failure of Freedom*.
13. These matters are discussed in volume 1 (1915) and volume 11 (1917) of Tsuda's *Bungaku ni Arawaretaru Waga Kokumin Shisō no Kenkyū* (A study of our national thought as expressed in literature).
14. Tsuda, *Shina Shisō to Nihon* (Chinese thought and Japan).
15. A representative work of Hani Gorō is *Nihon ni okeru Kindai Shisō no Zentei* (Precursors of modern thought in Japan).
16. On Ienaga, see Chapter 2, above.
17. Representative works of Muraoka include *Motoori Norinaga* and *Nihon Shisōshi Kenkyū* (Studies in the history of Japanese thought). A selection of his essays has recently been translated by Delmer Brown for the Japanese UNESCO series.
18. Biographical material on Watsuji has been drawn from his own writings, from the introductory notes to various volumes of the Watsuji Tetsurō *Zenshū*, and the article on Watsuji by Shida Shōzō in the *Asahi Journal* 5, no. 5 (1963).
19. *Nietzsche Kenkyū*; *Zenshū*, vol. 1. *Soren Kierkegaard*; *Zenshū*, vol. 1.
20. *Nihon Kodai Bunka* (Ancient Japanese culture);. *Zenshū*, vol. 3. *Genshi Bukkyō no Jissen Tetsugaku* (The practical philosophy of primitive Buddhism); *Zenshū*, vol. 5. *Koji Junrei* (Pilgrimages to ancient temples); *Zenshū*, vol. 2. Also *Nihon Seishinshi Kenkyū* and *Zoku Nihon Seishinshi Kenkyū* (Studies in

Japanese spiritual history); *Zenshū*, vol. 4, contain material on Buddhist as well as non-Buddhist aspects of ancient and medieval Japanese culture. *Polis-teki Ningen no Rinrigaku* (Ethics of the polis); *Zenshū*, vol. 7. (Parts of this appeared serially as early as 1936.) *Genshi Kirisutokyō no Bunkashi-teki Igi* (The significance of primitive Christianity in the history of culture); *Zenshū*, vol. 7.

21. *Confucius; Zenshū*, vol. 6.

22. *Nihon no Shindō; Amerika no Kokuminsei, Chikuma Shobō*, 1944. *Nihon no Shindō* is in vol. 14 of the *Zenshū; Amerika no Kokuminsei* in vol. 17.

23. Benedict, *Chrysanthemum and the Sword*. Incidentally the influence of Nietzsche and Dilthey lies behind both Benedict and Watsuji.

24. This would mean not a criticism of the war itself but of the direction of the war by the army bureaucrats who were probably seen by Watsuji as acting too much for themselves and not enough for the emperor. The *"shin"* in *"Nihon no Shindō"* is difficult to translate. While it means "subject" relative to the ruler, it implies "vassal" or "retainer" rather than common people. "Shindō" could therefore in the present context be translated "Way of the Officer" as well as "Way of the Subject."

25. Already in *Nihon Kodai Bunka* he had developed this position. He criticized Motoori's absolute irrational faith in Shinto myth and argued for the continuous philosophical reinterpretation of myth, only emperor worship (or reverence) remaining constant. See the discussion of faith and myth, *Nihon Kodai Bunka, Zenshū*, 3:260–79.

26. *Rinrigaku*, vol. 1, 1937; vol. 2, 1942; and vol. 3, 1949; *Zenshū*, vols. 10 and 11.

27. Watsuji discusses religious organization in *Rinrigaku*, pt. 3, ch. 6; the state in pt. 3, ch. 7; *Zenshū*, 10:519–625.

28. Shaw, *Man of Destiny*, 2:212–13.

29. For a discussion of Spengler's terminology and its context in German thought, see Kroeber and Kluckhohn, *Culture*, esp. p. 26.

30. *Zenshū*, 7:10–14.

31. Watsuji, *Nihon Seishinshi Kenkyū*, pp. 3–38.

32. See Watsuji, *Ningen no Gaku to shite no Rinrigaku*.

33. Watsuji, *Zoku Nihon Seishinshi Kenkyū*, pp. 338–83.

34. Various terms used at different times to denote "Japanese spirit."

35. Watsuji, *Zoku Nihon Seishinshi Kenkyū*, pp. 1–72.

36. Watsuji, "Bunkateki Sōzō ni Tazusawaru mono no Tachiba," first published in *Shisō*, October 1937, then reprinted in a collection of Watsuji's occasional writings, *Men to Persona*, published by Iwanami in December 1937; *Zenshū*, 17:441–44.

37. See Takeuchi, "Kindai no Chōkoku" in *Kindai Nihon Shisōshi Kōza* (Symposium on the history of modern Japanese thought), 7:227–81.

38. *Zenshū*, vol. 13.

39. Watsuji, *Gūzō Saikō* (Resurrection of idols), pp. 12–13.

40. *Zenshū*, 13:456.

41. Ibid., 1:8.

42. Ibid., 1:410.

43. Watsuji, *Gūzō Saikō*, p. 13.

44. Ibid., pp. 237ff.

45. For example, DeVos, "Relation of Guilt Toward Parents," pp. 287–331; Vogel, *Japan's New Middle Class.*

46. See Watsuji, *Nihon Kodai Bunka.*

47. One of Watsuji's Marxist critics, Tosaka Jun, found him especially dangerous just because he expressed "reactionary Japanism" in "a la mode, modern, chic scholarly methods." Tosaka, *Nihon Ideorogii-ron* (An essay on Japanese ideology).

48. *Fūdo* was first published in book form in 1935, though parts of it had appeared earlier in periodicals. In 1943 a revised edition was published that eliminated "traces of Leftist theory" that were "prevalent" in 1928 when the book was first written, according to Watsuji's preface to that edition. *Zenshū*, vol. 8. It was translated by Geoffrey Bownas for the Japanese UNESCO series and appeared in 1961 under the awkward title, *A Climate*, although it is clear from Bownas's preface that his own suggested title was the much more felicitous *Climate and Culture.*

49. This sort of thing called forth some sarcastic comments from Tosaka Jun as to the inherent superiority of the Japanese language to any other in intuitively expressing the truth (Tosaka, *Nihon Ideorogii-ron*).

50. Maruyama Masao's term. See his *Thought and Behavior in Modern Japanese Politics*, pp. 63 and 304.

51. Watsuji, *Sakoku: Nihon no Higeki* (The closing of the country: Japan's tragedy); *Zenshū*, 15:3.

52. Watsuji, *Nihon Rinri Shisōshi* (History of Japanese ethical thought), 2:695–793, *Zenshū*, vols. 12 and 13.

53. The appendix to vol. 2 of the *Zenshū* contains the major passages cut from the 1942 edition.

54. See the article on Watsuji by Shida Shōzō in the *Asahi Journal* 5, no. 5 (1963): 42.

55. The theoretical assumptions and terminology used in this paragraph are explained at greater length in Bellah, "Religious Evolution," pp. 358–74.

56. Abegglen, *Japanese Factory*; Vogel, *Japan's New Middle Class.*

CHAPTER 4: NOTES ON MARUYAMA MASAO

This review of *Studies in the Intellectual History of Tokugawa Japan* by Masao Maruyama (translated by Mikiso Hane) (Tokyo and Princeton, N.J.: University of Tokyo Press and Princeton University Press, 1974), was published in the *Journal of Japanese Studies* 1, no. 3 (1977): 177–83.

1. This remembrance of Maruyama was written for an issue of *Misuzu* (no. 427 [October 1996]: 11–13) devoted to his memory. I am indebted to the work of Andrew Barshay for some of my comments in this article.

CHAPTER 5: INTELLECTUAL AND SOCIETY IN JAPAN

This article was first published as "Intellectuals and Tradition," in *Daedalus* 101, no. 2 (spring 1972): 89–115. It was originally presented as a paper at a conference on intellectuals and tradition in Jerusalem in March 1971, sponsored by the Jerusalem Van Leer Foundation and organized by S. N. Eisenstadt.

1. On the relation between order in society and order in the soul in Plato, see Voegelin, *Order and History, III: Plato and Aristotle*, pt. 1.

2. I have relied on the paraphrase and commentary of Muraoka Tsunetsugu in his "Kenpō Jūshichi-ken no Kenkyū" (A study of the Seventeen-Article Constitution), pp. 7–71. A translation of the constitution can be found in Tsunoda, de Bary, and Keene, *Sources*, pp. 50–53.

3. Even J. H. Kamstra, in his *Encounter or Syncretism*, accepts the authenticity of this saying, pp. 379–81. Kamstra offers an extreme demythologization of Shōtoku and goes further in this direction than any Japanese scholar. For a reasoned defense of the authenticity of most of the texts attributed to Shōtoku, see Futaba, *Kodai Bukkyō Shisōshi Kenkyū* (A study of the history of ancient Buddhist thought).

4. Nakamura, *A History of the Development of Japanese Thought*, I:142.

5. McEwan, *Ogyū Sorai*, p. 33.

6. Dore's *Education in Tokugawa Japan* is an excellent description of scholarship and education in the Tokugawa period, and I have relied on it extensively in this section.

7. Ibid., pp. 317–22. I have given a summary figure where Dore gives a cautious series of estimates based on school attendance.

8. Hall, "Ikeda Mitsumasa and the Bizen Flood of 1654," pp. 65–66.

9. On the central significance of Sorai in Tokugawa thought, see above all the very influential book of Maruyama, *Nihon Seiji Shisōshi Kenkyū* (Studies in the history of Japanese political thought). This book has influenced not only my treatment of Sorai but my entire treatment of Tokugawa thought.

10. McEwan, *Ogyū Sorai*, p. 9. The three paragraphs are independent passages from different places in Sorai's writings and are not continuous.

11. We now have in English an excellent book on Norinaga, perhaps the best book on any premodern Japanese thinker: Matsumoto, *Motoori Norinaga*. Maruyama, *Nihon Seiji Shisōshi Kenkyū*, treats the relation between Sorai and Norinaga in ch. 1, sec 4.

12. Matsumoto, *Motoori Norinaga*, p. 32.

13. On Kokugaku at the end of the Tokugawa period and its influence among the upper stratum of peasants, see Sonoda, "Bakumatsu Kokugaku no Shisōshi-teki Mondai" (Problems in the history of Kokugaku thought at the end of the Tokugawa period), pp. 1–31.

14. See Matsumoto, *Motoori Norinaga*, esp. ch. 2 and conclusion. In the contrast between Sorai and Norinaga we already have the contrast between the bureaucratic model and the *Gemeinschaft* model of Japanese society, which will be discussed below.

15. On late Tokugawa political thought, see Harootunian, *Toward Restoration*.

16. For my knowledge of Yamagata Daini, I am indebted to Tetsuo Najita for his paper "Restorationism in the Political Thought of Yamagata Daini (1725–1767)," presented at the colloquium of the Center for Japanese and Korean Studies, University of California, Berkeley, December 2, 1970. His series of papers on the restorationist strand in Japanese thought, others of which will be cited below, have influenced my whole conception of the relation between thought and action in Japan.

17. Najita, "Oshio Heihachirō ( 1793–1837)," pp. 155–79.

18. Bellah, *Tokugawa Religion*, ch. 6 and appendix 1.

19. On these movements, see Yasumaru, "Nihon no Kindaika to Minshū Shisō" (Japanese modernization and popular thought), no. 78, pp. 1–10; no. 79, pp. 40–58. Yasumaru is rather critical of my argument in *Tokugawa Religion*, feeling that I attempt to explain too much with a notion of "traditional values" and ignore the particular historical circumstances of the various movements. Though there are important theoretical differences between us this article is an important supplement to my book.

20. Nakane, *Japanese Society*, is a somewhat revised translation of *Tate-Shakai no Ningen-kankei—Tanitsu Shakai no Riron* (Human relations in a vertical society—A theory of homogeneous society).

21. Fukuzawa, *Encouragement of Learning*, p. 1.

22. Ibid., p. 2.

23. Ibid., p. 23.

24. Irokawa, *Zōhō Meiji Seishinshi* (A history of Meiji consciousness). See also his *Meiji no Bunka* (Meiji culture); and *Minshū Kempō no sōzō* (Creation of a popular constitution). The latter contains drafts of constitutions drawn up in the local areas in the 1870s and 1880s. I have profited from several conversations with Professor Irokawa during his stay in Berkeley in January and February of 1971.

25. Craig, "Fukuzawa Yukichi," p. 117.

26. Ibid., pp. 133, 134–35.

27. Scheiner, *Christian Converts*, esp. ch. 8, "Loyalty and Criticism."

28. Pyle, *New Generation in Meiji Japan*.

29. Kaji, "Introduction of French Political Ideas," p. 67.

30. See the collection of writings edited by Hidaka Rokurō, *Kindai-shugi* (Modernism). This collection features such writers as Otsuka Hisao and Maruyama Masao. For a vigorous if somewhat wide of the mark attack on this school, see Irokawa, *Meiji no Bunka*, ch. 8, "Seishin kōzō to shite Tennōsei" (The emperor system as a spiritual structure). Irokawa accuses the modernists of elitism in their critique of Japanese *Gemeinschaft*.

31. Wray has an interesting discussion of the left-wing socialist Asō Hisashi in this context in his "Asō Hisashi and the Search for Renovation in the 1930's," pp. 55–99. The right-wing socialist Abe Isō took up the slogan of "a second restoration" in the period 1929–30. See Tsunoda, de Bary, and Keene, *Sources*, pp. 816–20.

32. Nishida Kitarō spoke of the imperial house as the "contradictory identity of subjective unity and the multiplicity of individuals." Quoted by Ueyama, *Kindai Nihon Shisōshi Kōza* (Symposium on the history of modern Japanese thought), 4:80. Nishida argued, "It was neither the whole opposing the individual nor the individual opposing the whole, but rather that with the Imperial Household as the center, the individual and the whole mutually negate themselves." Quoted by Arima, *Failure of Freedom*, p. 11. Okakura Tenshin took a similar view. He always insisted on the aspects of harmony, oneness, and *advaita* as basic in Japanese culture and society. He said, "The true infinity is the circle, not the extended line. Every organism implies a subordination of parts to a whole. Real equality lies in the due fulfillment of the respective function of each part." Quoted by Maruyama, "Fukuzawa, Uchimura, and Okakura," p. 14.

33. Lois M. Greenwood, a graduate student at Berkeley, has underlined this aspect of Uchimura's behavior in a very interesting paper, "Uchimura Kanzō: A Study in Japanese Identity," unpublished.

34. Patricia Golden Steinhoff has discussed this aspect of *tenkō* in her 1969 Harvard doctoral dissertation on the subject.

35. Two suggestive efforts to account for the appeal of Marxism in modern Japan are that of Albert M. Craig in Fairbank, Reischauer, and Craig, *East Asia*, pp. 552–54; and Okada in the introduction to vol. 2, no. 1, of the *Journal of Social and Political Ideas in Japan*, devoted to the subject of Japanese Intellectuals, p. 4.

36. Wilson, *Radical Nationalist in Japan*, p. 69.

37. An extraordinarily interesting discussion of Nakano is to be found in Tetsuo Najita's unpublished paper, "Nakano Seigo and the Spirit of the Meiji Restoration in Twentieth Century Japan."

38. See the article that appeared just two months before his death: Mishima, "Kakumei no Tetsugaku to shite no Yōmeigaku" (Wang Yang-ming teaching as a revolutionary philosophy).

39. Kawabata, *Japan, the Beautiful, and Myself;* I have taken the liberty of altering Seidensticker's translation of the poem.

CHAPTER 6: THE JAPANESE EMPEROR
AS A MOTHER FIGURE

Shortly after I came to Berkeley in 1967 I gave this paper as a talk at a colloquium organized by the Center for Japanese and Korean Studies. The paper has subsequently been circulated privately and even cited by others, but this is its first publication.

CHAPTER 7. CONTINUITY AND CHANGE
IN JAPANESE SOCIETY

This essay was published in a volume in honor of Talcott Parsons, *Stability and*

*Social Change,* ed. Bernard Barber and Alex Inkeles (Boston: Little, Brown), 1971.

1. This article has been influenced by two recent books: *Japanese Society* by Ishida Takeshi of Tokyo University; and *Tate Shakai no Ningen Kankei* (Human relationships in a vertical society) by Nakane Chie, also of Tokyo University. Professor Nakane's book has been published in translation by the University of California Press under the title *Japanese Society.* Among many other books that might be mentioned one perhaps stands out: Maruyama Masao's *Nihon no Shishō* (Japanese thought). The title essay was published originally in 1957.
2. Tanizaki, *The Makioka Sisters;* and Murasaki, *The Tale of Genji.*
3. See Beardsley, "Japan Before History."
4. See Parsons, "Christianity and Modern Industrial Society"; Parsons, "Christianity"; and Parsons, *Societies.*
5. Bellah, *Tokugawa Religion,* chs. 1 and 2.
6. Huntsberry, "Religion and Value&nbhy;Formation in Japan."
7. Vogel, *Japan's New Middle Class.* The analysis of Nakane Chie (see n. 1, above) also confirms the continuation of the earlier pattern into the contemporary period.
8. Bellah, "Values and Social Change in Modern Japan," pp. 32–33.
9. Ibid., pp. 34–39.
10. On early Japanese social and political organization, see the extremely helpful book by Hall, *Government and Local Power in Japan, 500 to 1700.*
11. On this point, see Huntsberry, "Religion and Value&nbhy;Formation in Japan."
12. Ibid., p. 12.
13. Ibid., p. 13.
14. In "Nihon Bunka no Tokushitsu" (The characteristics of Japanese culture), p. 476. This article is actually an interview with Miki Kiyoshi and was published in Miki's collected works rather than of Nishida's. Its omission from the collected works of Nishida may be because its editors felt the words were not necessarily Nishida's or it may be that the nationalist sentiment in this interview, stronger than in most of Nishida's writings, was offensive to the editors. Maruyama, *Nihon no Shisō,* pp. 11ff.
15. Maruyama, *Nihon no Shisō,* pp. 2ff.
16. Nakane, *Tate Shakai no Ningen Kankei,* esp. chs. 3 and 4.
17. Ibid., pp. 49ff.
18. See Chapter 6, above, on the Japanese emperor as a mother&nbhy;figure. On the whole question of the feminine dimension of Japanese culture, see Huntsberry, "Religion and Value&nbhy;Formation in Japan"; and Matsumoto, *Motoori Norinaga.*
19. On the relation between family structure and achievement in Japan, see Kamishima Jirō, *Kindai Nihon no Seishin Kōzō* (The spiritual structure of modern Japan), pt. 3; and DeVos, "Relation of Guilt Toward Parents."
20. Ienaga, *Nihon Shisō&nbhy;shi ni okeru Shūkyōteki Shizenkan no*

234 / Notes to Pages 195–207

*Tenkai* (The development of the religious view of nature in the history of Japanese thought).

21. See the introduction to Miner, *Japanese Poetic Diaries*. Miner's suggestive treatment of poetic diaries has quite general implications for the place of the aesthetic in Japanese life.

22. See Seidensticker, *Kafū the Scribbler*, ch. 8.

23. S. N. Eisenstadt in a talk at the Institute of International Studies, University of California, Berkeley, in July 1969 emphasized the dominance of the nation-state model in most existing conceptions of modernization and the many ways in which non-Western polities differ from that model.

24. See Ishida, *Meiji Seiji Shisō-shi Kenkyū* (Studies in the history of Meiji political thought), pt. 1.

25. Maruyama, *Nihon no Shisō*, intro.

26. See Takeda, *Ningenkan no Sokoku* (Conflicting views of man), for the similarities and differences between Japanese traditional thought and Christianity as they appeared in the Meiji period.

27. Carlo Caldarola is making an extremely interesting study of the contemporary Nonchurch Christians in a doctoral dissertation in sociology at the University of California, now in progress.

28. Miki expounded his views in a number of books the most comprehensive and influential of which was *Kōsōryoku no Ronri* (The logic of the power of the imagination), vol. 8 of Miki *Kiyoshi Zenshū* (Collected works). This work was first published serially from 1937 to 1943. Miki died in prison in 1945 but has enjoyed a great postwar vogue.

29. A convenient summary of some of these issues in postwar thought can be found in Matsumoto Sannosuke's introduction to the August 1966 issue of the *Journal of Social and Political Ideas in Japan* 4, no. 2: 2–19.

30. Patricia Golden Steinhoff has treated these documents extensively in a 1969 doctoral dissertation on *tenkō* (recantation) submitted for a degree in sociology at Harvard University.

31. See Oda, "Meaning of 'Meaningless Death.'" This is a translation of an article that appeared in *Tenbō* (January 1965).

32. On this point, see Matsumoto, "Contemporary Japan"; and Ishida, *Gendai Soshiki-ron* (Contemporary organization theory).

33. See Ishida, *Japanese Society*, ch. 9.

34. See Matsumoto, Introduction. Takeuchi Yoshimi has been especially influential in applying this lesson of the Chinese Revolution to Japan.

# Bibliography

Abé, Ryūichi. 1999. *The Weaving of the Mantra: Kūkai and the Construction of Esoteric Buddhist Discourses*. New York: Columbia University Press.

Abegglen, James C. 1958. *The Japanese Factory*. Glencoe, Ill.: Free Press.

Arima, Tatsuo. 1969. *Failure of Freedom*. Cambridge, Mass.: Harvard University Press.

Armstrong, Robert Cornell. 1914. *Light from the East: Studies in Japanese Confucianism*. Toronto: University of Toronto Press.

Arnason, Johann P. 1998. Comparing Japan: The Return to Asia. *Japanstudien. Jahrbuch des Deutschen Instituts für Japanstudien der Philipp Franz von Siebold Stiftung*, Band 10.

——. 1997. *Social Theory and Japanese Experience: The Dual Civilization*. London: Kegan Paul International.

Barber, Bernard, and Alex Inkeles, eds. 1971. *Stability and Social Change*. Boston: Little, Brown.

Barshay, Andrew. Forthcoming. *The Social Sciences in Japan*.

——. 1989. The Problem of the Emperor System in Japanese Social Science. A paper prepared for the Regional Seminar of the Center for Japanese Studies at the University of California, Berkeley, on "Reflections on Tennosei: Culture, Politics and Japan's Emperor."

——. 1988. *State and Intellectual in Imperial Japan*. Berkeley and Los Angeles: University of California Press.

Beardsley, Richard K. 1955. Japan Before History. *Far Eastern Quarterly* 14, no. 3: 317–46.

Bellah, Robert N. 2001. Epilogue: Meaning and Modernity: America and the World. In *Meaning and Modernity*, ed. Richard Madsen et al. Berkeley and Los Angeles: University of California Press.

——. 1999. Max Weber and World-Denying Love: A Look at the Historical Sociology of Religion. *Journal of the American Academy of Religion* 67, no. 2: 277–304.

——. 1996. Maruyama Masao as Scholar and Friend. *Misuzu* 427: 11–13.

———. 1977. Review of Maruyama Masao. *Studies in the Intellectual History of Tokugawa Japan. Journal of Japanese Studies* 1, no. 3: 177–83.

———. [1970] 1991. *Beyond Belief: Essays on Religion in a Post-Traditional World*. Berkeley and Los Angeles: University of California Press.

———. 1967. Civil Religion in America. *Daedalus* 96, no. 1: 1–21

———. 1965. Ienaga Saburō and the Search for Meaning in Modern Japan. In *Changing Japanese Attitudes Toward Modernization*, ed. Marius Jansen, pp. 369–423. Princeton, N.J.: Princeton University Press.

———. 1964. Religious Evolution. *American Sociological Review* 29: 358–74.

———. 1962. Values and Social Change in Modern Japan. *Asian Cultural Studies* 3: 13–56.

———. 1957. *Tokugawa Religion*. Glencoe, Ill.: Free Press.

Benedict, Ruth. 1946. *The Chrysanthemum and the Sword*. Boston: Houghton Mifflin.

Bielefeldt, Carl W. 1972. *Shōbōgenzō-sansuikyō*. M.A. Thesis. University of California at Berkeley.

Blacker, Carmen. 1964. *The Japanese Enlightenment*. Oxford: Oxford University Press.

Bloom, Alfred. 1968. *The Life of Shinran Shōnin: The Journey to Self-Acceptance*. Leiden: Brill.

———. 1965. *Shinran's Gospel of Pure Grace*. The Association for Asian Studies: Monographs and Papers 20.

Blyth, R. H. 1952. *Haiku*, vol. I. Tokyo: Hokuseido.

Broadbent, Jeffrey. 1998. *Environmental Politics in Japan: Networks of Power and Protest*. Cambridge: Cambridge University Press.

Collins, Randall. 1999. *Macrohistory: Essays in Sociology in the Long Run*. Stanford, Calif.: Stanford University Press.

Conze, Edward. 1967. *Buddhist Thought in India*. Ann Arbor: University of Michigan Press.

Craig, Albert M. 1968. Fukuzawa Yukichi: The Philosophical Foundations of Meiji Nationalism. In *Political Development in Modern Japan*, ed. Robert E. Ward. Princeton, N.J.: Princeton University Press.

———. 1961. *Chūshū in the Meiji Restoration*. Cambridge, Mass.: Harvard University Press.

Craig, Albert M., John Fairbank, and Edwin Reischauer. 1965. *East Asia: The Great Transformation*. Boston: Houghton Mifflin.

Craig, Albert M., and Donald H. Shively, eds. 1970. *Personality in Japanese History*. Berkeley and Los Angeles: University of California Press.

Dale, Peter N. 1988. *The Myth of Japanese Uniqueness Revisited*. Nissan Occasional Papers.

———. 1986. *The Myth of Japanese Uniqueness*. London and Sydney: Croom, Held.

Davis, Winston. 1983. Pilgrimage and World Renewal: A Study of Religion and Social Values in Tokugawa Japan, Part 1. *History of Religions* 23, no. 2: 97–116; Part II, *History of Religions* 23, no. 3 (1984): 197–221.

DeVos, George. 1964. Role Narcissism and the Etiology of Japanese Suicide. Mimeo.

———. 1960. The Relation of Guilt Toward Parents to Achievement and Arranged Marriage Among the Japanese. *Psychiatry* 23, no. 3: 287–301.

Dōgen. 1971. *Bendowa.* Trans. Abe Masao and Norman Waddell. *The Eastern Buddhist* (New Series) 4, no. 1: 124–57.

Dore, R. P. 1965. *Education in Tokugawa Japan.* Berkeley and Los Angeles: University of California Press.

Dower, John W. 1999. *Embracing Defeat: Japan in the Wake of World War II.* New York: W. W. Norton.

———. 1990. The Useful War. *Daedalus* 119, no. 3: 49–70.

Eisenstadt, S. N. 2002. Mirror-Image Modernities: Contrasting Religious Premises of Japanese and U.S. Modernity. In *Meaning and Modernity: Religion, Polity, and Self,* ed. Madsen et al. Berkeley and Los Angeles: University of California Press

———. 2000. Trust and Institutional Dynamics in Japan: The Construction of Generalized Particularistic Trust. *Japanese Journal of Political Science* 1, no. 1: 53–72.

———. 1997. *Japanese Civilization.* Chicago: University of Chicago Press.

———. 1986. *The Origins and Diversity of Axial Age Civilizations.* Albany: State University of New York Press.

Elison, George. 1973. *Deus Destroyed.* Cambridge, Mass.: Harvard University Press.

Fairbank, John K., Edwin O. Reischauer, and Albert M. Craig. 1973. *East Asia: Tradition and Transformation.* Boston: Houghton Mifflin.

Field, Norma. 1991. *In the Realm of the Dying Emperor: A Portrait of Japan at Century's End.* New York: Pantheon.

Foard, James H. 1998. What One Kamakura Story Does: Practice, Place, and Text in the Account of Ippen at Kumano. In *Re-Visioning "Kamakura" Buddhism,* ed. Richard K. Payne. Honolulu: University of Hawaii Press.

Frank, Andre Gunder. 1998. *ReOrient: Global Economy in the Asian Age.* Berkeley and Los Angeles: University of California Press.

Fujitani, Takashi. 1996. *Splendid Monarchy: Power and Pageantry in Modern Japan.* Berkeley and Los Angeles: University of California Press.

Fukuzawa Yukichi. 1969. *An Encouragement of Learning.* Trans. David A. Dilworth and Umeyo Hirano. Tokyo: Sophia University Press.

Futaba Kenkō. 1962. *Kodai Bukkyō Shisōshi Kenkyū* (A study of the history of ancient Buddhist thought). Kyoto: Nagata Bunshōdō.

———. 1962. *Shinran no Kenkyū* (Shinran studies). Kyoto: Hyakkaen.

Garon, Sheldon. 1997. *Molding Japanese Minds: The State in Everyday Life.* Princeton, N.J.: Princeton University Press.

Gluck, Carol. 1985. *Japan's Modern Myths: Ideology in the Late Meiji Period.* Princeton, N.J.: Princeton University Press.

Grapard, Allan. 1992. *The Protocol of the Gods: A Study of the Kasuga Cult in Japanese History.* Berkeley and Los Angeles: University of California Press.

————. 1988. Institution, Ritual, and Ideology: The Twenty-Two Shrine-Temple Multiplexes of Heian Japan. *History of Religions* 22, no. 3: 246–69.

Groner, Paul. 2000. *Saichō: The Establishment of the Japanese Tendai School.* Honolulu: University of Hawaii Press.

Hakeda, Yoshito S. 1972. *Kūkai: Major Works Translated, with an Account of his Life and a Study of his Thought.* New York: Columbia University Press.

Hall, John Whitney. 1970. Ikeda Mitsumasa and the Bizen Flood of 1654. In *Personality in Japanese History,* ed. Albert M. Craig and Donald H. Shively. Berkeley and Los Angeles: University of California Press, A Publication of the Center for Japanese and Korean Studies.

————. 1966. *Government and Local Power in Japan, 500 to 1700.* Princeton, N.J.: Princeton University Press.

Hani Gorō. 1949. *Nihon ni okeru Kindai Shisō no Zentei* (Precursors of modern thought in Japan). Tokyo: Iwanami.

Hardacre, Helen. 1989. *Shinto and the State, 1868–1988.* Princeton, N.J.: Princeton University Press.

Harootunian, Harry. 2000. *History's Disquiet: Modernity, Cultural Practice, and the Question of Everyday Life.* New York: Columbia University Press.

————. 2000. *Overcome by Modernity: History, Culture, and Community in Interwar Japan.* Princeton, N.J.: Princeton University Press.

————. 1970. *Toward Restoration: The Growth of Political Consciousness in Tokugawa Japan.* Berkeley and Los Angeles: University of California Press.

Hidaka Rokurō, ed. 1964. *Gendai Nihon Shisō Taikei* (An outline of contemporary Japanese thought). Tokyo: Chikuma Shōbō.

————. 1964. *Kindai-shugi* (Modernism). Tokyo: Chikuma Shōbō.

Hobsbawm, Eric, and Terence Ranger, eds. 1983. *The Invention of Tradition.* Cambridge: Cambridge University Press.

Hoston, Germaine A. 1994. *The State, Identity, and the National Question in China and Japan.* Princeton, N.J.: Princeton University Press.

————. 1986. *Marxism and the Crisis of Development in Prewar Japan.* Princeton, N.J.: Princeton University Press.

Huntsberry, Randall. 1968. Religion and Value-Formation in Japan. Ph.D. dissertation in Comparative Religion. Harvard University.

Ienaga Saburō. 1977. *Nihon dōtoku shisōshi* (A history of Japanese ethical thought). Tokyo: Iwanami.

————. 1961. *Shin Nihonshi* (A new history of Japan). Tokyo: Sanseido.

————. 1960. *Ueki Emori kenkyū* (A study of Ueki Emori).

————. 1959. *Kokumin no Nihonshi* (A people's history of Japan). Tokyo: Bunichi Shuppan.

————. 1957. *Nihon no kindai shigaku* (The modern study of history in Japan).

————. 1955. *Kakumei shisō no senkusha* (A pioneer of revolutionary thought). Tokyo: Iwanami.

————. 1955. *Sūki naru shisōka no shōgai* (The checkered career of a thinker). Tokyo: Iwanami.

————. 1954. *Rekishi no kiki ni menshite* (Facing historical crisis).

————. 1953. *History of Japan.* Tokyo: Japan Tourist Library.

————. 1953. *Nihon kindai shisōshi kenkyū* (Studies in the history of modern thought). Tokyo: Tokyo Daigaku Shuppankai.

————. 1950. *Kindai Seishin to Sono Genkai* (The modern spirit and its limitations). Tokyo: Kadokawa.

————. 1950. *Shinkokushi gaisetsu* (An outline of a new national history).

————. 1948. Atarashii shisōshi no kōsō (The conception of a new history). *Kokumin no rekishi* 2, no. 9: 14–18.

————. 1948. *Gairai bunka sesshushi ron* (Essay on the history of the reception of foreign culture).

————. 1948. Nihon shisōshigaku no kako to shōrai (The past and future of the history of Japanese thought). In *Nihon shisōshi no shomondai*, pp. 149–239. Tokyo: Saito Shoten.

————. 1947. *Chūsei Bukkyō shisōshi kenkyū* (Studies in medieval Buddhist thought). Kyoto: Hozokan.

————. 1944. *Nihon Shisō-shi ni okeru Shūkyōteki Shizenkan no Tenkai* (The development of the religious view of nature in the history of Japanese thought). Tokyo: Sōgensha.

————. 1942. *Jōdai Bukkyō shisōshi kenkyū* (Studies in ancient Buddhist thought). Tokyo: Unebi Shobo.

————. 1940. *Nihon shisōshi ni okeru hitei no ronri no hattatsu* (The development of the logic of negation in the history of Japanese thought). Tokyo: Shinsensha.

Ikegami, Eiko. 1995. *The Taming of the Samurai: Honorific Individualism and the Making of Modern Japan.* Cambridge, Mass.: Harvard University Press.

Inden, Ronald B. 1990. *Imagining India.* Cambridge, Mass.: Blackwell.

Inoue Tetsujirō. 1925. *Waga Kokutai to Kokumin Dōtoku* (Our Kokutai and national morality). Tokyo: Kōbundō.

————. 1891. *Chokugo Engi* (Commentary on the rescript). Tokyo: Keigyōsha.

Irokawa Daikichi. 1970. *Meiji no Bunka* (Meiji culture). Tokyo: Iwanami.

————. 1970. *Minshū Kempō no sōzō* (Creation of a popular constitution). Tokyo: Hyōronsha.

————. 1968. *Zōhō Meiji Seishinshi* (A history of Meiji consciousness). Tokyo: Kōga Shobō.

Ishida Takeshi. 1989. The Emperor Problem in a Historical Perspective. In *The Emperor System as a Japan Problem: The Case of Meiji Gakuin University,* ed. Sakamoto Yoshikazu, pp. 47–56. International Peace Research Institute Meigaku, Occasional Papers Series Number 5.

————. 1971. *Japanese Society.* New York: Random House.

————. 1961. *Gendai Soshiki-ron* (Contemporary organization theory). Tokyo: Iwanami.

————. 1954. *Meiji Seiji Shisō-shi Kenkyū* (Studies in the history of Meiji political thought). Tokyo: Miraisha.

Jansen, Marius B. 2000. *The Making of Modern Japan.* Cambridge, Mass.: Harvard University Press.

Jaspers, Karl. 1953. *The Origin and Goal of History.* London: Routledge and Kegan Paul.

Johnson, Chalmers. 1982. *MITI and the Japanese Miracle: The Growth of Industrial Policy, 1925–1975.* Stanford, Calif.: Stanford University Press.

Kaji Ryūichi. 1966. The Introduction of French Political Ideas—Nakae Chomin: The Man and His Thought. *Philosophical Studies of Japan* 7: 53–71.

Kamishima Jirō. 1961. *Kindai Nihon no Seishin Kōzō* (The spiritual structure of modern Japan). Tokyo: Iwanami.

Kamstra, J. H. 1967. *Encounter or Syncretism: The Initial Growth of Japanese Buddhism.* Leiden: Brill.

Kasulis, Thomas P. Kūkai (774–835): Philosophizing in the Archaic. In *Myth and Philosophy,* ed. Frank E. Reynolds and David Tracy. Albany: State University of New York Press.

Katsumata Shizuo, and Martin Collcutt. 1981. The Development of Sengoku Law. In *Japan Before Tokugawa: Political Consolidation and Economic Growth, 1500–1650,* ed. John Whitney Hall, Nagahara Keiji, and Kozo Yamamura. Princeton, N.J.: Princeton University Press.

Kawabata Yasunari. 1969. *Japan, the Beautiful, and Myself.* Trans. E. G. Seidensticker. Tokyo: Kodansha.

Keene, Donald. 1969. *The Japanese Discovery of Europe, 1720–1830.* Stanford, Calif.: Stanford University Press.

———. 1954. Hirata Atsutane and Western Learning. *T'oung Pao* 42: 353–80.

Kluckhohn, Clyde, and Alfred L. Kroeber. 1952. *Culture: A Critical Review of Concepts and Definitions.* Papers of the Peabody Museum of American Archaeology and Ethnology, Harvard University, vol. 47, no. 1.

Kobayashi Issa. 1960. *Oraga Haru* (The year of my life). Trans. Nobuyuki Yuasa. Berkeley and Los Angeles: University of California Press.

Koschmann, J. Victor. 1996. *Revolution and Subjectivity in Postwar Japan.* Chicago: University of Chicago Press.

Lifton, Robert Jay. 1962. Youth and History: Individual Change in Postwar Japan. *Daedalus* 95, no. 1: 172–97.

Lipset, Seymour Martin. 1993. Pacific Divide: American Exceptionalism and Japanese Uniqueness. *International Journal of Public Opinion Research* 5, no. 2: 121–66.

MacKenzie, Lewis. 1957. *The Autumn Wind: A Selection from the Poems of Issa.* London: John Murray.

Madsen, Richard, William Sullivan, Ann Swidler, and Steven Tipton, eds. 2002. *Meaning and Modernity: Religion, Polity, and Self.* Berkeley and Los Angeles: University of California Press.

Maruyama Masao. 1988. The Structure of Matsurigoto: The *basso ostinato* of Japanese Political Life. In *Themes and Theories in Modern Japanese History,* ed. Sue Henny and Jean-Pierre Lehmann. London: Athlone Press.

———. 1974. *Studies in the Intellectual History of Tokugawa Japan.* Trans. Mikiso Hane. Princeton, N.J.: Princeton University Press.

———. 1966. Fukuzawa, Uchimura, and Okakura—Meiji Intellectuals and Westernization. *The Developing Economies* 4, no. 4: 594–611.

————. 1963. *Thought and Behavior in Modern Japanese Politics.* Oxford: Oxford University Press.

————. 1961. *Nihon no Shishō* (Japanese thought). Tokyo: Iwanami.

————. 1952. *Nihon Seiji Shisōshi Kenkyū* (Studies in the history of Japanese political thought). Tokyo: Tokyo University Press.

Matsumoto Sannosuke. 1966. Introduction. *Journal of Social and Political Ideas in Japan* 4, no. 3: 2–19.

Matsumoto, Shigeru. 1970. *Motoori Norinaga.* Cambridge, Mass.: Harvard University Press.

Matsumoto, Yoshiharu Scott. 1960. Contemporary Japan: The Individual and the Group. *Transactions of the American Philosophical Society* 50, no. 1.

McEwan, J. R. 1962. *The Political Writings of Ogyū Sorai.* Cambridge: Cambridge University Press.

McMullin, Neil. 1984. *Buddhism and the State in Sixteenth-Century Japan.* Princeton, N.J.: Princeton University Press.

Miki Kiyoshi. 1968. *Nihon Bunka no Tokushitsu* (The characteristics of Japanese culture). In *Miki Kiyoshi Zenshū* 17, p. 476. Tokyo: Iwanami.

————. 1967. *Kōsōryoku no Ronri* (The logic of the power of the imagination). In *Miki Kiyoshi Zenshū* (Collected works of Miki Kiyoshi) 8. Tokyo: Iwanami.

————. 1967. *Ningengaku no Marukusu-teki Keitei* (The Marxist form of anthropology). In *Miki Kiyoshi Zenshū* 3. Tokyo: Iwanami.

————. 1967. *Rekishi Tetsugaku* (Philosophy of history). In *Miki Kiyoshi Zenshū* 6. Tokyo: Iwanami.

Miner, Earl. 1969. *Japanese Poetic Diaries.* Berkeley and Los Angeles: University of California Press.

Mishima Yukio. 1970. *Kakumei no Tetsugaku to shite no Yômeigaku* (Wang Yang-ming teaching as a revolutionary philosophy). *Shokun* (September).

Miyake Hitoshi. 2001. *Shugendō: Essays on the Structure of Japanese Folk Religion.* Ann Arbor: Center for Japanese Studies, University of Michigan.

Moore, Barrington. 1988. Japanese Peasant Protests and Revolts in Comparative Historical Perspective. *International Review of Social History* 33, pt. 3.

Morris, Ivan. 1963. Theory and Psychology of Ultra-Nationalism. In *Thought and Behaviour in Modern Japanese Politics,* by Maruyama Masao. Oxford: Oxford University Press.

Muraoka Tsunetsugu. 1957. Kenpō Jūshichi-ken no Kenkyū (A study of the Seventeen-Article Constitution). In *Nihon Shisōshi no Shomondai* (Problems in the history of Japanese thought), pp. 7–71. Tokyo: Sobunsha.

————. 1927. *Motoori Norinaga.* Tokyo: Iwanami.

————. 1927–48. *Nihon Shisōshi Kenkyū* (Studies in the history of Japanese thought). 4 volumes. Tokyo: Iwanami.

Murasaki Shikibu. 1960. *The Tale of Genji.* Trans. Arthur Waley. New York: Modern Library.

Najita, Tetsuo. 2000. On History and Politics in the Thought of Maruyama Masao. The Maruyama Masao Lecture. University of California, Berkeley.

————. 2000. Some Comments on the Theme of Translation in Ogyū Sorai

(1666–1728) and Ogata Kōan (1810–1863). Seminar Presentation, Center for Japanese Studies. University of California, Berkeley.

———. 1999. Ambiguous Encounters: Ogata Kōan and International Studies in Late Tokugawa Osaka. In *Osaka: The Merchant's Capital of Early Modern Japan*, ed. James L. McClain and Wakita Osamu. Ithaca, N.Y. and Osaka: Cornell University Press/Osaka University Press.

———. 1998. *Tokugawa Political Writings*. Cambridge: Cambridge University Press.

———. 1987. *Visions of Virtue: The Kaitokudō Merchant Academy of Osaka*. Chicago: University of Chicago Press.

———. 1970. *Japanese Society*. Berkeley and Los Angeles: University of California Press.

———. 1970. Oshio Heihachirō (1793–1837). In *Personality in Japanese History*, ed. Albert M. Craig and Donald H. Shively, pp. 155–79. Berkeley and Los Angeles: University of California Press.

———. 1970. *Restorationism in the Political Thought of Yamagata Daini (1725–1767)*. Presented at a colloquium of the Center for Japanese and Korean Studies, University of California, Berkeley, December 2.

Nakamura Hajime. 1969. *A History of the Development of Japanese Thought from A.D. 592 to 1868*. Tokyo: Kokusai Bunka Shinkokai.

———. 1964. *The Ways of Thinking of Eastern Peoples*. Hawaii: East-West Center Press.

Nakane Chie. 1967. *Tate-Shakai no Ningen-kankei—Tanitsu Shakai no Riron* (Human relations in a vertical society—A theory of homogeneous society). Tokyo: Kōdansha.

Natsume Soseki. 1979. My Individualism. *Monumenta Nipponica*. 4, no. 1: 26–46.

Nishida Kitarō. 1968. *Nihon Bunka no Tokushitsu* (The characteristics of Japanese culture), an interview with Miki Kiyoshi. In *Miki Kiyoshi Zenshū* (Collected works of Miki Kiyoshi) 17. Tokyo: Iwanami.

———. 1958. *The Intelligibility and the Philosophy of Nothingness*. Trans. Robert Schinzinger. Tokyo: Maruzen.

———. 1947. *Tetsugaku no kompon mondai* (The basic problems of philosophy). Tokyo: Kangensha.

Oda, Makoto. 1966. The Meaning of "Meaningless Death." *Journal of Social and Political Ideas in Japan* 4, no. 2: 75–85.

Okada, Yuzuru. 1966. Introduction. *Journal of Social and Political Ideas in Japan* 2, no. 14: 97–110.

Ooms, Herman. 1985. *Tokugawa Ideology: Early Constructs, 1570–1680*. Princeton, N.J.: Princeton University Press.

———. 1975. *Charismatic Bureaucrat: A Political Biography of Matsudaira Sadanobu, 1758–1829*. Chicago: Chicago University Press.

Ōtsuka, Hisao. 1976. *Max Weber on the Spirit of Capitalism*. Tokyo: Institute of Developing Economies.

Parsons, Talcott. 1968. Christianity. *International Encyclopedia of the Social Sciences*. New York: Macmillan.

————. 1966. *Societies: Evolutionary and Comparative Perspectives.* Englewood Cliffs, N.J.: Prentice-Hall.

————. 1963. Christianity and Modern Industrial Society. In *Sociological Theory, Values and Sociocultural Change,* ed. Edward Tiryakian. New York: Free Press.

Payne, Richard K. ed. 1998. *Re-Visioning "Kamakura" Buddhism.* Honolulu: University of Hawaii Press.

Pyle, Kenneth B. 1969. *The New Generation in Meiji Japan: Problems of Cultural Identity, 1885–1895.* Stanford, Calif.: Stanford University Press.

Rubin, Jay. 1979. Soseki on Individualism. *Monumenta Nipponica.* 4, no. 1: 21–25.

Sakamoto Yoshikazu, ed. 1989. *The Emperor System as a Japan Problem: The Case of Meiji Gakuin University.* International Peace Research Institute Meigaku, Occasional Papers Series Number 5.

Samuel, Geoffrey. 1993. *Civilized Shamans: Buddhism in Tibetan Societies.* Washington, D.C.: Smithsonian Institution Press.

Scheiner, Irwin. 1970. *Christian Converts and Social Protest in Meiji Japan.* Berkeley and Los Angeles: University of California Press.

Seidensticker, Edward. 1965. *Kafū the Scribbler.* Stanford, Calif.: Stanford University Press.

Shaw, George Bernard. 1942. The Man of Destiny. In *Plays: Pleasant and Unpleasant* II: 212–13. New York: Dodd, Mead.

Shida Shōzō. 1963. *Asahi Journal* 5, no. 5

Sonoda Minoru. 1966. Bakumatsu Kokugaku no Shisōshi-teki Mondai (Problems in the history of Kokugaku thought at the end of the Tokugawa period). *Kokugakuin Daigaku Nihon Bunka Kenkyūsho Kiyō* no. 18: 1–31.

Stone, Jacqueline I. 1999. *Original Enlightenment and the Transformation of Medieval Japanese Buddhism.* Honolulu: University of Hawaii Press.

Suzuki, D. T. 1971. *Mysticism, Christian and Buddhist.* New York: Harper and Row.

Takeda Kiyoko. 1959. *Ningenkan no Sokoku* (Conflicting views of man). Tokyo: Kōbundō.

Takeuchi Yoshimi. 1959. Kindai no Chōkoku (Overcoming the modern). *Kindai Nihon Shisōshi Kōza* (Symposium on the history of modern Japanese thought) 7: 227–81. Tokyo: Chikuma Shobō.

Tambiah, Stanley. 1985. *Culture, Thought, and Social Action: An Anthropological Perspective.* Cambridge, Mass.: Harvard University Press.

————. 1976. *World Conqueror and World Renouncer: A Study of Buddhism and Polity in Thailand Against a Historical Background.* Cambridge: Cambridge University Press.

Tanabe Hajime. 1933. *Tetsugaku tsūron* (An introduction to philosophy).

Tanizaki Junichiro. 1957. *The Makioka Sisters.* Trans. Edward G. Seidensticker. New York: Alfred A. Knopf.

Tosaka Jun. 1935. *Nihon Ideorogii-ron* (An essay on Japanese ideology). Tokyo: Hakuyōsha.

Tsuda Sōkichi. 1948. *Polis-teki Ningen no Rinrigaku* (Ethics of the polis). Tokyo: Hakujitsu Shōin.

———. 1939. *Shina Shisō to Nihon* (Chinese thought and Japan). Tokyo: Iwanami.

———. 1915. *Bungaku ni Arawaretaru Waga Kokumin Shisō no Kenkyū* (A study of our national thought as expressed in literature). Tokyo: Rakuyōdō.

Tsunoda, Ryusaku, William de Bary, and Donald Keene. 1958. *Sources of the Japanese Tradition*. New York: Columbia University Press.

Ueyama Shumpei. 1959. *Kindai Nihon Shisōshi Kōza* (Symposium on the history of modern Japanese thought). Tokyo: Chikuma Shobō.

Viglielmo, Valdo. 1955. *The Later Natsume Sōseki*. Doctoral dissertation in Far Eastern Languages, Harvard University.

Vlastos, Stephen. 1998. *Mirror of Modernity: Invented Traditions of Modern Japan*. Berkeley and Los Angeles: University of California Press.

Voegelin, Eric. 1957. *Order and History, III: Plato and Aristotle*. Baton Rouge: Louisiana State University Press.

Vogel, Ezra. 1963. *Japan's New Middle Class*. Berkeley and Los Angeles: University of California Press.

Wakabayashi, Bob Tadashi. 1986. *Anti-Foreignism and Western Learning in Early-Modern Japan*. Cambridge, Mass.: Harvard University Press.

Watsuji Tetsurō. 1988. *Climate and Culture*. Trans. Geoffrey Bownas. New York: Greenwood Press.

———. 1961–63. *Zenshū*. 20 vols. Tokyo: Iwanami.

———. 1952. *Nihon Rinri Shisōshi* (History of Japanese ethical thought). Tokyo: Iwanami.

———. 1951. *Sakoku: Nihon no Higeki* (The closing of the country: Japan's tragedy). Tokyo: Chikuma Shobō.

———. 1949. *Rinrigaku* (Ethics). Vol. 3. Tokyo: Iwanami.

———. 1948. *Polis-teki Ningen no Rinrigaku* (Ethics of the polis). Tokyo: Iwanami.

———. 1944. *Nihon no Shindō* (The way of the subject in Japan). Tokyo: Chikuma Shobō.

———. 1942. *Rinrigaku* (Ethics). Vol. 2. Tokyo: Iwanami.

———. 1938. *Confucius*. Tokyo: Iwanami.

———. 1937. *Men to Persona* ("Men" [J. face, mask] and "Persona"). Tokyo: Iwanami.

———. 1937. *Rinrigaku* (Ethics). Vol. 1. Tokyo: Iwanami.

———. 1935. *Zoku Nihon Seishinshi Kenkyū* (Studies in Japanese spiritual history). Tokyo: Iwanami.

———. 1931. *Ningen no Gaku to shite no Rinrigaku* (Ethics as anthropology). Tokyo: Iwanami.

———. 1927. *Genshi Bukkyō no Jissen Tetsugaku* (The practical philosophy of primitive Buddhism). Tokyo: Iwanami.

———. 1926. *Genshi Kirisutokyō no Bunkashi-teki Igi* (The significance of primitive Christianity in the history of culture). Tokyo: Iwanami.

———. 1926. *Nihon Seishinshi Kenkyū* (Studies in Japanese history). Tokyo: Iwanami.

———. 1920. *Koji Junrei* (Pilgrimages to ancient temples). Tokyo: Iwanami.

———. 1920. *Nihon Kodai Bunka* (Ancient Japanese culture). Tokyo: Iwanami.

———. 1918. *Gūzō Saikō* (Resurrection of idols). Tokyo: Iwanami.

———. 1915. *Soren Kierkegaard*. Tokyo: Iwanami.

———. 1913. *Nietzsche Kenkyū* (A study of Nietzsche). Tokyo: Iwanami.

Weber, Max. 1930. *The Protestant Ethic and the Spirit of Capitalism*. New York: Scribners.

Wheatley, Paul, and Thomas See. 1978. *From Court to Capital: A Tentative Interpretation of the Origins of the Japanese Urban Tradition*. Chicago: University of Chicago Press.

Wilson, George M. 1969. *Radical Nationalist in Japan: Kita Ikki, 1883–1937*. Cambridge, Mass.: Harvard University Press.

Wray, William D. 1970. Asō Hisashi and the Search for Renovation in the 1930s. *Papers on Japan* 5: 55–99. Cambridge, Mass.: Harvard East Asian Research Center.

Yasumaru Yoshio. 1965. Nihon no Kindaika to Minshū Shisō (Japanese modernization and popular thought). *Nihonshi Kenkyū* (Japanese historical studies) no. 78: 1–10; no. 79: 40–58.

Yoshino, Kosaku. 1992. *Cultural Nationalism in Contemporary Japan: A Sociological Inquiry*. London: Routledge.

# Index

| Compositor: | BookMatters |
|---|---|
| Text: | 10/13 Aldus |
| Display: | Aldus |
| Printer and Binder: | Integrated Book Technology, Inc. |

One of the most influential sociologists living today, Robert N. Bellah began his career as a Japan specialist and has continued to contribute to the field over the past thirty years. *Imagining Japan* is a collection of some of his most important writings, including essays that consider the entire sweep of Japanese history and the character of Japanese society and religion. Combining intellectual rigor, broad scholarship, and ethical commitment, this book also features a new and extensive introduction that brings together intellectual and institutional dimensions of Japanese history.

Bellah shows that characterizing Japan has been a challenge for Japanese and for foreigners for quite some time. Imagining Japan involves thinking historically, asking how Japanese society and culture have developed over the last millennium and a half, and thinking comparatively, asking where Japan fits in comparison with other societies and cultures. The task has always been controversial: What is the Japanese tradition? Is it unitary or plural? What are its tensions and contradictions? Is it unique? In these pages the reader will meet apologists and critics, traditionalists and reformers. Every culture is engaged in a process of constant self-interpretation and self-transformation. This book argues that the "Japanese difference" is only one of degree and that Japanese culture is intelligible within the normal range of human cultural variation. It is thus not only a description of Japan but an exercise in imagining.

"Bellah is a sociologist with a grand vision of history, deeply concerned with the twists and turns of religious values, weaving pre-modern religious thinking into the debates of modernization and modernity. He takes a reflective turn with *Imagining Japan*, evidencing his profound concern with religious evolution." **TETSUO NAJITA**, University of Chicago

"One of the most original attempts to understand some of the psychological and symbolic roots of the central problems in Japanese history. Bellah masterfully brings together intellectual and institutional dimensions of Japan, making a very important contribution to Japanese Studies." **S. N. EISENSTADT**, author of *Japanese Civilization: A Comparative View*

**ROBERT N. BELLAH** is Elliott Professor of Sociology, Emeritus, at the University of California, Berkeley. He is author of *Beyond Belief* (California, 1991) and *Tokugawa Religion: The Cultural Roots of Modern Japan* (1985), and coauthor of *Habits of the Heart* (California, 1985).

ISBN-13: 978-0-520-23598-4
ISBN-10: 0-520-23598-3

UNIVERSITY OF CALIFORNIA PRESS
BERKELEY 94720   www.ucpress.edu